ARCHER & ARMSTRONG

THE ONE PERCENT
AND OTHER TALES

FRED VAN LENTE | RAY FAWKES | KARL BOLLERS | CLAYTON HENRY | JOE EISMA

CONTENTS

Collection Cover Art: Pere Pérez

Editor: Josh Johns
Editor-in-Chief: Warren Simons

VALIANT

Peter Cuneo
Chairman

Dinesh Shamdasani
CEO & Chief Creative Officer

Gavin Cuneo
Chief Operating Officer & CFO

Fred Pierce
Publisher

Warren Simons
VP Editor-in-Chief

Walter Black
VP Operations

Hunter Gorinson
Director of Marketing, Communications & Digital Media

Atom! Freeman
Matthew Klein
Andy Liegl
Sales Managers

Josh Johns
Digital Sales & Special Projects Manager

Travis Escarfullery
Jeff Walker
Production & Design Managers

Alejandro Arbona
Editor

Kyle Andrukiewicz
Tom Brennan
Associate Editors

Peter Stern
Publishing & Operations Manager

Chris Daniels
Marketing Coordinator

Danny Khazem
Operations Coordinator

Ivan Cohen
Collection Editor

Steve Blackwell
Collection Designer

Rian Hughes/Device
Trade Dress & Book Design

Russell Brown
President, Consumer Products, Promotions and Ad Sales

Jason Kothari
Vice Chairman

Archer & Armstrong®: The One Percent and Other Tales. Published by Valiant Entertainment LLC. Office of Publication: 424 West 33rd Street, New York, NY 10001.
First Printing. ISBN: 9781939346537.

ARCHER & ARMSTRONG

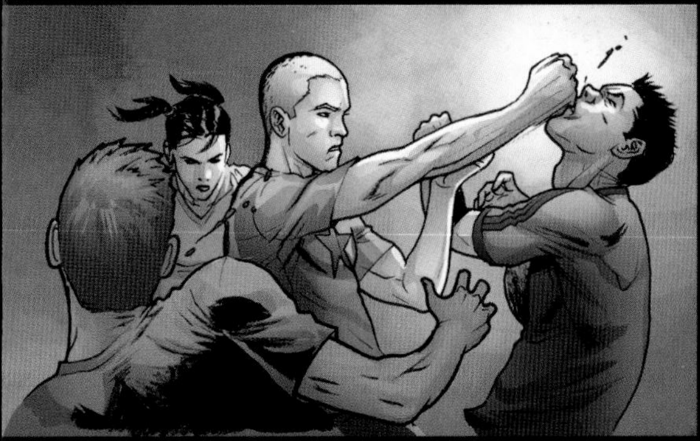

Archer, born with the ability to mimic any skill, trained long and hard to become an assassin for his family's Sect.

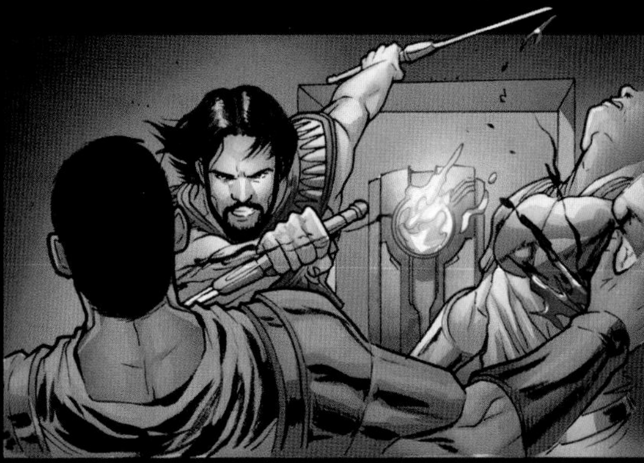

Armstrong, born with incredible strength, rebelled against his family and became "cursed" with immortality.

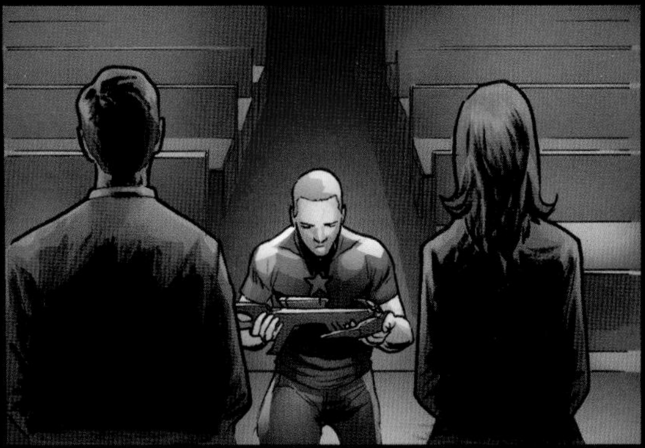

Archer's strong sense of duty made him say, "Yes! Of course!" when his parents asked him to murder Armstrong on behalf of the Sect.

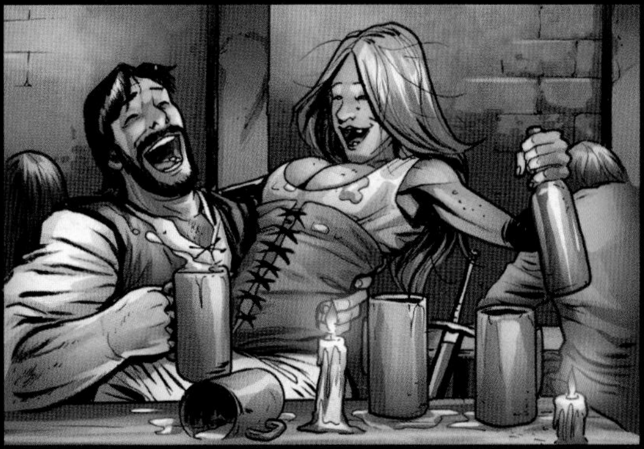

Armstrong's strong sense of hedonism made him say, "Just one more, I swear," and is the only man to have the same venereal disease for 5,000 years.

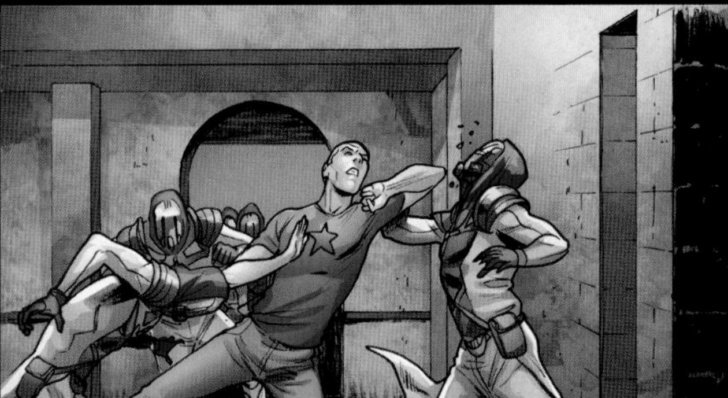

Archer learned that Armstrong wasn't so bad, that the Sect was evil, and so partnered with his immortal buddy to travel the world on conspiracy-busting adventures.

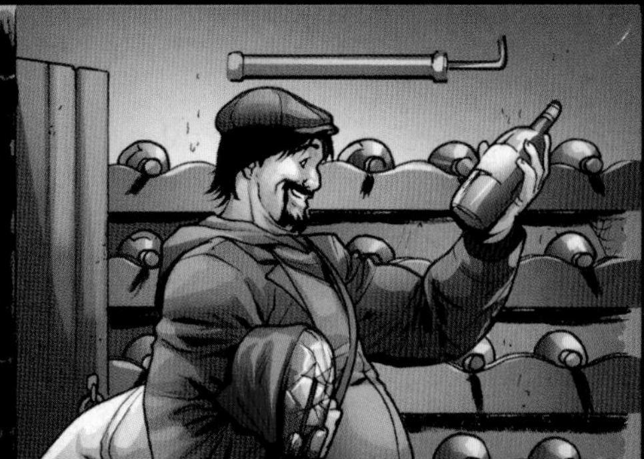

Armstrong learned ... uh ... oh, screw it, who are we kidding. Armstrong didn't learn a damn thing.

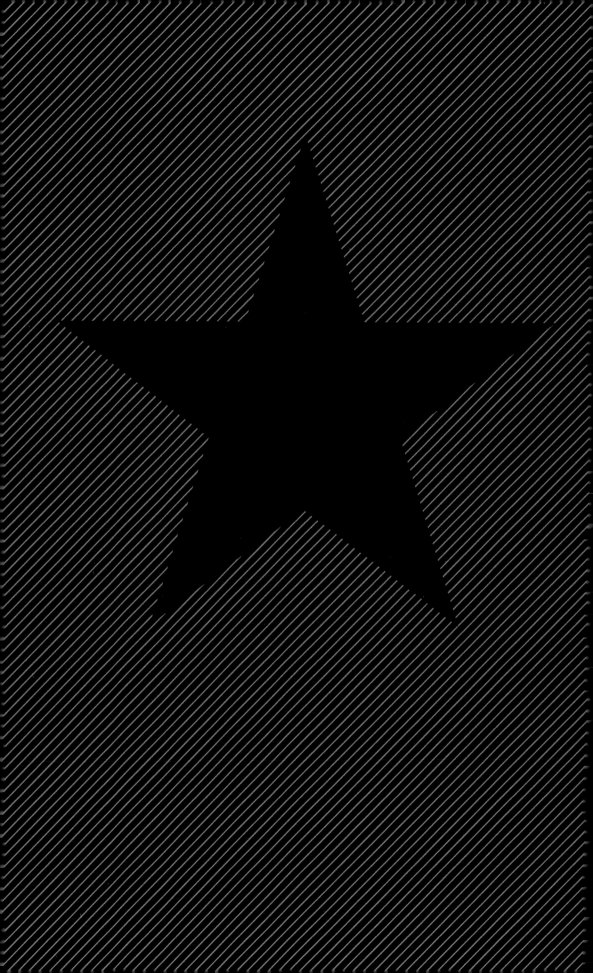

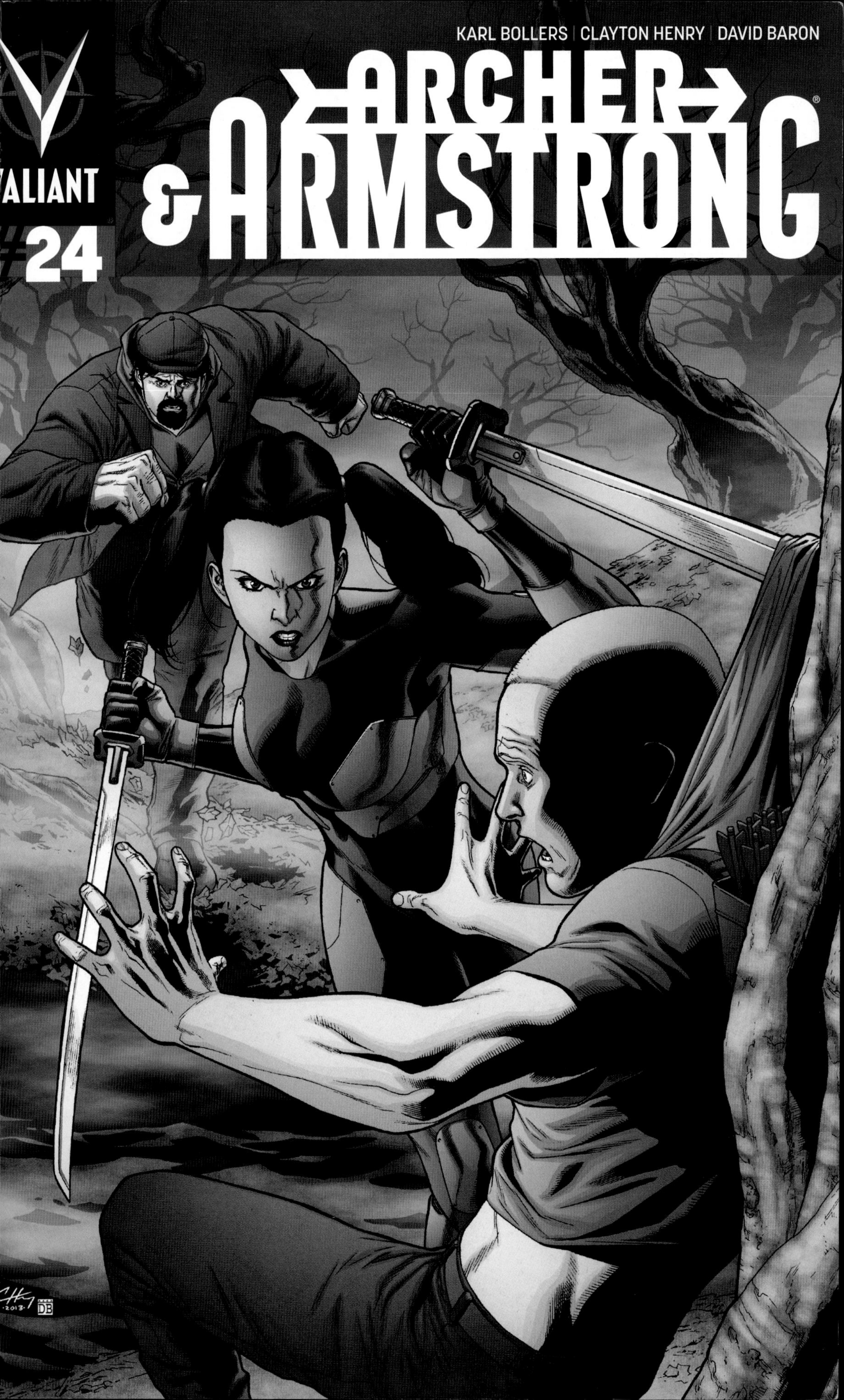

KARL BOLLERS | CLAYTON HENRY | DAVID BARON
ARCHER & ARMSTRONG
VALIANT
#24

ARCHER & ARMSTRONG

OUR STORY SO FAR...

Three brothers—Ivar, Gilad, and Aram—stole an immensely powerful weapon called the Boon from a mysterious land known as the Faraway. Though they were successful in their thievery, it came at a tremendous price: the youngest of the brothers, Gilad, died during their journey. Driven to desperation by his brother's death, Ivar activated the Boon in hopes of a miracle. The resulting explosion not only devastated much of the ancient world, but also made Aram immortal, leaving him to wander the Earth for all recorded history.

Enter youthful idealist Obadiah Archer. Unbeknownst to Obadiah, he was adoptedand raised by an evil organization calledthe Sect. Archer's uncanny ability to mimic any skill made him an invaluable asset to his adoptive parents' mission: kill Aram Anni-Padda (today known as Armstrong) and retrieve the Boon. To make a long story short, things did not go as planned. Archer eventually turned on his parents, assisting Armstrong in destroying the Boon and forming an unlikely friendship with the drunken immortal in the process.

While Archer and Armstrong set their sights on heroism and high adventure, Archer's adopted sister (and on-again, off-again love interest), Mary-Maria Archer, had other plans. Mary-Maria successfully took over a faction of the Sect called the Sisters of Perpetual Darkness, and has since set her sights on thwarting Archer and Armstrong's plans and destroying the Sisters' rival factions!

This is just a regular Tuesday for her...

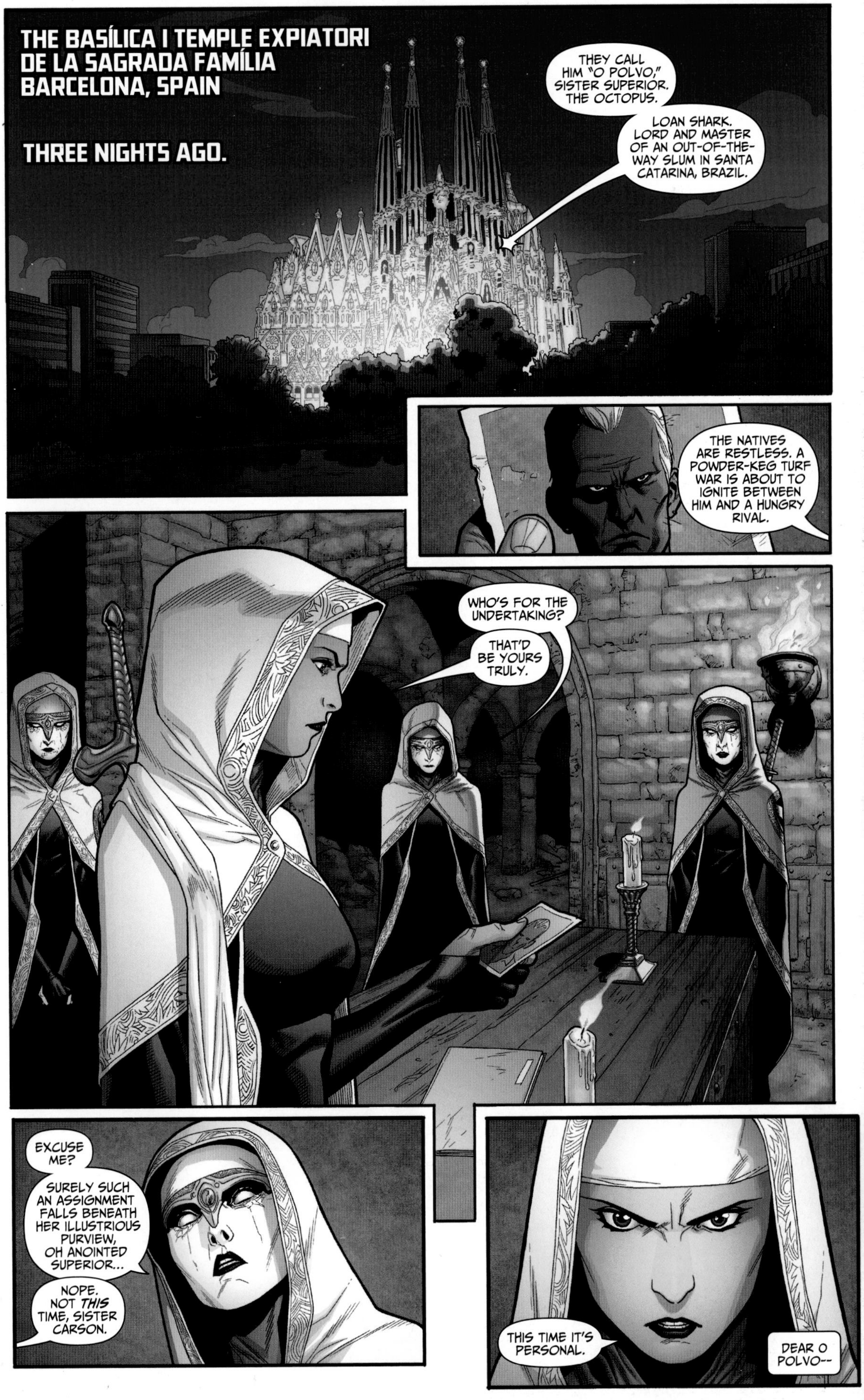
THE BASÍLICA I TEMPLE EXPIATORI DE LA SAGRADA FAMÍLIA
BARCELONA, SPAIN
THREE NIGHTS AGO.
THEY CALL HIM "O POLVO," SISTER SUPERIOR. THE OCTOPUS.
LOAN SHARK. LORD AND MASTER OF AN OUT-OF-THE-WAY SLUM IN SANTA CATARINA, BRAZIL.
THE NATIVES ARE RESTLESS. A POWDER-KEG TURF WAR IS ABOUT TO IGNITE BETWEEN HIM AND A HUNGRY RIVAL.
WHO'S FOR THE UNDERTAKING?
THAT'D BE YOURS TRULY.
EXCUSE ME?
SURELY SUCH AN ASSIGNMENT FALLS BENEATH HER ILLUSTRIOUS PURVIEW, OH ANOINTED SUPERIOR...
NOPE. NOT *THIS* TIME, SISTER CARSON.
THIS TIME IT'S PERSONAL.
DEAR O POLVO--

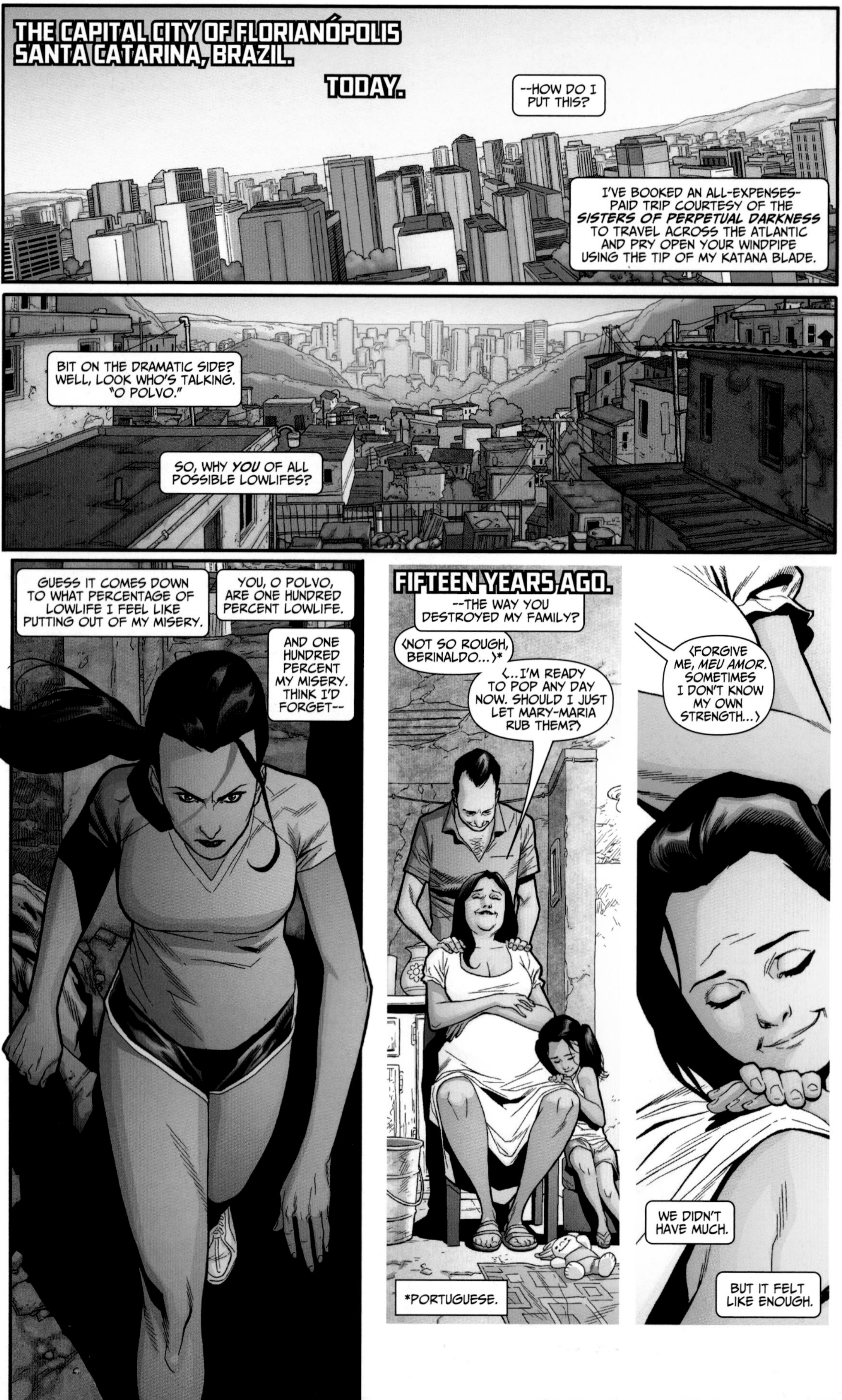
THE CAPITAL CITY OF FLORIANÓPOLIS SANTA CATARINA, BRAZIL.
TODAY.
--HOW DO I PUT THIS?
I'VE BOOKED AN ALL-EXPENSES-PAID TRIP COURTESY OF THE SISTERS OF PERPETUAL DARKNESS TO TRAVEL ACROSS THE ATLANTIC AND PRY OPEN YOUR WINDPIPE USING THE TIP OF MY KATANA BLADE.
BIT ON THE DRAMATIC SIDE? WELL, LOOK WHO'S TALKING. "O POLVO."
SO, WHY YOU OF ALL POSSIBLE LOWLIFES?
GUESS IT COMES DOWN TO WHAT PERCENTAGE OF LOWLIFE I FEEL LIKE PUTTING OUT OF MY MISERY.
YOU, O POLVO, ARE ONE HUNDRED PERCENT LOWLIFE.
AND ONE HUNDRED PERCENT MY MISERY. THINK I'D FORGET--
FIFTEEN YEARS AGO.
--THE WAY YOU DESTROYED MY FAMILY?
‹NOT SO ROUGH, BERINALDO...›*
‹...I'M READY TO POP ANY DAY NOW. SHOULD I JUST LET MARY-MARIA RUB THEM?›
*PORTUGUESE.
‹FORGIVE ME, MEU AMOR. SOMETIMES I DON'T KNOW MY OWN STRENGTH...›
WE DIDN'T HAVE MUCH.
BUT IT FELT LIKE ENOUGH.

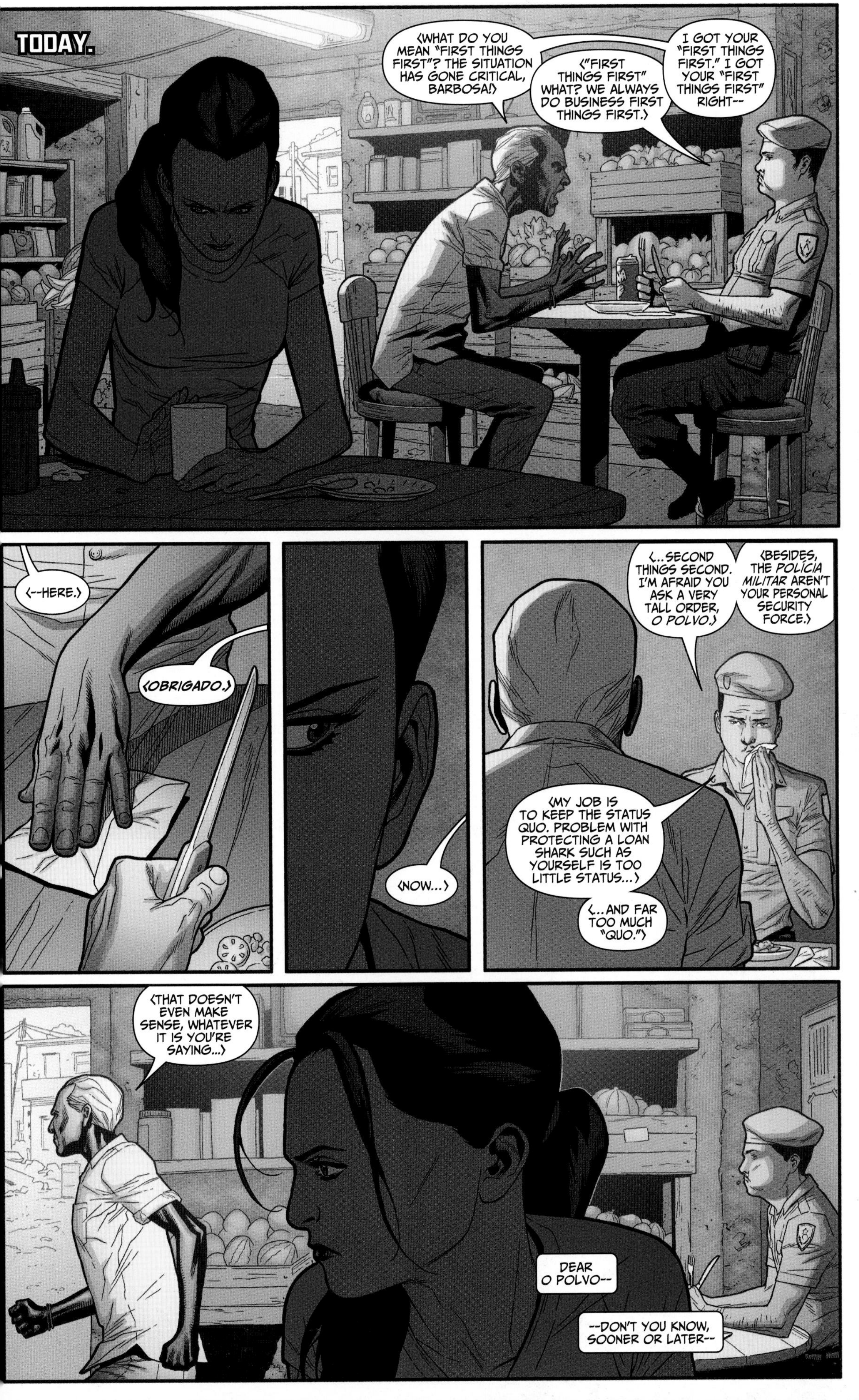

TODAY.
‹WHAT DO YOU MEAN "FIRST THINGS FIRST"? THE SITUATION HAS GONE CRITICAL, BARBOSA!›
‹"FIRST THINGS FIRST" WHAT? WE ALWAYS DO BUSINESS FIRST THINGS FIRST.›
I GOT YOUR "FIRST THINGS FIRST." I GOT YOUR "FIRST THINGS FIRST" RIGHT--
‹--HERE.›
‹OBRIGADO.›
‹NOW...›
‹..SECOND THINGS SECOND. I'M AFRAID YOU ASK A VERY TALL ORDER, *O POLVO*.›
‹BESIDES, THE *POLÍCIA MILITAR* AREN'T YOUR PERSONAL SECURITY FORCE.›
‹MY JOB IS TO KEEP THE STATUS QUO. PROBLEM WITH PROTECTING A LOAN SHARK SUCH AS YOURSELF IS TOO LITTLE STATUS...›
‹...AND FAR TOO MUCH "QUO."›
‹THAT DOESN'T EVEN MAKE SENSE, WHATEVER IT IS YOU'RE SAYING...›
DEAR O POLVO--
--DON'T YOU KNOW, SOONER OR LATER--

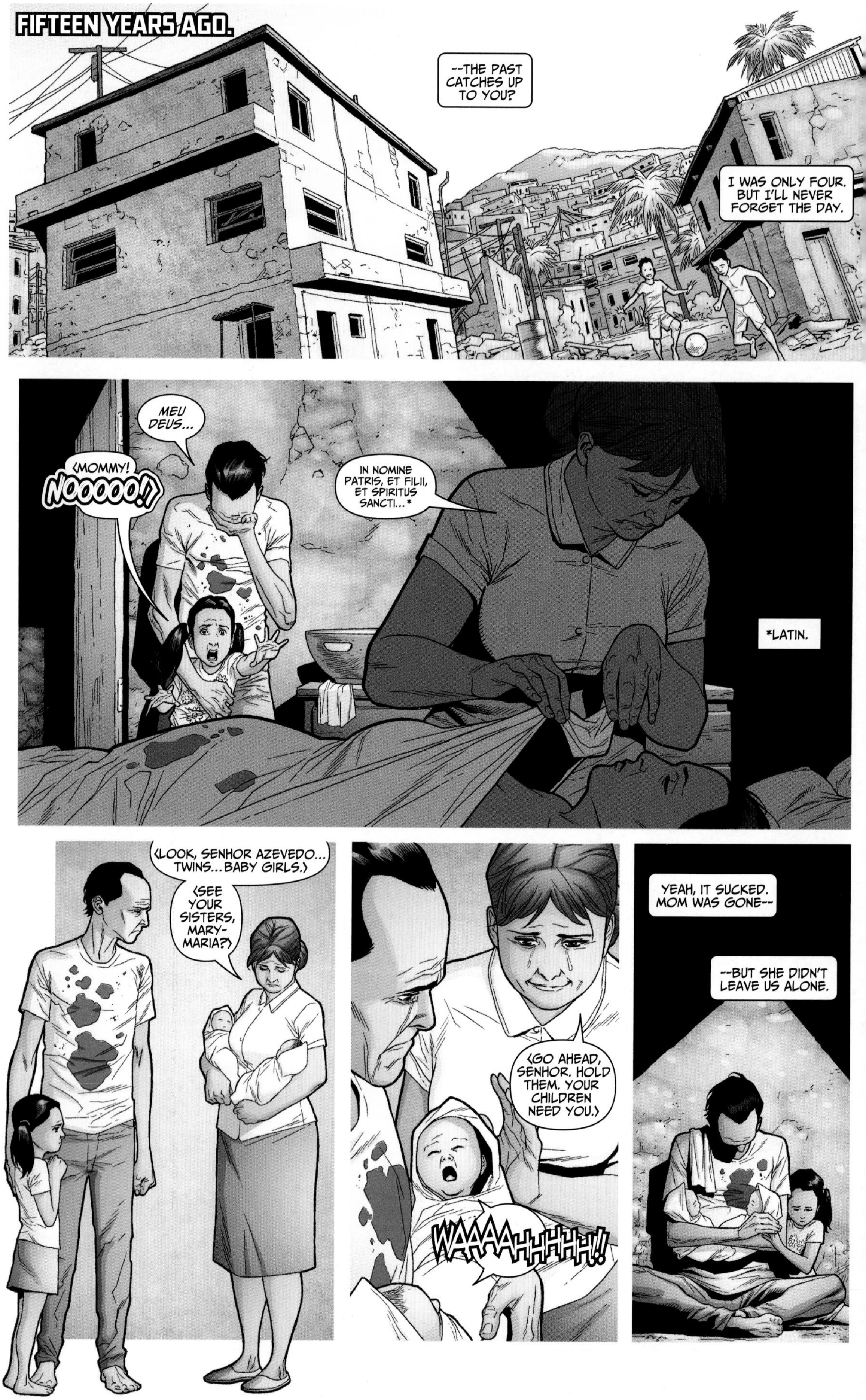
FIFTEEN YEARS AGO.
--THE PAST CATCHES UP TO YOU?
I WAS ONLY FOUR. BUT I'LL NEVER FORGET THE DAY.
MEU DEUS...
‹MOMMY! NOOOOO!!›
IN NOMINE PATRIS, ET FILII, ET SPIRITUS SANCTI...*
*LATIN.
‹LOOK, SENHOR AZEVEDO... TWINS... BABY GIRLS.›
‹SEE YOUR SISTERS, MARY-MARIA?›
‹GO AHEAD, SENHOR. HOLD THEM. YOUR CHILDREN NEED YOU.›
WAAAAHHHHH!!
YEAH, IT SUCKED. MOM WAS GONE--
--BUT SHE DIDN'T LEAVE US ALONE.

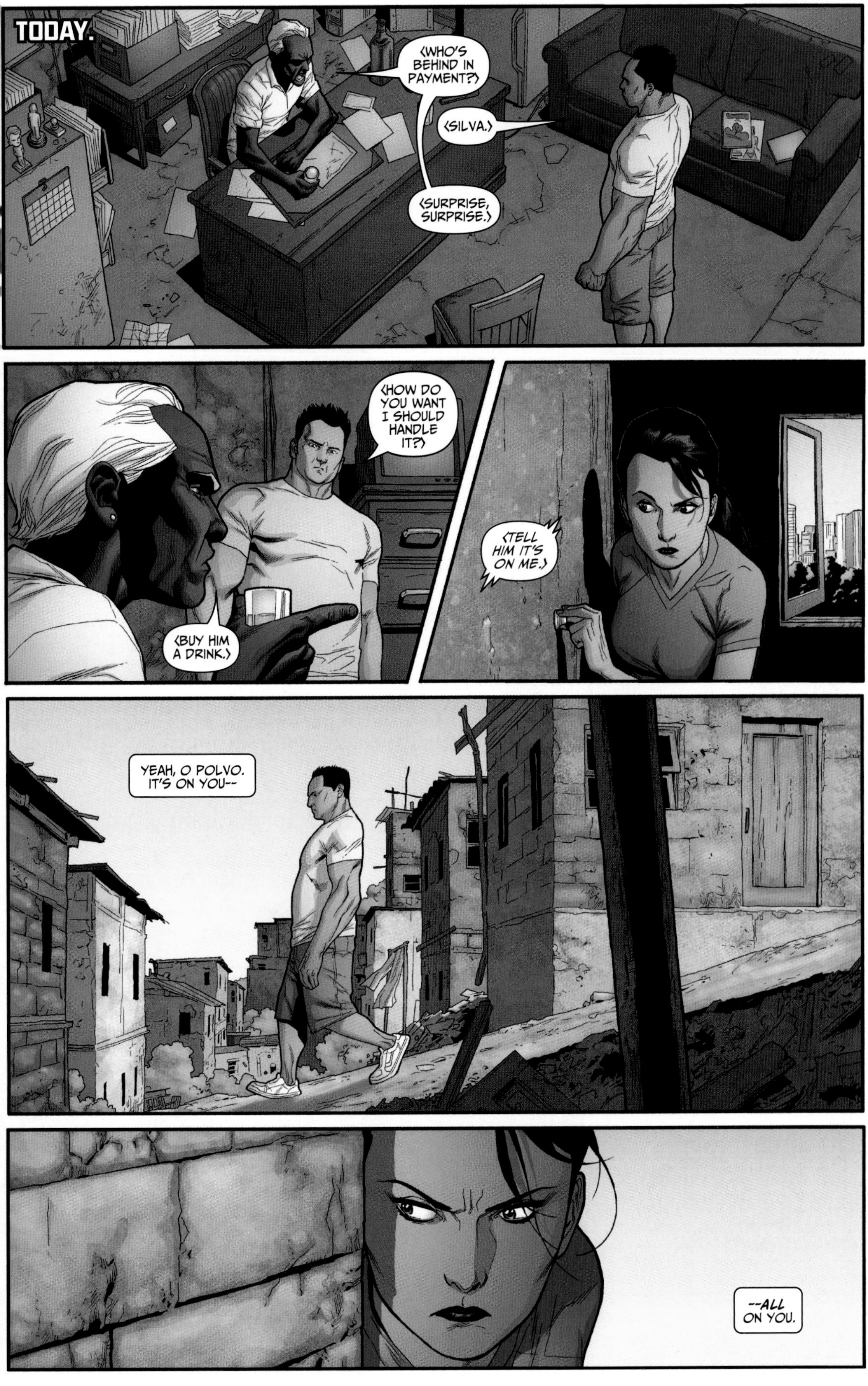
TODAY.
<WHO'S BEHIND IN PAYMENT?>
<SILVA.>
<SURPRISE, SURPRISE.>
<HOW DO YOU WANT I SHOULD HANDLE IT?>
<BUY HIM A DRINK.>
<TELL HIM IT'S ON ME.>
YEAH, O POLVO. IT'S ON YOU--
--ALL ON YOU.

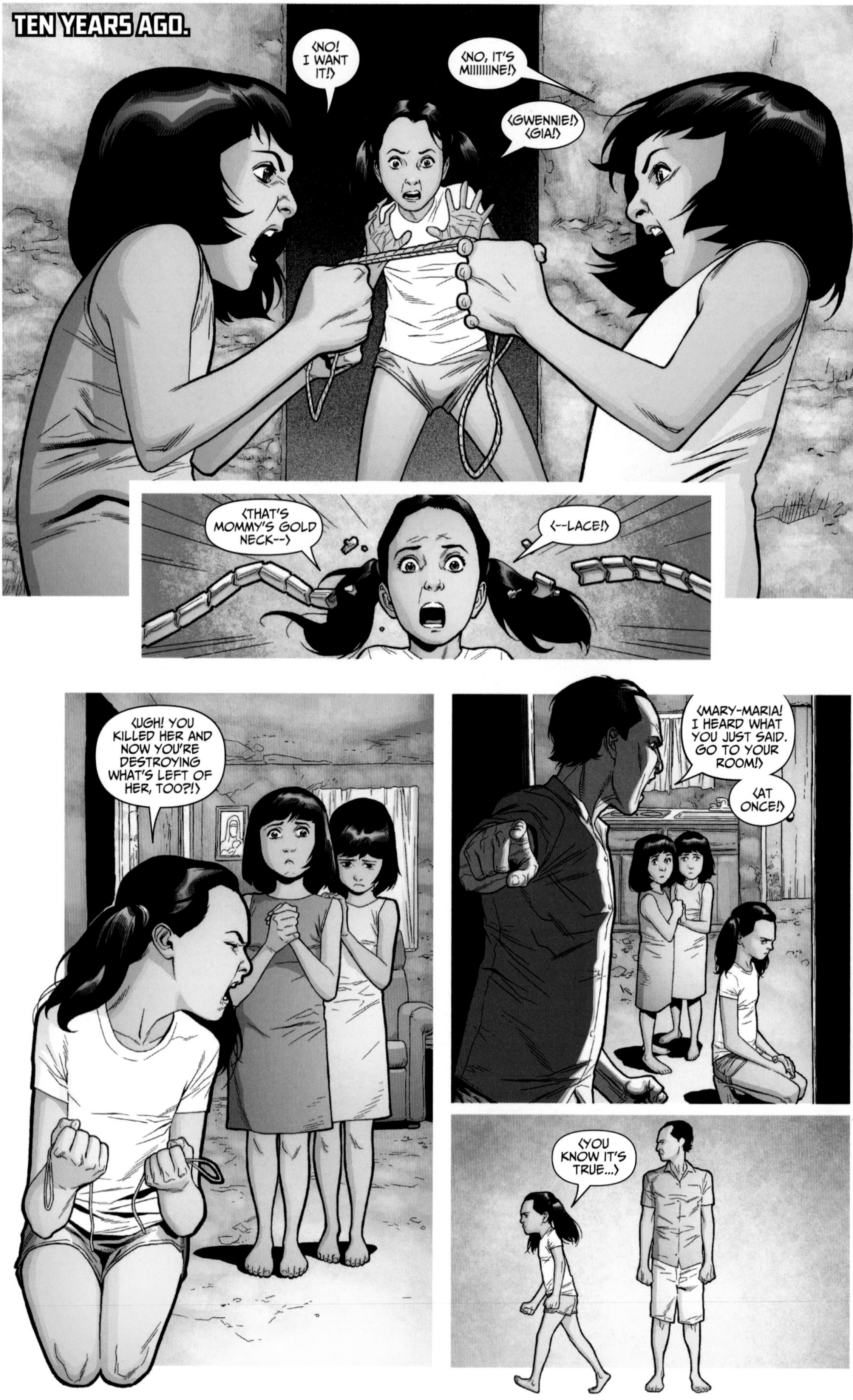
TEN YEARS AGO.
<NO! I WANT IT!>
<NO, IT'S MIIIIIINE!>
<GWENNIE!> <GIA!>
<THAT'S MOMMY'S GOLD NECK-->
<--LACE!>
<UGH! YOU KILLED HER AND NOW YOU'RE DESTROYING WHAT'S LEFT OF HER, TOO?!>
<MARY-MARIA! I HEARD WHAT YOU JUST SAID. GO TO YOUR ROOM!>
<AT ONCE!>
<YOU KNOW IT'S TRUE...>

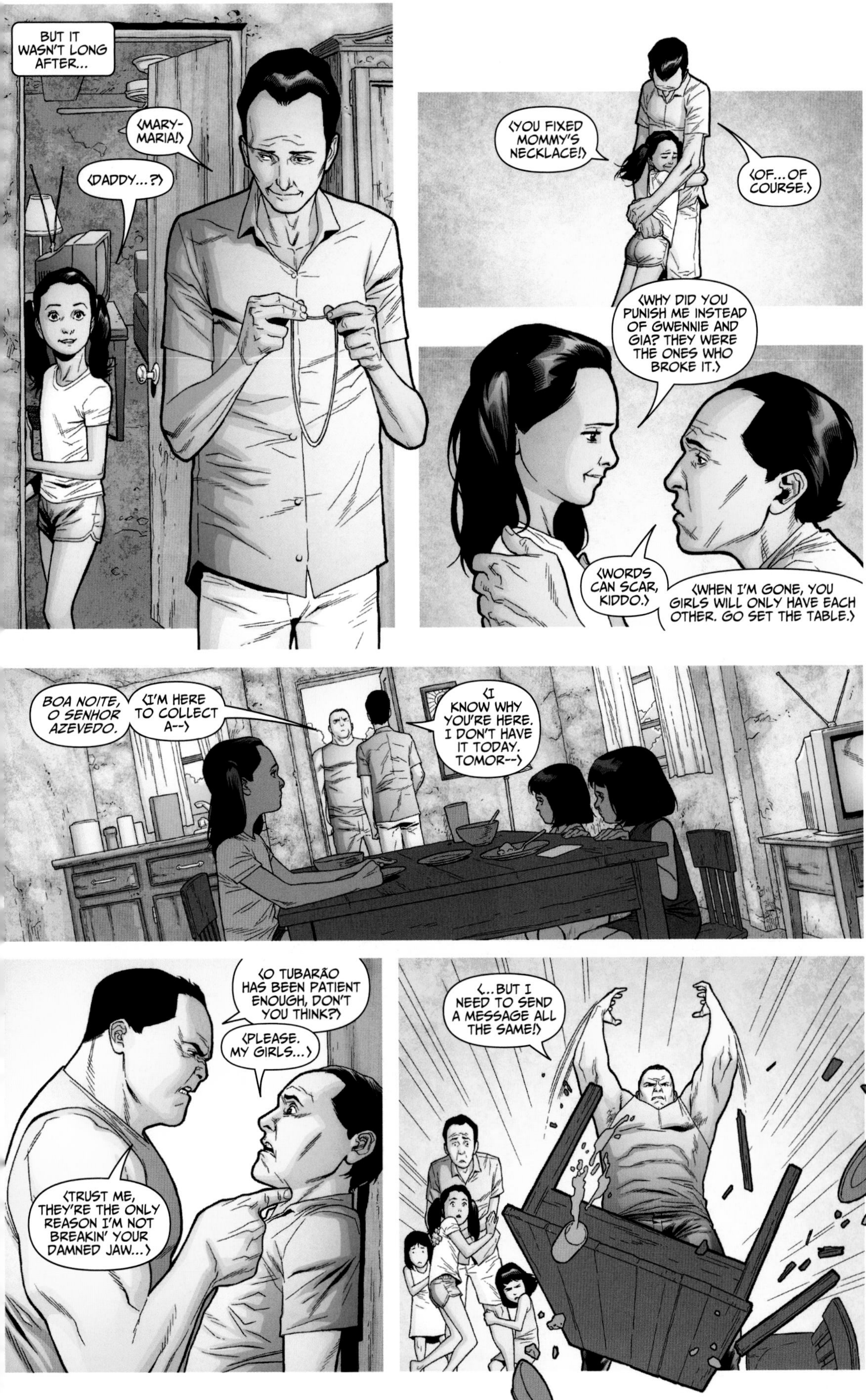
BUT IT WASN'T LONG AFTER...
⟨MARY-MARIA!⟩
⟨DADDY...?⟩
⟨YOU FIXED MOMMY'S NECKLACE!⟩
⟨OF...OF COURSE.⟩
⟨WHY DID YOU PUNISH ME INSTEAD OF GWENNIE AND GIA? THEY WERE THE ONES WHO BROKE IT.⟩
⟨WORDS CAN SCAR, KIDDO.⟩
⟨WHEN I'M GONE, YOU GIRLS WILL ONLY HAVE EACH OTHER. GO SET THE TABLE.⟩
BOA NOITE, O SENHOR AZEVEDO.
⟨I'M HERE TO COLLECT A--⟩
⟨I KNOW WHY YOU'RE HERE. I DON'T HAVE IT TODAY. TOMOR--⟩
⟨O TUBARÃO HAS BEEN PATIENT ENOUGH, DON'T YOU THINK?⟩
⟨PLEASE. MY GIRLS...⟩
⟨TRUST ME, THEY'RE THE ONLY REASON I'M NOT BREAKIN' YOUR DAMNED JAW...⟩
⟨...BUT I NEED TO SEND A MESSAGE ALL THE SAME!⟩

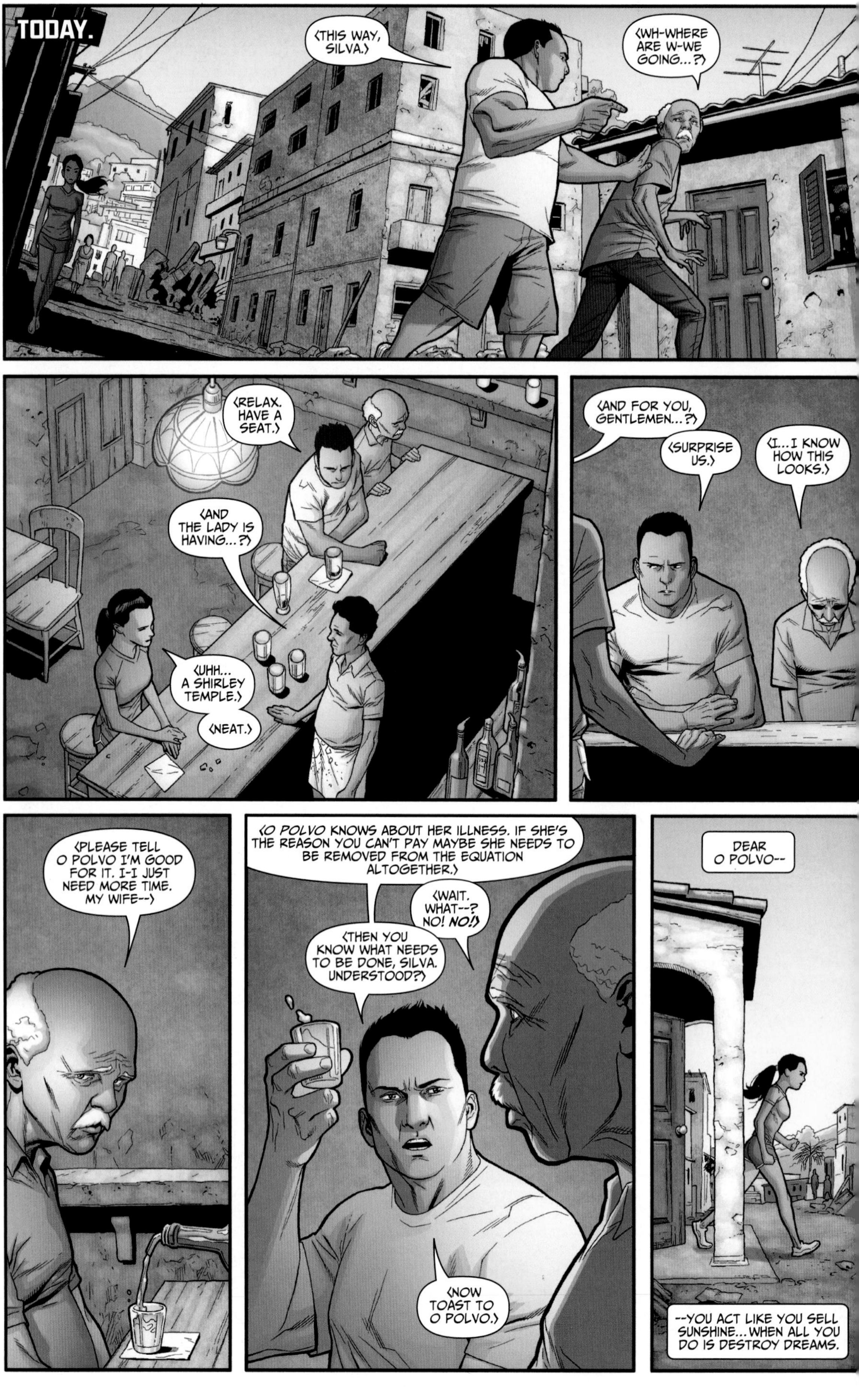
TODAY.
<THIS WAY, SILVA.>
<WH-WHERE ARE W-WE GOING...?>
<RELAX. HAVE A SEAT.>
<AND THE LADY IS HAVING...?>
<UHH... A SHIRLEY TEMPLE.>
<NEAT.>
<AND FOR YOU, GENTLEMEN...?>
<SURPRISE US.>
<I...I KNOW HOW THIS LOOKS.>
<PLEASE TELL O POLVO I'M GOOD FOR IT. I-I JUST NEED MORE TIME. MY WIFE-->
<*O POLVO* KNOWS ABOUT HER ILLNESS. IF SHE'S THE REASON YOU CAN'T PAY MAYBE SHE NEEDS TO BE REMOVED FROM THE EQUATION ALTOGETHER.>
<WAIT. WHAT--? NO! ***NO!***>
<THEN YOU KNOW WHAT NEEDS TO BE DONE, SILVA. UNDERSTOOD?>
<NOW TOAST TO O POLVO.>
DEAR O POLVO--
--YOU ACT LIKE YOU SELL SUNSHINE...WHEN ALL YOU DO IS DESTROY DREAMS.

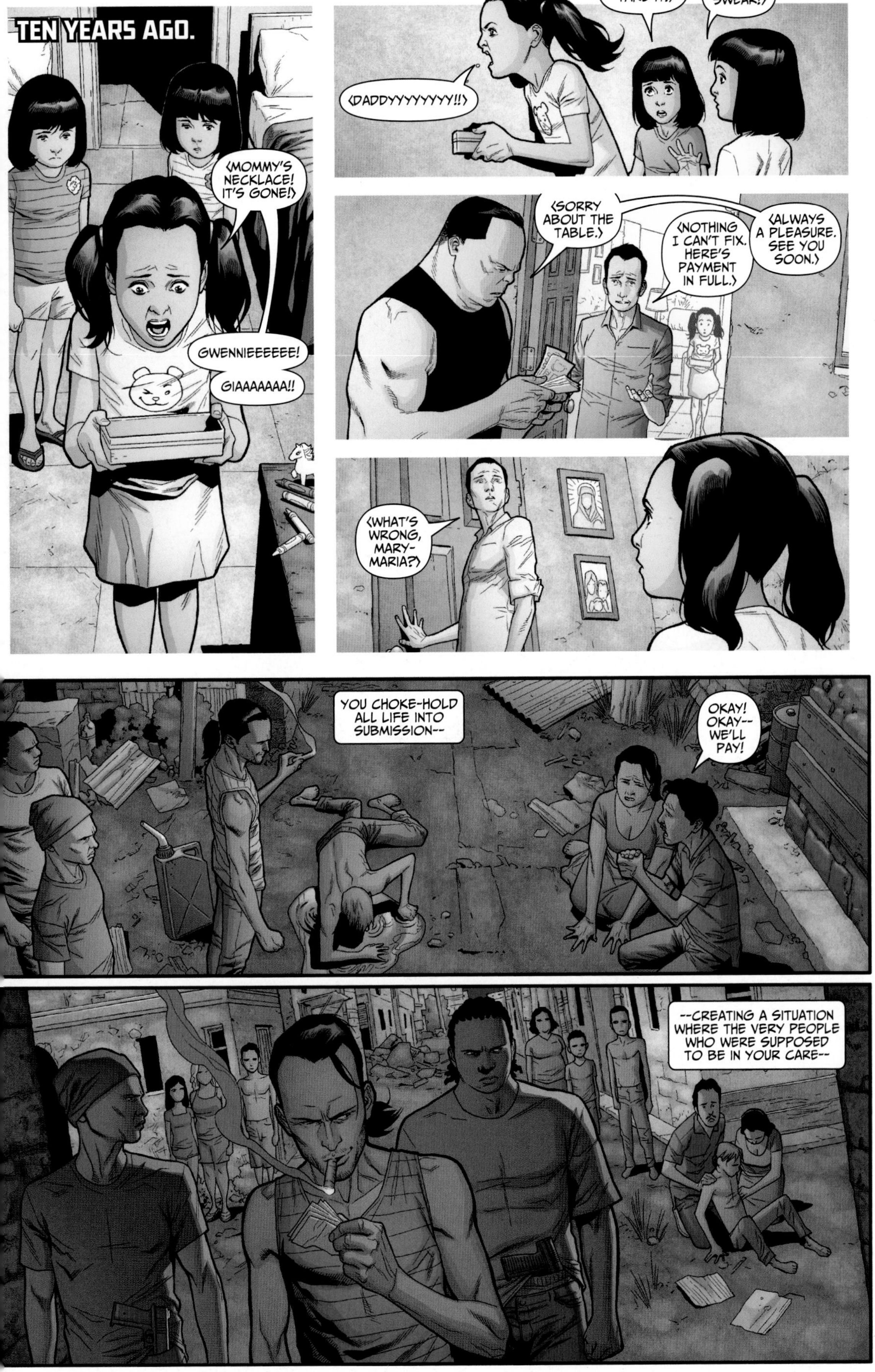
TEN YEARS AGO.
‹MOMMY'S NECKLACE! IT'S GONE!›
GWENNIEEEEEE!
GIAAAAAAA!!
‹DADDYYYYYYYY!!›
‹WE DIDN'T TAKE IT!›
‹WE SWEAR!›
‹SORRY ABOUT THE TABLE.›
‹NOTHING I CAN'T FIX. HERE'S PAYMENT IN FULL.›
‹ALWAYS A PLEASURE. SEE YOU SOON.›
‹WHAT'S WRONG, MARY-MARIA?›
YOU CHOKE-HOLD ALL LIFE INTO SUBMISSION--
OKAY! OKAY--WE'LL PAY!
--CREATING A SITUATION WHERE THE VERY PEOPLE WHO WERE SUPPOSED TO BE IN YOUR CARE--

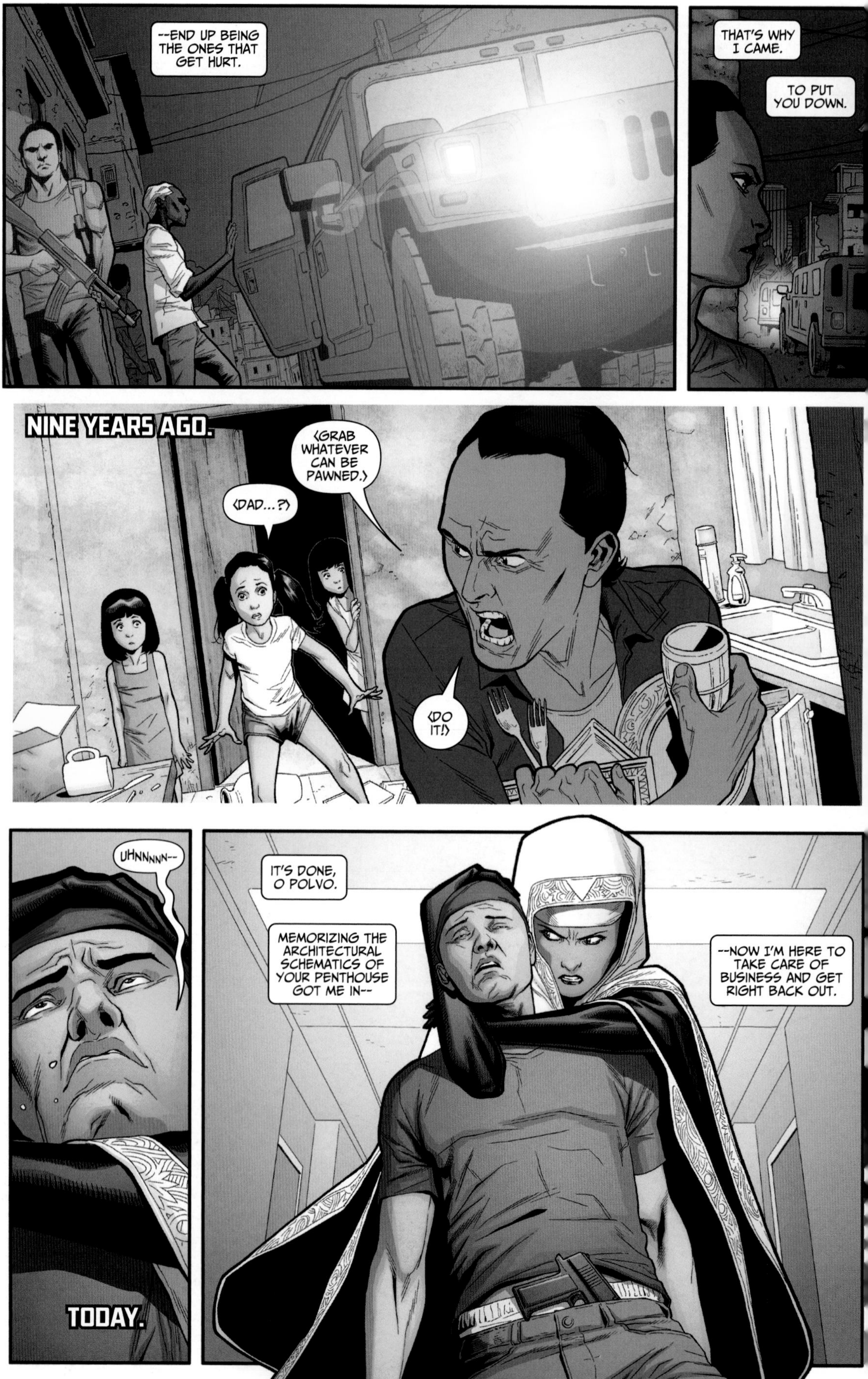
--END UP BEING THE ONES THAT GET HURT.
THAT'S WHY I CAME.
TO PUT YOU DOWN.
NINE YEARS AGO.
‹DAD...?›
‹GRAB WHATEVER CAN BE PAWNED.›
‹DO IT!›
UHNNNNN--
TODAY.
IT'S DONE, O POLVO.
MEMORIZING THE ARCHITECTURAL SCHEMATICS OF YOUR PENTHOUSE GOT ME IN--
--NOW I'M HERE TO TAKE CARE OF BUSINESS AND GET RIGHT BACK OUT.

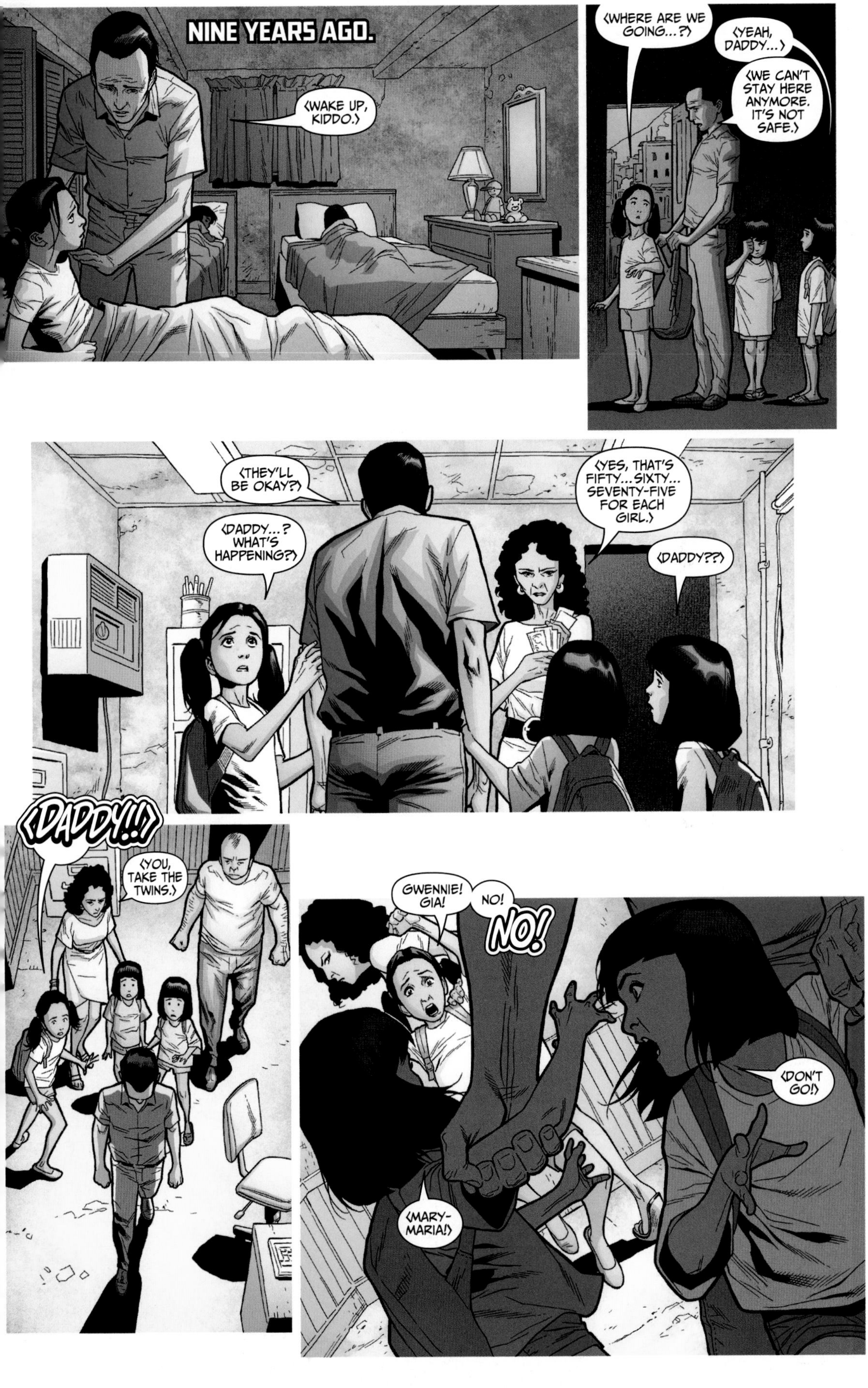
NINE YEARS AGO.
⟨WAKE UP, KIDDO.⟩
⟨WHERE ARE WE GOING...?⟩
⟨YEAH, DADDY...⟩
⟨WE CAN'T STAY HERE ANYMORE. IT'S NOT SAFE.⟩
⟨THEY'LL BE OKAY?⟩
⟨DADDY...? WHAT'S HAPPENING?⟩
⟨YES, THAT'S FIFTY... SIXTY... SEVENTY-FIVE FOR EACH GIRL.⟩
⟨DADDY??⟩
⟨DADDY!!⟩
⟨YOU, TAKE THE TWINS.⟩
GWENNIE! GIA!
NO!
NO!
⟨DON'T GO!⟩
⟨MARY-MARIA!⟩

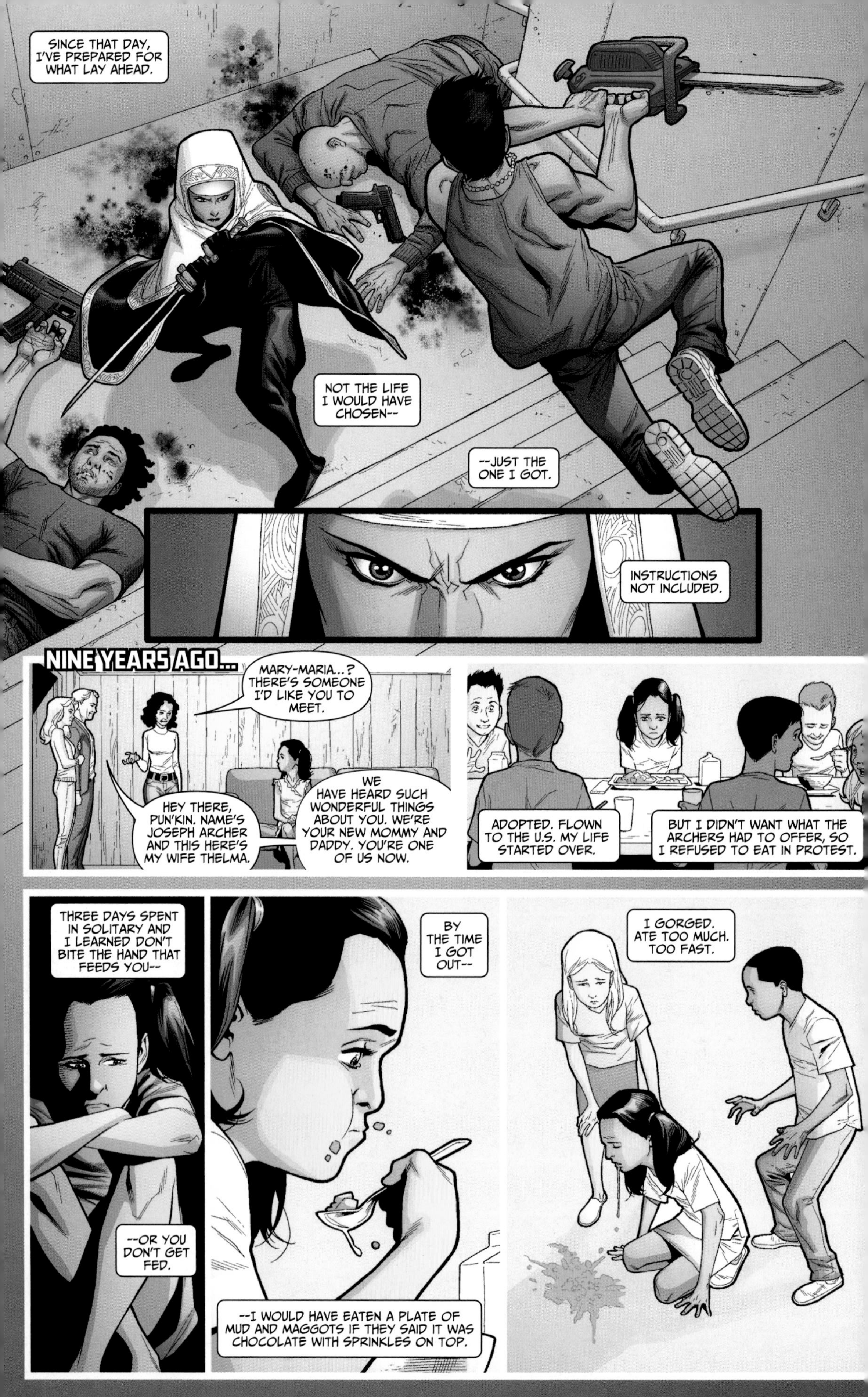
SINCE THAT DAY, I'VE PREPARED FOR WHAT LAY AHEAD.
NOT THE LIFE I WOULD HAVE CHOSEN--
--JUST THE ONE I GOT.
INSTRUCTIONS NOT INCLUDED.
NINE YEARS AGO...
MARY-MARIA...? THERE'S SOMEONE I'D LIKE YOU TO MEET.
HEY THERE, PUN'KIN. NAME'S JOSEPH ARCHER AND THIS HERE'S MY WIFE THELMA.
WE HAVE HEARD SUCH WONDERFUL THINGS ABOUT YOU. WE'RE YOUR NEW MOMMY AND DADDY. YOU'RE ONE OF US NOW.
ADOPTED. FLOWN TO THE U.S. MY LIFE STARTED OVER.
BUT I DIDN'T WANT WHAT THE ARCHERS HAD TO OFFER, SO I REFUSED TO EAT IN PROTEST.
THREE DAYS SPENT IN SOLITARY AND I LEARNED DON'T BITE THE HAND THAT FEEDS YOU--
--OR YOU DON'T GET FED.
BY THE TIME I GOT OUT--
--I WOULD HAVE EATEN A PLATE OF MUD AND MAGGOTS IF THEY SAID IT WAS CHOCOLATE WITH SPRINKLES ON TOP.
I GORGED. ATE TOO MUCH. TOO FAST.

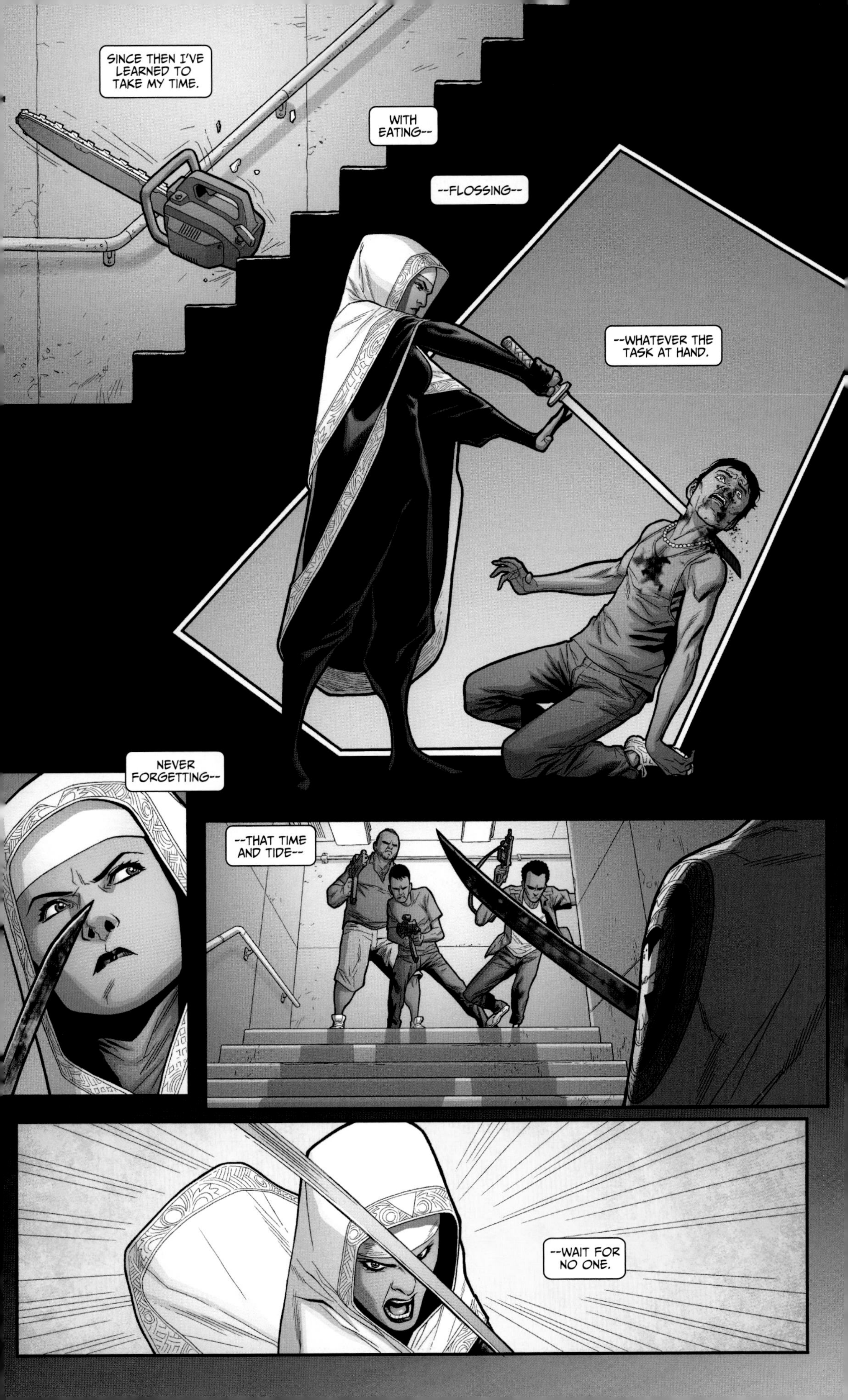
SINCE THEN I'VE LEARNED TO TAKE MY TIME.
WITH EATING--
--FLOSSING--
--WHATEVER THE TASK AT HAND.
NEVER FORGETTING--
--THAT TIME AND TIDE--
--WAIT FOR NO ONE.

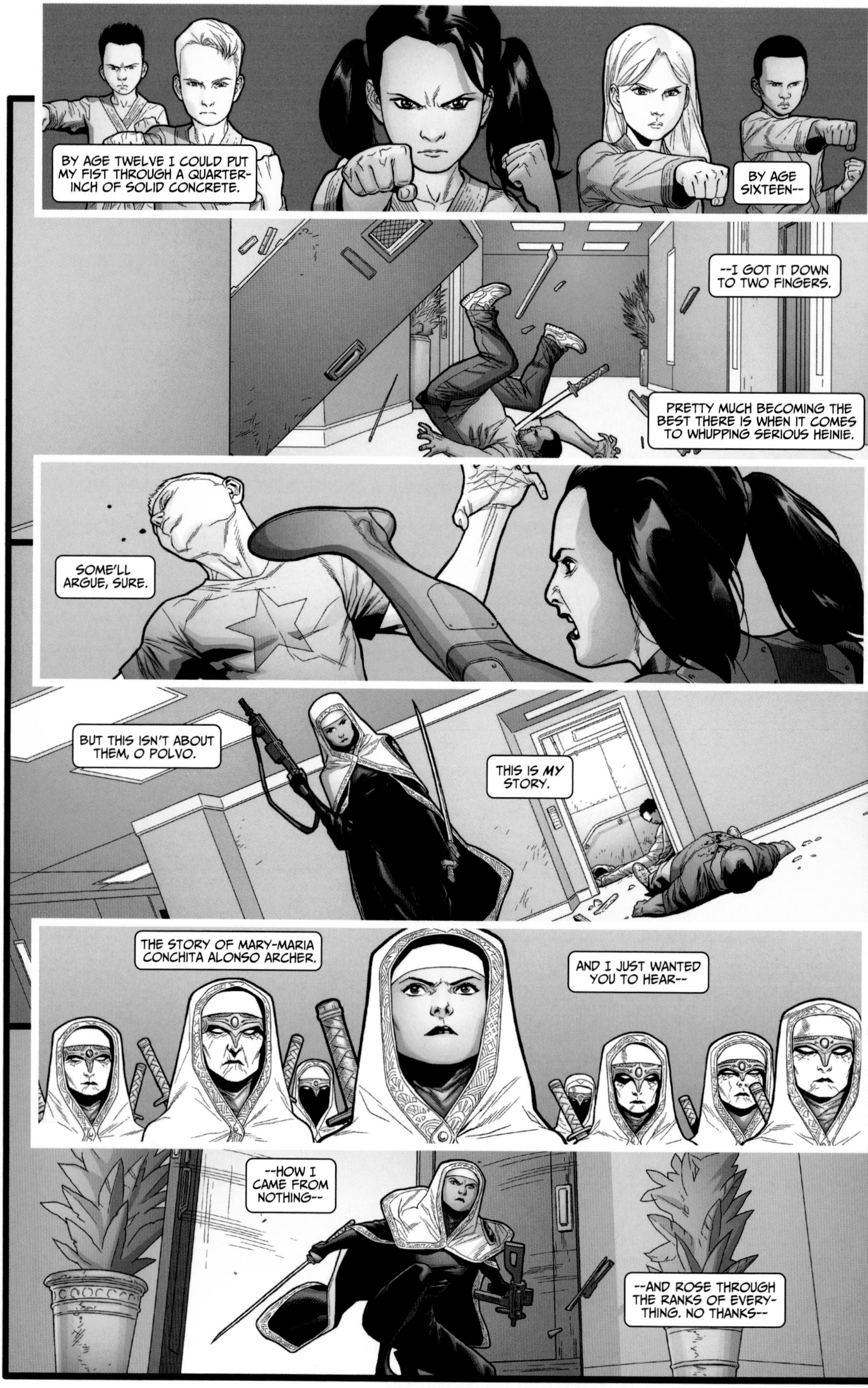
BY AGE TWELVE I COULD PUT MY FIST THROUGH A QUARTER-INCH OF SOLID CONCRETE.
BY AGE SIXTEEN--
--I GOT IT DOWN TO TWO FINGERS.
PRETTY MUCH BECOMING THE BEST THERE IS WHEN IT COMES TO WHUPPING SERIOUS HEINIE.
SOME'LL ARGUE, SURE.
BUT THIS ISN'T ABOUT THEM, O POLVO.
THIS IS MY STORY.
THE STORY OF MARY-MARIA CONCHITA ALONSO ARCHER.
AND I JUST WANTED YOU TO HEAR--
--HOW I CAME FROM NOTHING--
--AND ROSE THROUGH THE RANKS OF EVERY-THING. NO THANKS--

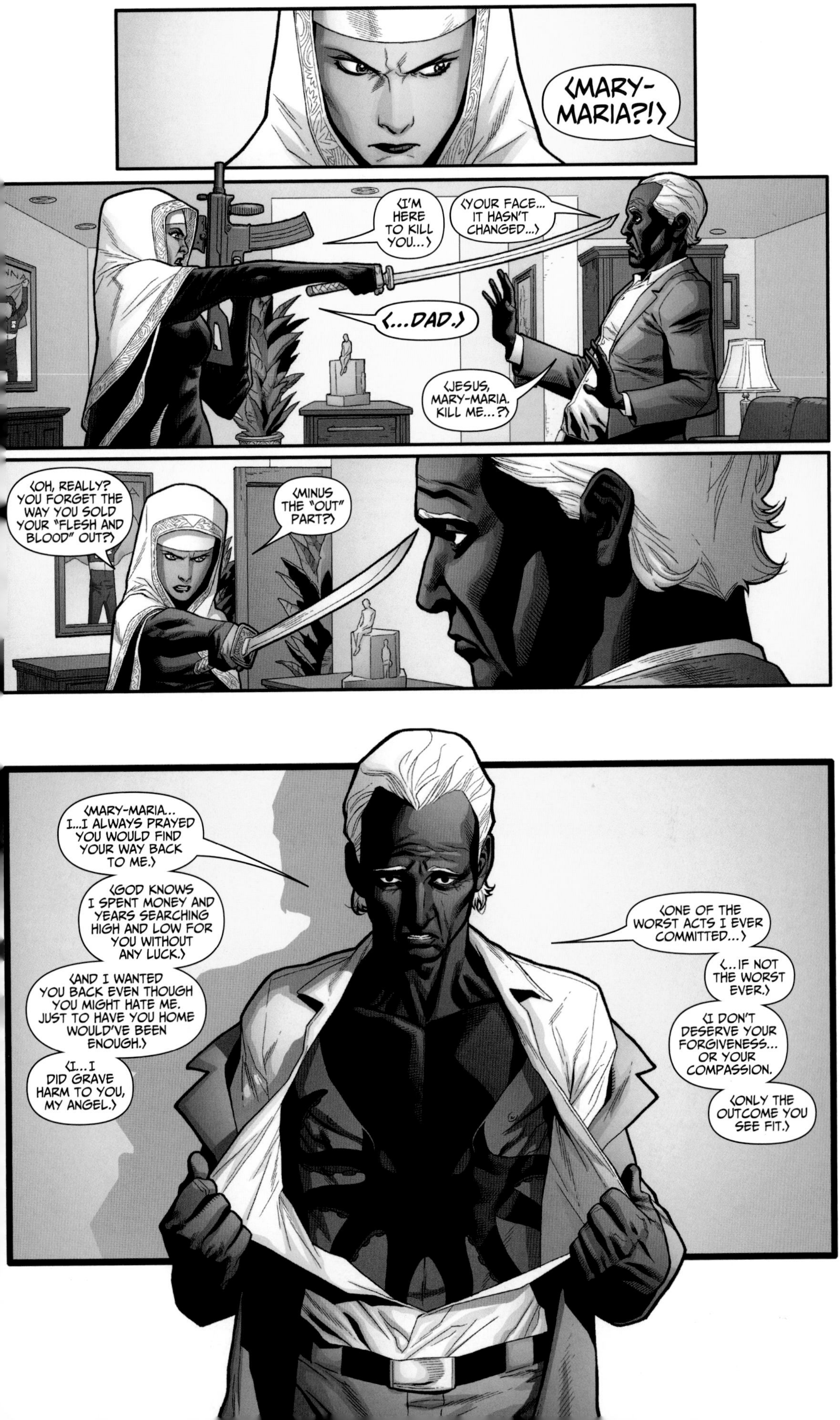

⟨MARY-MARIA?!⟩
⟨I'M HERE TO KILL YOU...⟩
⟨YOUR FACE... IT HASN'T CHANGED...⟩
⟨...DAD.⟩
⟨JESUS, MARY-MARIA. KILL ME...?⟩
⟨OH, REALLY? YOU FORGET THE WAY YOU SOLD YOUR "FLESH AND BLOOD" OUT?⟩
⟨MINUS THE "OUT" PART?⟩
⟨MARY-MARIA... I...I ALWAYS PRAYED YOU WOULD FIND YOUR WAY BACK TO ME.⟩
⟨GOD KNOWS I SPENT MONEY AND YEARS SEARCHING HIGH AND LOW FOR YOU WITHOUT ANY LUCK.⟩
⟨AND I WANTED YOU BACK EVEN THOUGH YOU MIGHT HATE ME. JUST TO HAVE YOU HOME WOULD'VE BEEN ENOUGH.⟩
⟨I...I DID GRAVE HARM TO YOU, MY ANGEL.⟩
⟨ONE OF THE WORST ACTS I EVER COMMITTED...⟩
⟨...IF NOT THE WORST EVER.⟩
⟨I DON'T DESERVE YOUR FORGIVENESS... OR YOUR COMPASSION.
⟨ONLY THE OUTCOME YOU SEE FIT.⟩

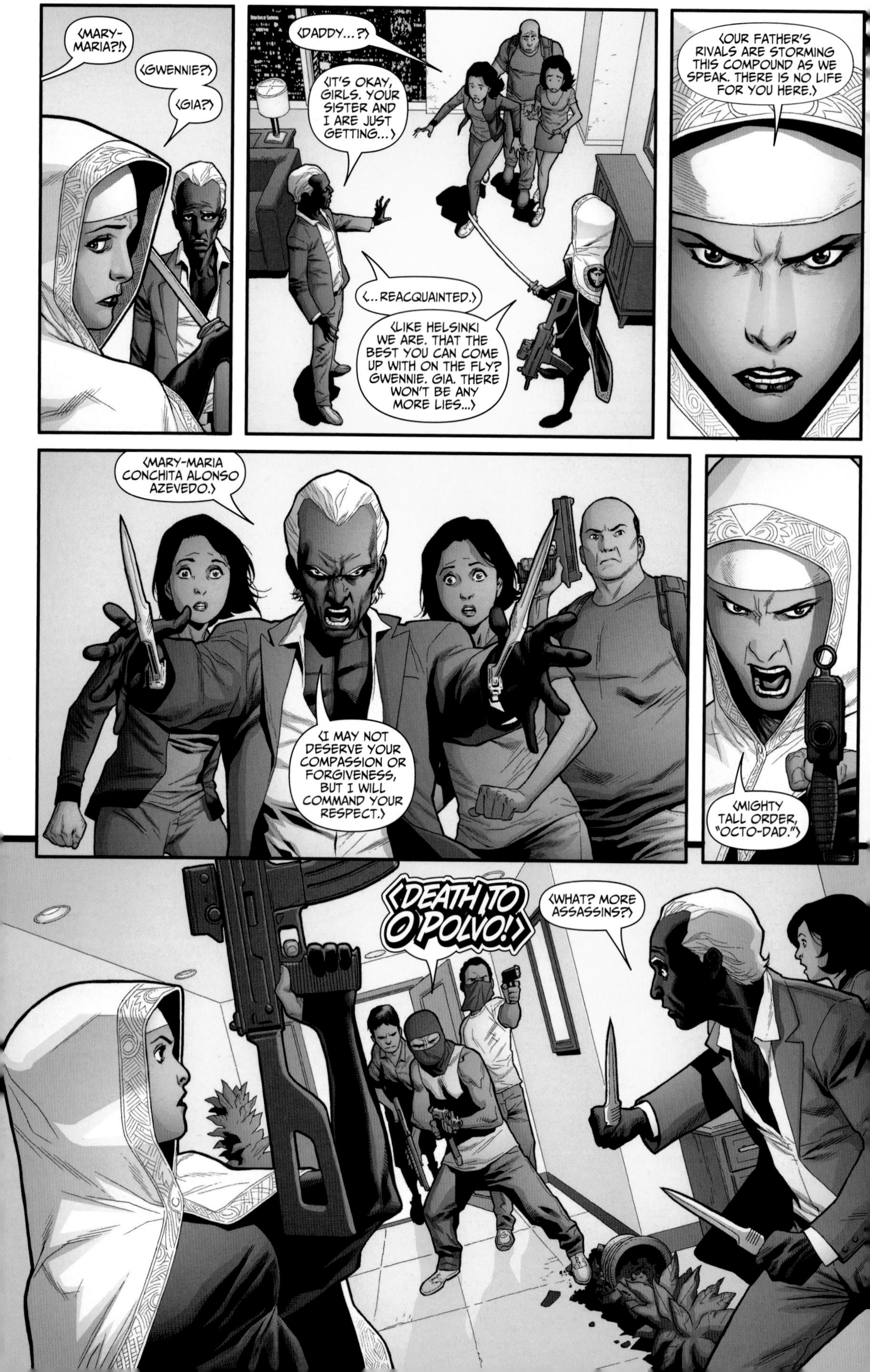

<MARY-MARIA?!>
<GWENNIE?>
<GIA?>
<DADDY...?>
<IT'S OKAY, GIRLS. YOUR SISTER AND I ARE JUST GETTING...>
<...REACQUAINTED.>
<LIKE HELSINKI WE ARE. THAT THE BEST YOU CAN COME UP WITH ON THE FLY? GWENNIE. GIA. THERE WON'T BE ANY MORE LIES...>
<OUR FATHER'S RIVALS ARE STORMING THIS COMPOUND AS WE SPEAK. THERE IS NO LIFE FOR YOU HERE.>
<MARY-MARIA CONCHITA ALONSO AZEVEDO.>
<I MAY NOT DESERVE YOUR COMPASSION OR FORGIVENESS, BUT I WILL COMMAND YOUR RESPECT.>
<MIGHTY TALL ORDER, "OCTO-DAD.">
<DEATH TO O POLVO!>
<WHAT? MORE ASSASSINS?>

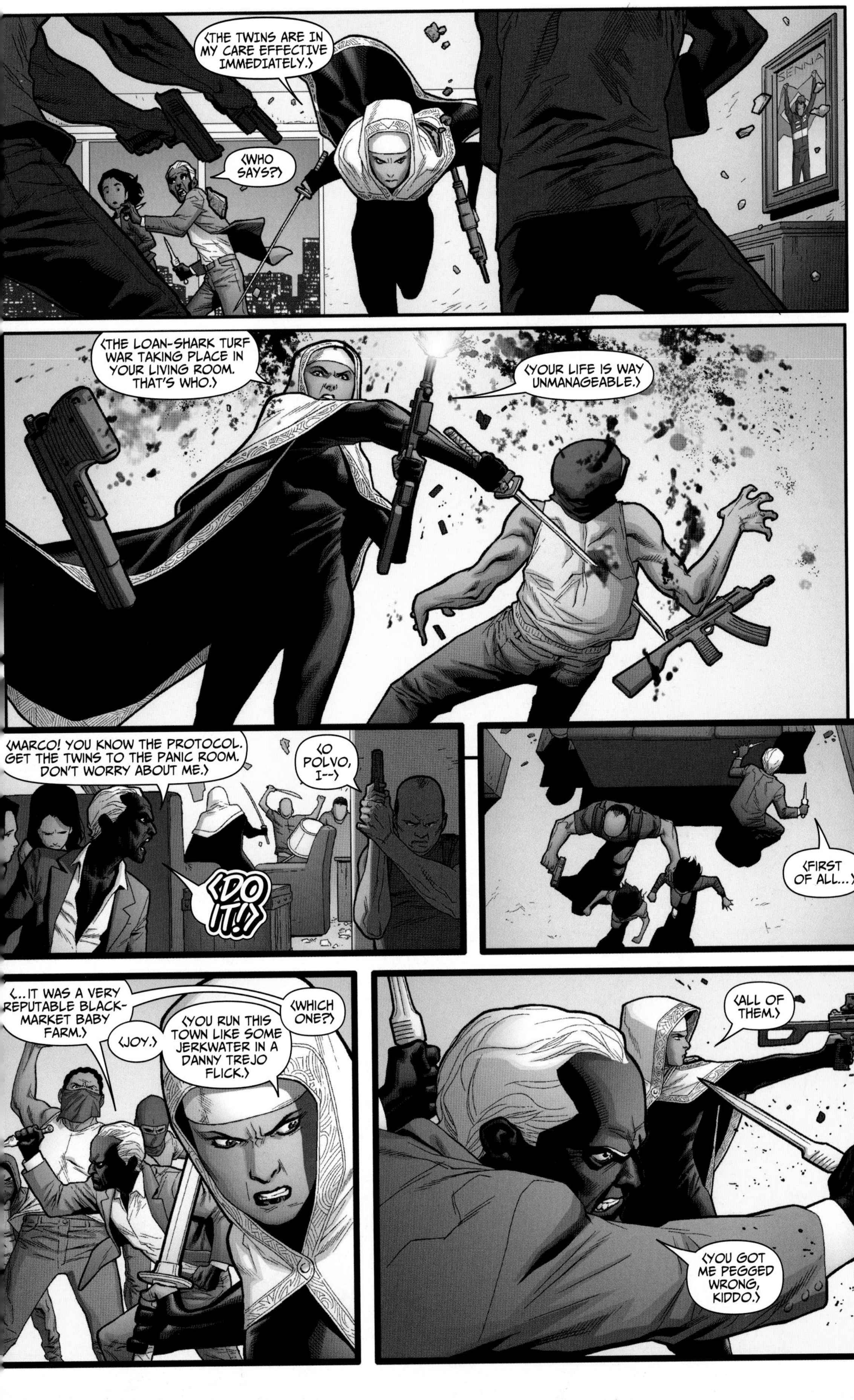
‹THE TWINS ARE IN MY CARE EFFECTIVE IMMEDIATELY.›
‹WHO SAYS?›
‹THE LOAN-SHARK TURF WAR TAKING PLACE IN YOUR LIVING ROOM. THAT'S WHO.›
‹YOUR LIFE IS WAY UNMANAGEABLE.›
‹MARCO! YOU KNOW THE PROTOCOL. GET THE TWINS TO THE PANIC ROOM. DON'T WORRY ABOUT ME.›
‹O POLVO, I--›
‹DO IT!›
‹FIRST OF ALL...›
‹...IT WAS A VERY REPUTABLE BLACK-MARKET BABY FARM.›
‹JOY.›
‹WHICH ONE?›
‹YOU RUN THIS TOWN LIKE SOME JERKWATER IN A DANNY TREJO FLICK.›
‹ALL OF THEM.›
‹YOU GOT ME PEGGED WRONG, KIDDO.›

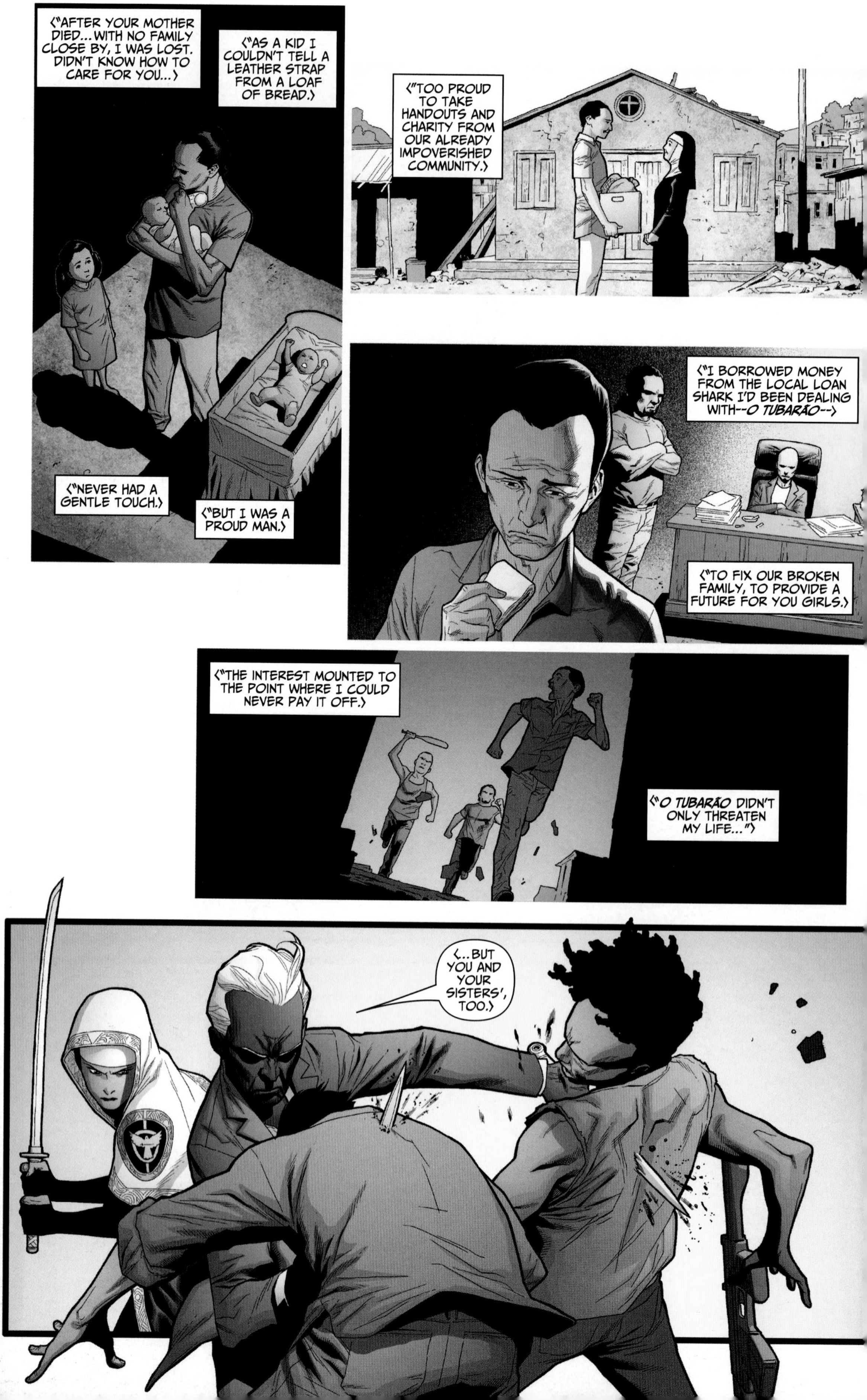
‹"AFTER YOUR MOTHER DIED...WITH NO FAMILY CLOSE BY, I WAS LOST. DIDN'T KNOW HOW TO CARE FOR YOU...›
‹"AS A KID I COULDN'T TELL A LEATHER STRAP FROM A LOAF OF BREAD.›
‹"NEVER HAD A GENTLE TOUCH.›
‹"BUT I WAS A PROUD MAN.›
‹"TOO PROUD TO TAKE HANDOUTS AND CHARITY FROM OUR ALREADY IMPOVERISHED COMMUNITY.›
‹"I BORROWED MONEY FROM THE LOCAL LOAN SHARK I'D BEEN DEALING WITH--*O TUBARÃO*--›
‹"TO FIX OUR BROKEN FAMILY, TO PROVIDE A FUTURE FOR YOU GIRLS.›
‹"THE INTEREST MOUNTED TO THE POINT WHERE I COULD NEVER PAY IT OFF.›
‹"*O TUBARÃO* DIDN'T ONLY THREATEN MY LIFE..."›
‹...BUT YOU AND YOUR SISTERS', TOO.›

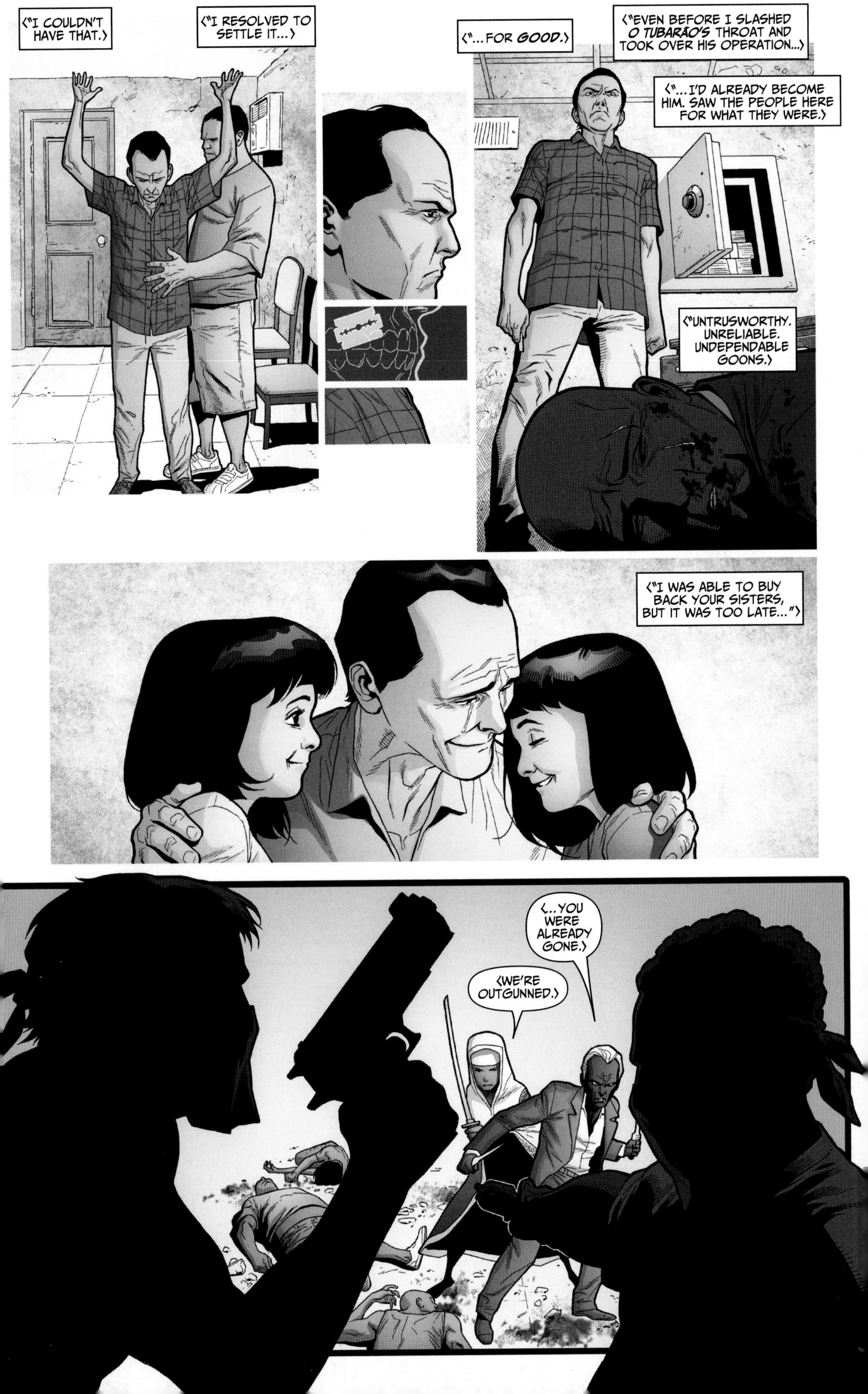

<"I COULDN'T HAVE THAT.>
<"I RESOLVED TO SETTLE IT...>
<"...FOR GOOD.>
<"EVEN BEFORE I SLASHED O TUBARÃO'S THROAT AND TOOK OVER HIS OPERATION...>
<"...I'D ALREADY BECOME HIM. SAW THE PEOPLE HERE FOR WHAT THEY WERE.>
<"UNTRUSWORTHY. UNRELIABLE. UNDEPENDABLE GOONS.>
<"I WAS ABLE TO BUY BACK YOUR SISTERS, BUT IT WAS TOO LATE...">
<...YOU WERE ALREADY GONE.>
<WE'RE OUTGUNNED.>

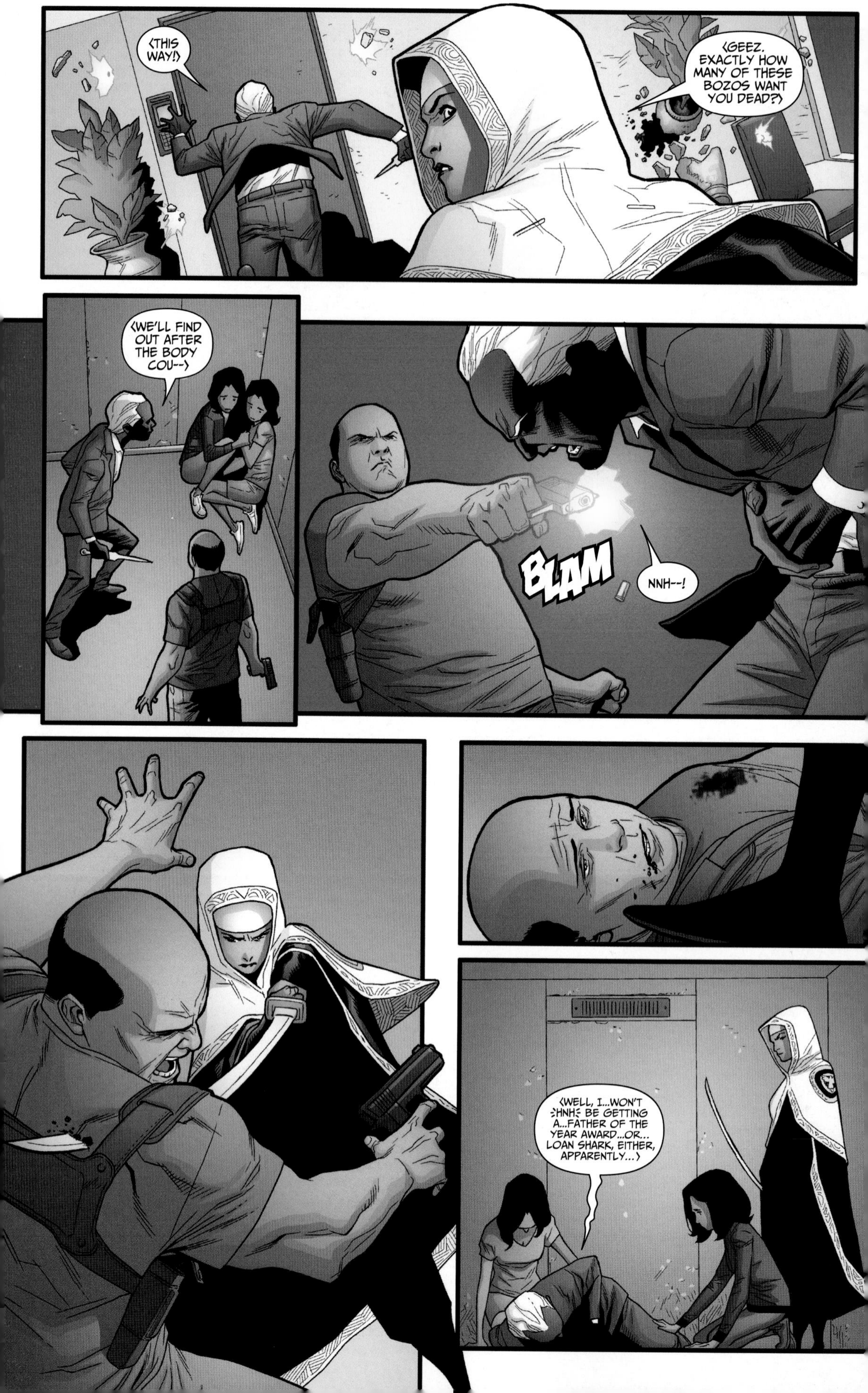

‹THIS WAY!›
‹GEEZ. EXACTLY HOW MANY OF THESE BOZOS WANT YOU DEAD?›
‹WE'LL FIND OUT AFTER THE BODY COU--›
BLAM
NNH--!
‹WELL, I...WON'T ≈HNH≈ BE GETTING A...FATHER OF THE YEAR AWARD...OR... LOAN SHARK, EITHER, APPARENTLY...›

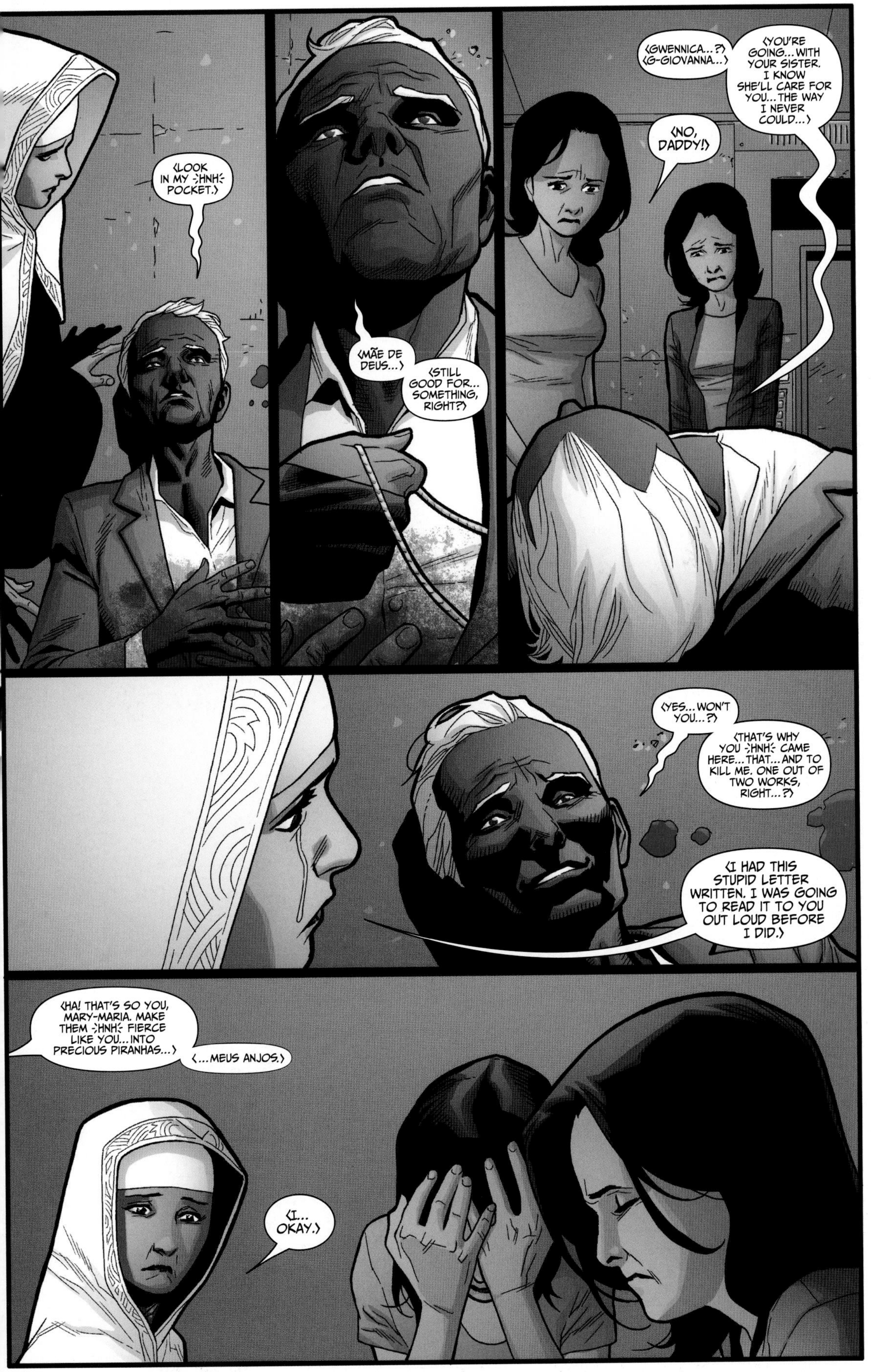
<LOOK IN MY -HNH- POCKET.>
<MÃE DE DEUS...>
<STILL GOOD FOR... SOMETHING, RIGHT?>
<GWENNICA...?> <G-GIOVANNA...>
<YOU'RE GOING... WITH YOUR SISTER. I KNOW SHE'LL CARE FOR YOU... THE WAY I NEVER COULD...>
<NO, DADDY!>
<YES... WON'T YOU...?>
<THAT'S WHY YOU -HNH- CAME HERE... THAT... AND TO KILL ME. ONE OUT OF TWO WORKS, RIGHT...?>
<I HAD THIS STUPID LETTER WRITTEN. I WAS GOING TO READ IT TO YOU OUT LOUD BEFORE I DID.>
<HA! THAT'S SO YOU, MARY-MARIA. MAKE THEM -HNH- FIERCE LIKE YOU... INTO PRECIOUS PIRANHAS...>
<...MEUS ANJOS.>
<I... OKAY.>

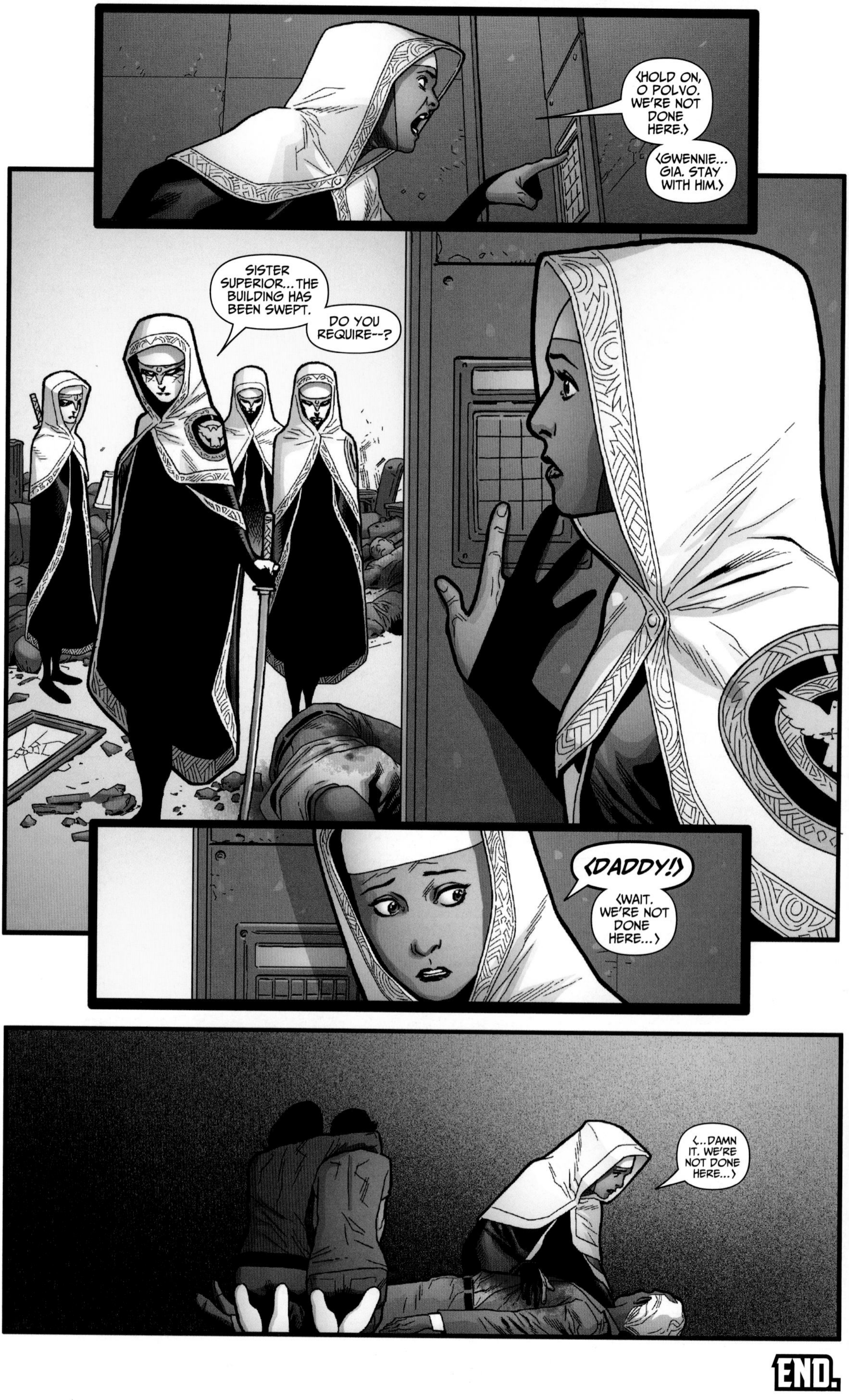

‹HOLD ON, O POLVO. WE'RE NOT DONE HERE.›
‹GWENNIE... GIA. STAY WITH HIM.›
SISTER SUPERIOR...THE BUILDING HAS BEEN SWEPT.
DO YOU REQUIRE--?
‹DADDY!›
‹WAIT. WE'RE NOT DONE HERE...›
‹...DAMN IT. WE'RE NOT DONE HERE...›
END.

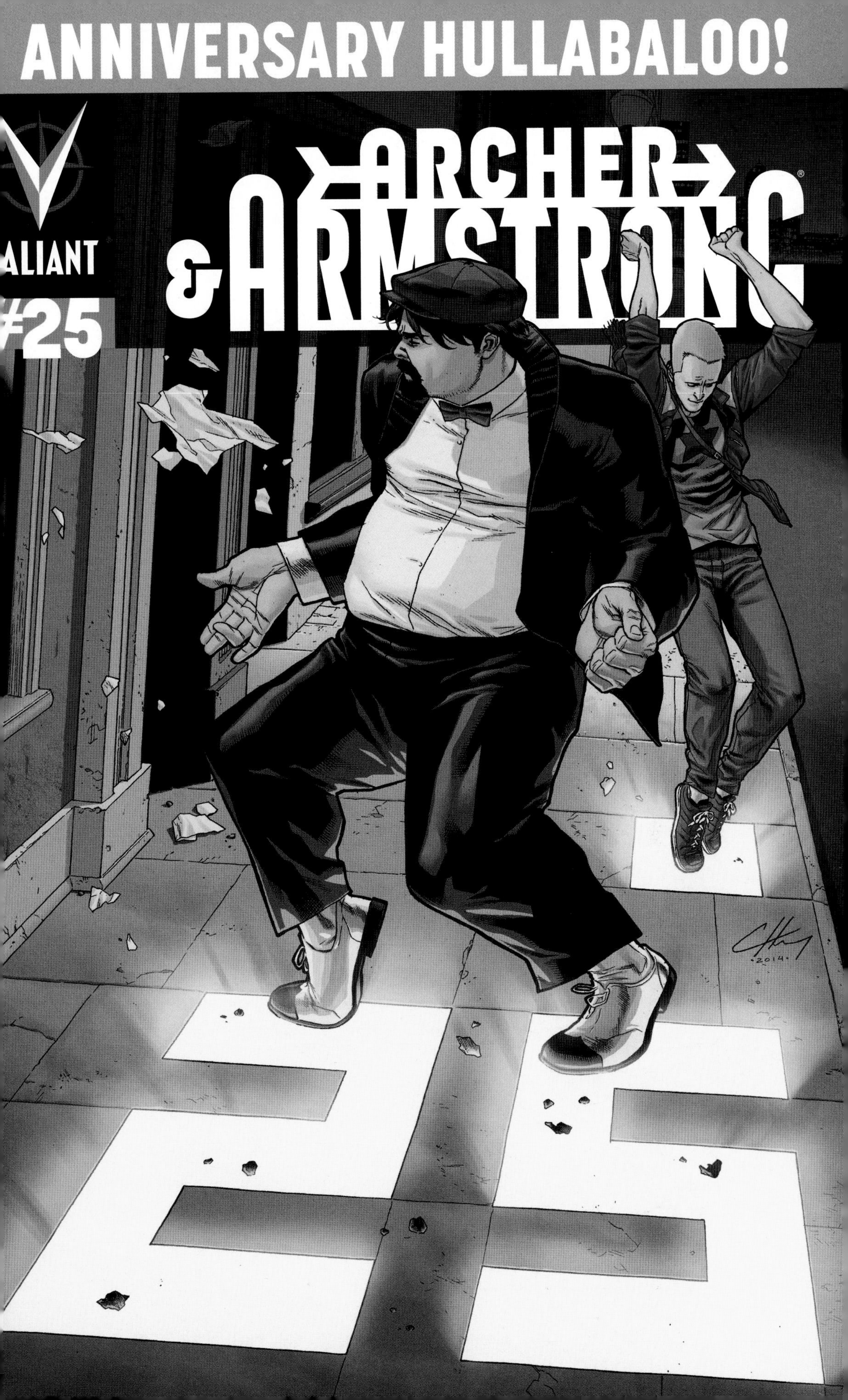

ANNIVERSARY HULLABALOO!
VALIANT
ARCHER & ARMSTRONG
#25
2014

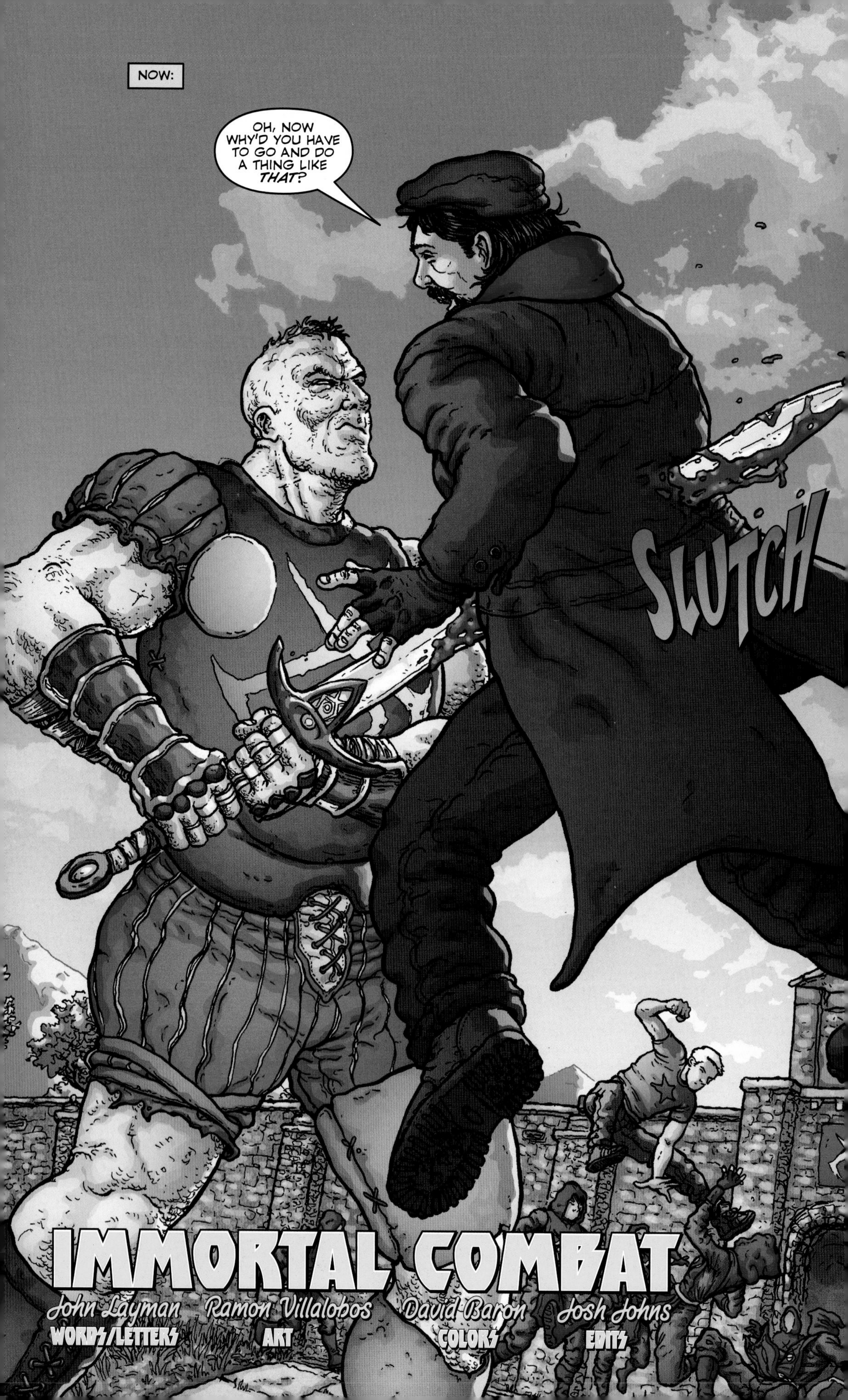
NOW:
OH, NOW WHY'D YOU HAVE TO GO AND DO A THING LIKE *THAT*?
SLUTCH
IMMORTAL COMBAT
John Layman WORDS/LETTERS
Ramon Villalobos ART
David Baron COLORS
Josh Johns EDITS

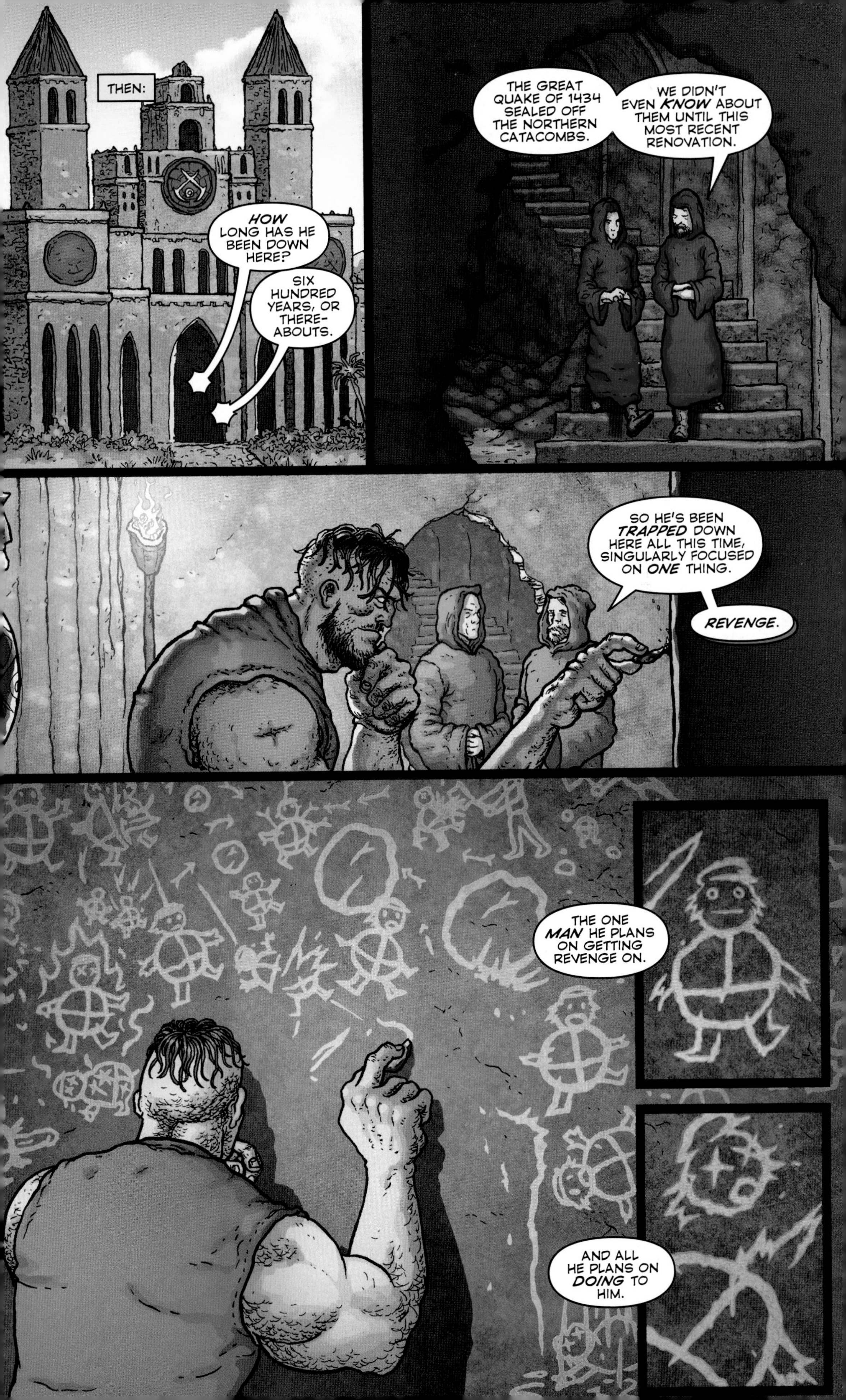
THEN:
HOW LONG HAS HE BEEN DOWN HERE?
SIX HUNDRED YEARS, OR THERE-ABOUTS.
THE GREAT QUAKE OF 1434 SEALED OFF THE NORTHERN CATACOMBS.
WE DIDN'T EVEN KNOW ABOUT THEM UNTIL THIS MOST RECENT RENOVATION.
SO HE'S BEEN TRAPPED DOWN HERE ALL THIS TIME, SINGULARLY FOCUSED ON ONE THING.
REVENGE.
THE ONE MAN HE PLANS ON GETTING REVENGE ON.
AND ALL HE PLANS ON DOING TO HIM.

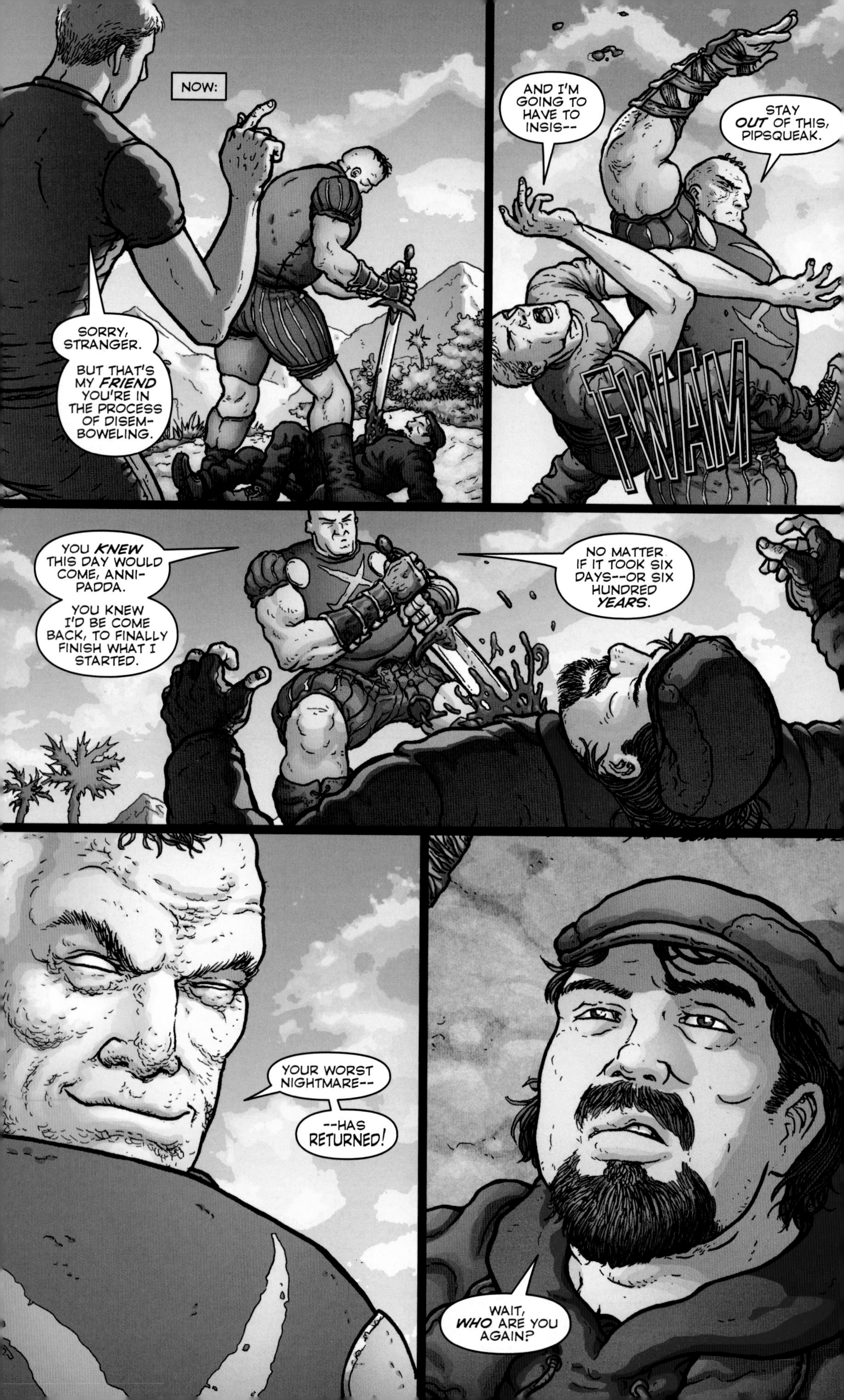
NOW:
SORRY, STRANGER.
BUT THAT'S MY FRIEND YOU'RE IN THE PROCESS OF DISEMBOWELING.
AND I'M GOING TO HAVE TO INSIS--
STAY OUT OF THIS, PIPSQUEAK.
FWAM
YOU KNEW THIS DAY WOULD COME, ANNI-PADDA.
YOU KNEW I'D BE COME BACK, TO FINALLY FINISH WHAT I STARTED.
NO MATTER IF IT TOOK SIX DAYS--OR SIX HUNDRED YEARS.
YOUR WORST NIGHTMARE--
--HAS RETURNED!
WAIT, WHO ARE YOU AGAIN?

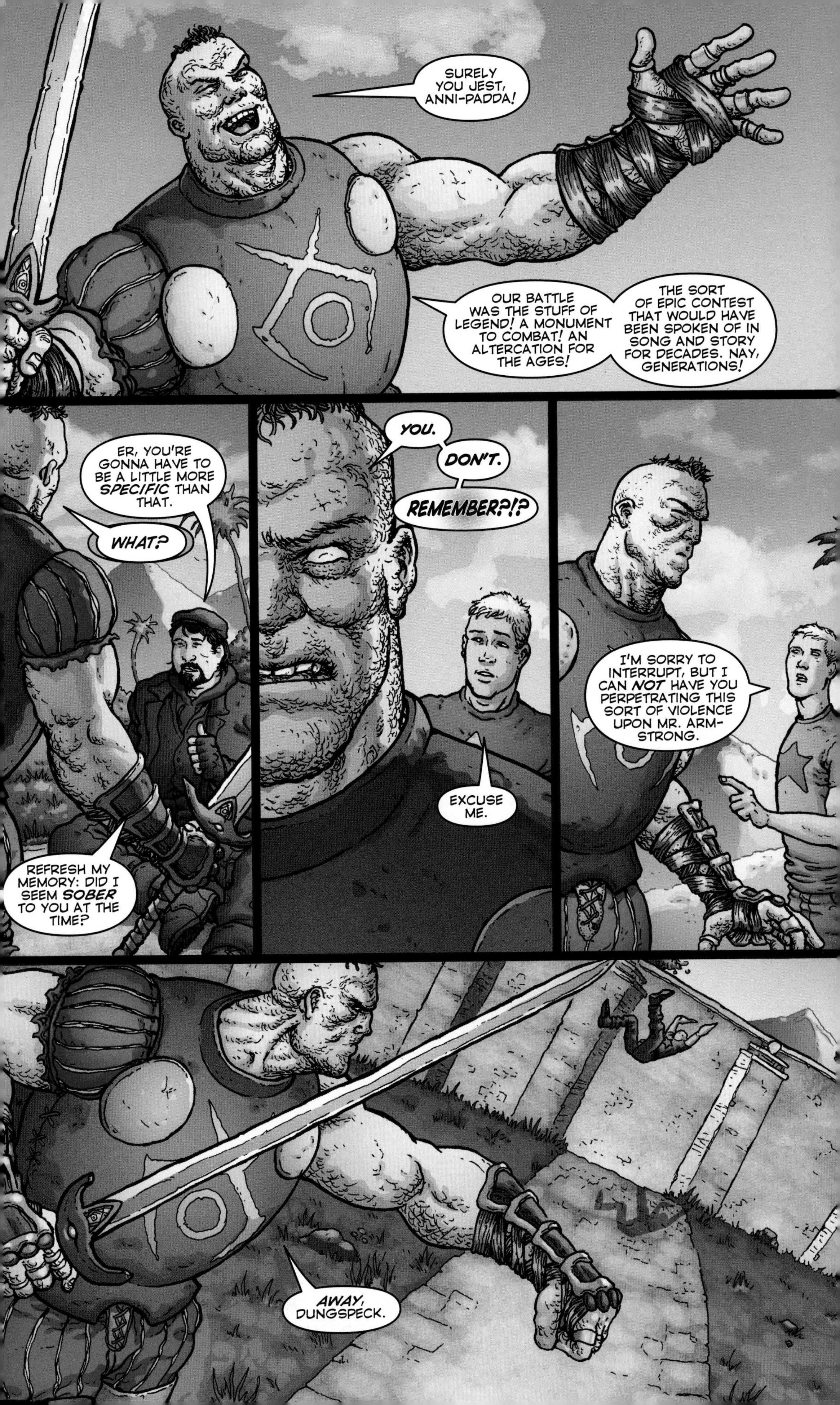
SURELY YOU JEST, ANNI-PADDA!
OUR BATTLE WAS THE STUFF OF LEGEND! A MONUMENT TO COMBAT! AN ALTERCATION FOR THE AGES!
THE SORT OF EPIC CONTEST THAT WOULD HAVE BEEN SPOKEN OF IN SONG AND STORY FOR DECADES. NAY, GENERATIONS!
ER, YOU'RE GONNA HAVE TO BE A LITTLE MORE *SPECIFIC* THAN THAT.
WHAT?
REFRESH MY MEMORY: DID I SEEM *SOBER* TO YOU AT THE TIME?
YOU.
DON'T.
REMEMBER?!?
EXCUSE ME.
I'M SORRY TO INTERRUPT, BUT I CAN *NOT* HAVE YOU PERPETRATING THIS SORT OF VIOLENCE UPON MR. ARM-STRONG.
AWAY, DUNGSPECK.

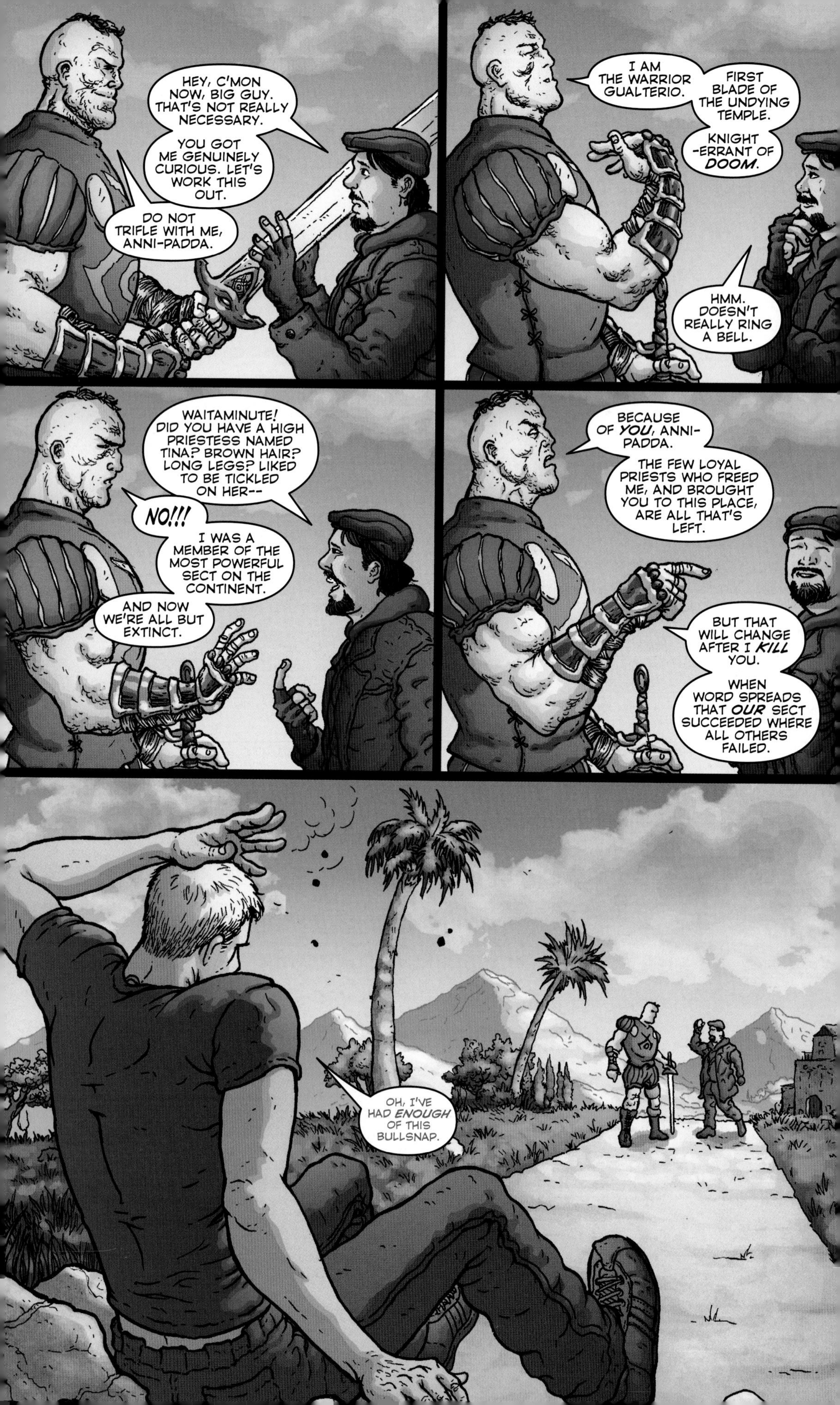
HEY, C'MON NOW, BIG GUY. THAT'S NOT REALLY NECESSARY.
YOU GOT ME GENUINELY CURIOUS. LET'S WORK THIS OUT.
DO NOT TRIFLE WITH ME, ANNI-PADDA.
I AM THE WARRIOR GUALTERIO.
FIRST BLADE OF THE UNDYING TEMPLE.
KNIGHT -ERRANT OF DOOM.
HMM. DOESN'T REALLY RING A BELL.
WAITAMINUTE! DID YOU HAVE A HIGH PRIESTESS NAMED TINA? BROWN HAIR? LONG LEGS? LIKED TO BE TICKLED ON HER--
NO!!!
I WAS A MEMBER OF THE MOST POWERFUL SECT ON THE CONTINENT.
AND NOW WE'RE ALL BUT EXTINCT.
BECAUSE OF YOU, ANNI-PADDA.
THE FEW LOYAL PRIESTS WHO FREED ME, AND BROUGHT YOU TO THIS PLACE, ARE ALL THAT'S LEFT.
BUT THAT WILL CHANGE AFTER I KILL YOU.
WHEN WORD SPREADS THAT OUR SECT SUCCEEDED WHERE ALL OTHERS FAILED.
OH, I'VE HAD ENOUGH OF THIS BULLSNAP.

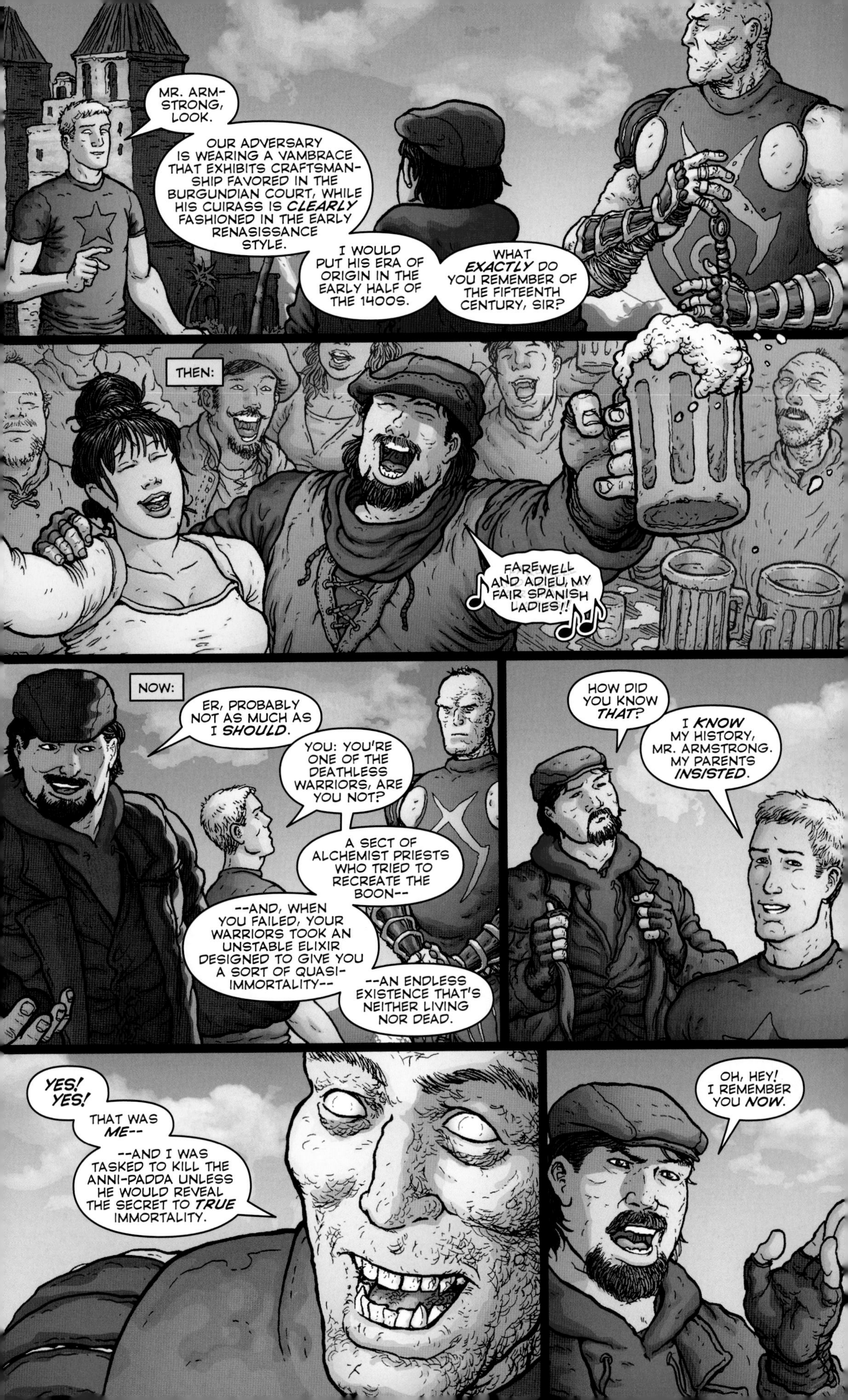

MR. ARM-STRONG, LOOK.
OUR ADVERSARY IS WEARING A VAMBRACE THAT EXHIBITS CRAFTSMANSHIP FAVORED IN THE BURGUNDIAN COURT, WHILE HIS CUIRASS IS *CLEARLY* FASHIONED IN THE EARLY RENASISSANCE STYLE.
I WOULD PUT HIS ERA OF ORIGIN IN THE EARLY HALF OF THE 1400S.
WHAT *EXACTLY* DO YOU REMEMBER OF THE FIFTEENTH CENTURY, SIR?
THEN:
FAREWELL AND ADIEU, MY FAIR SPANISH LADIES!!
NOW:
ER, PROBABLY NOT AS MUCH AS I *SHOULD*.
YOU: YOU'RE ONE OF THE DEATHLESS WARRIORS, ARE YOU NOT?
A SECT OF ALCHEMIST PRIESTS WHO TRIED TO RECREATE THE BOON--
--AND, WHEN YOU FAILED, YOUR WARRIORS TOOK AN UNSTABLE ELIXIR DESIGNED TO GIVE YOU A SORT OF QUASI-IMMORTALITY--
--AN ENDLESS EXISTENCE THAT'S NEITHER LIVING NOR DEAD.
HOW DID YOU KNOW *THAT*?
I *KNOW* MY HISTORY, MR. ARMSTRONG. MY PARENTS *INSISTED*.
YES! YES!
THAT WAS *ME*--
--AND I WAS TASKED TO KILL THE ANNI-PADDA UNLESS HE WOULD REVEAL THE SECRET TO *TRUE* IMMORTALITY.
OH, HEY! I REMEMBER YOU *NOW*.

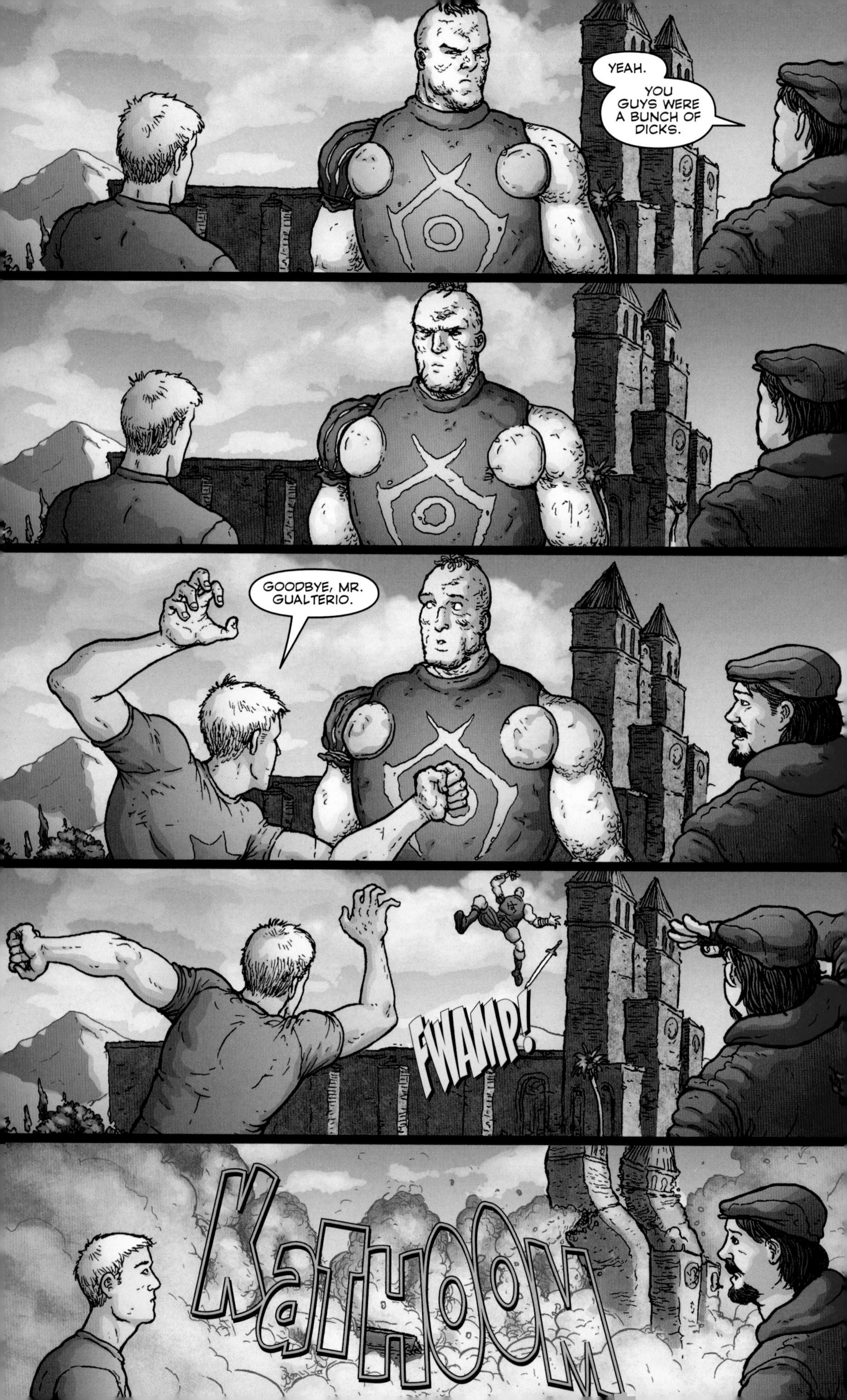
YEAH.
YOU GUYS WERE A BUNCH OF DICKS.
GOODBYE, MR. GUALTERIO.
FWAMP!
KATHOOOM

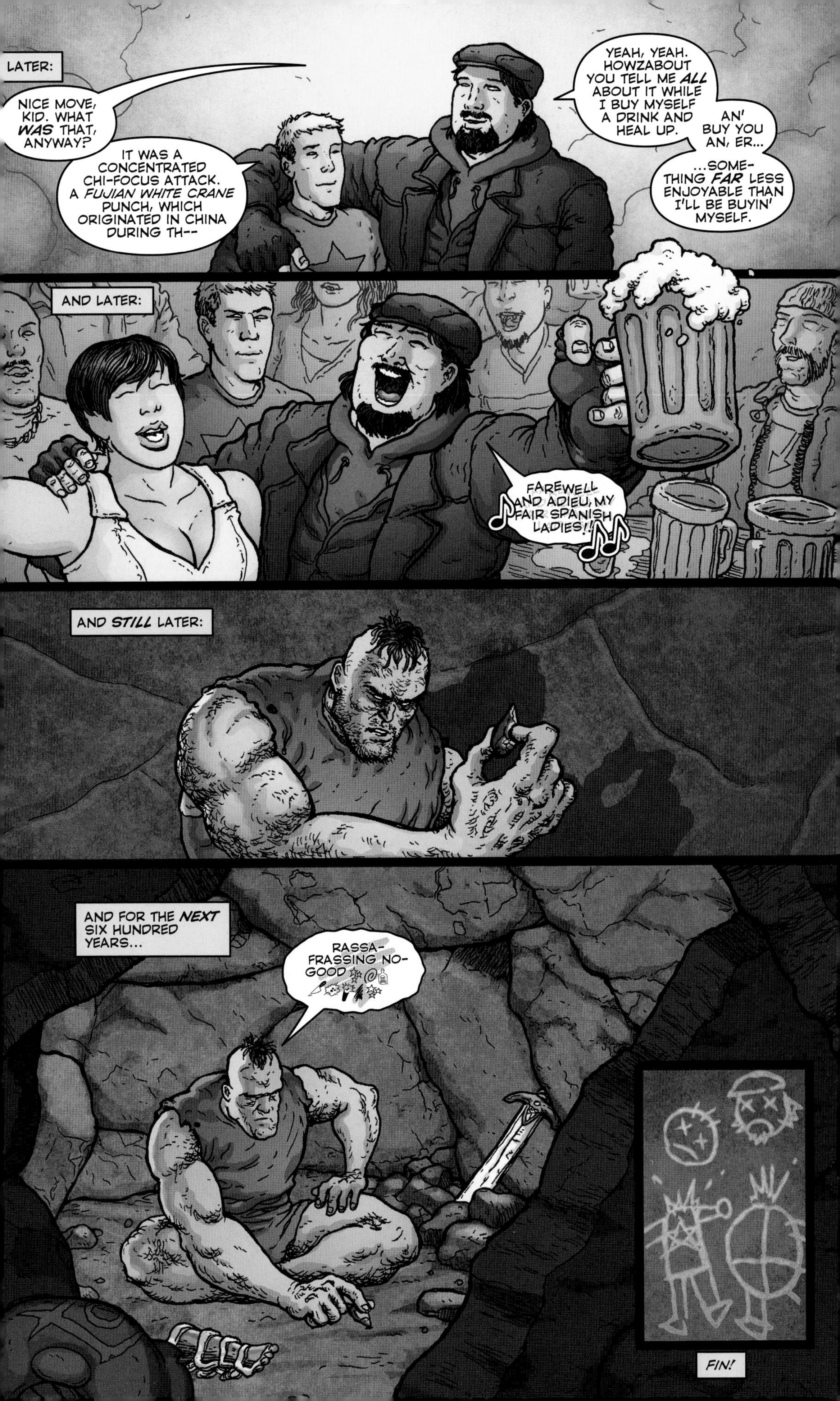
LATER:
NICE MOVE, KID. WHAT WAS THAT, ANYWAY?
IT WAS A CONCENTRATED CHI-FOCUS ATTACK. A FUJIAN WHITE CRANE PUNCH, WHICH ORIGINATED IN CHINA DURING TH--
YEAH, YEAH. HOWZABOUT YOU TELL ME ALL ABOUT IT WHILE I BUY MYSELF A DRINK AND HEAL UP.
AN' BUY YOU AN, ER...
...SOMETHING FAR LESS ENJOYABLE THAN I'LL BE BUYIN' MYSELF.
AND LATER:
FAREWELL AND ADIEU, MY FAIR SPANISH LADIES!!
AND STILL LATER:
AND FOR THE NEXT SIX HUNDRED YEARS...
RASSA-FRASSING NO-GOOD
FIN!

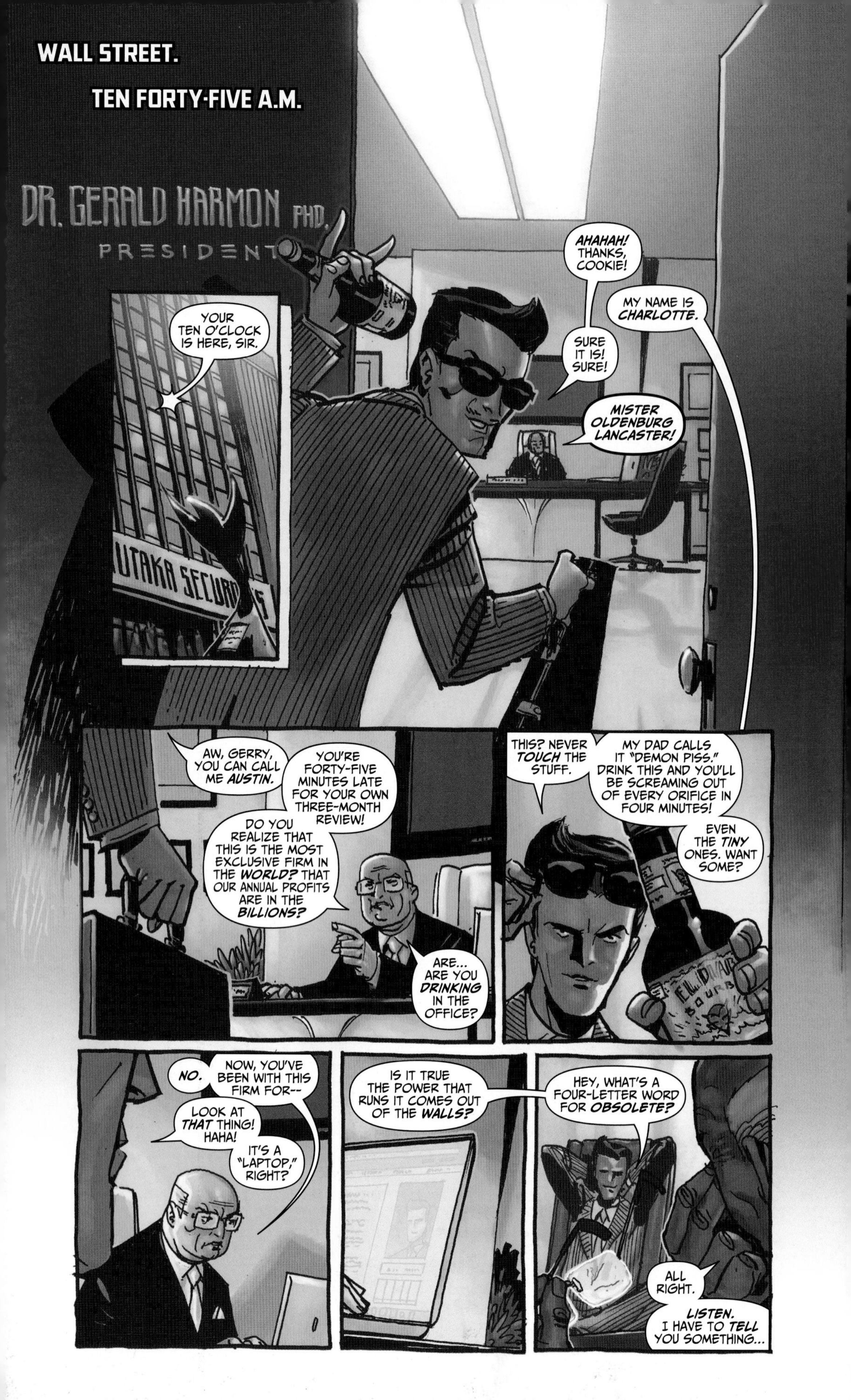
WALL STREET.
TEN FORTY-FIVE A.M.
DR. GERALD HARMON PHD.
PRESIDENT
YOUR TEN O'CLOCK IS HERE, SIR.
AHAHAH! THANKS, COOKIE!
MY NAME IS CHARLOTTE.
SURE IT IS! SURE!
MISTER OLDENBURG LANCASTER!
UTAKA SECURITIES
AW, GERRY, YOU CAN CALL ME AUSTIN.
YOU'RE FORTY-FIVE MINUTES LATE FOR YOUR OWN THREE-MONTH REVIEW!
DO YOU REALIZE THAT THIS IS THE MOST EXCLUSIVE FIRM IN THE WORLD? THAT OUR ANNUAL PROFITS ARE IN THE BILLIONS?
ARE... ARE YOU DRINKING IN THE OFFICE?
THIS? NEVER TOUCH THE STUFF.
MY DAD CALLS IT "DEMON PISS." DRINK THIS AND YOU'LL BE SCREAMING OUT OF EVERY ORIFICE IN FOUR MINUTES!
EVEN THE TINY ONES. WANT SOME?
NO.
NOW, YOU'VE BEEN WITH THIS FIRM FOR--
LOOK AT THAT THING! HAHA!
IT'S A "LAPTOP," RIGHT?
IS IT TRUE THE POWER THAT RUNS IT COMES OUT OF THE WALLS?
HEY, WHAT'S A FOUR-LETTER WORD FOR OBSOLETE?
ALL RIGHT.
LISTEN. I HAVE TO TELL YOU SOMETHING...

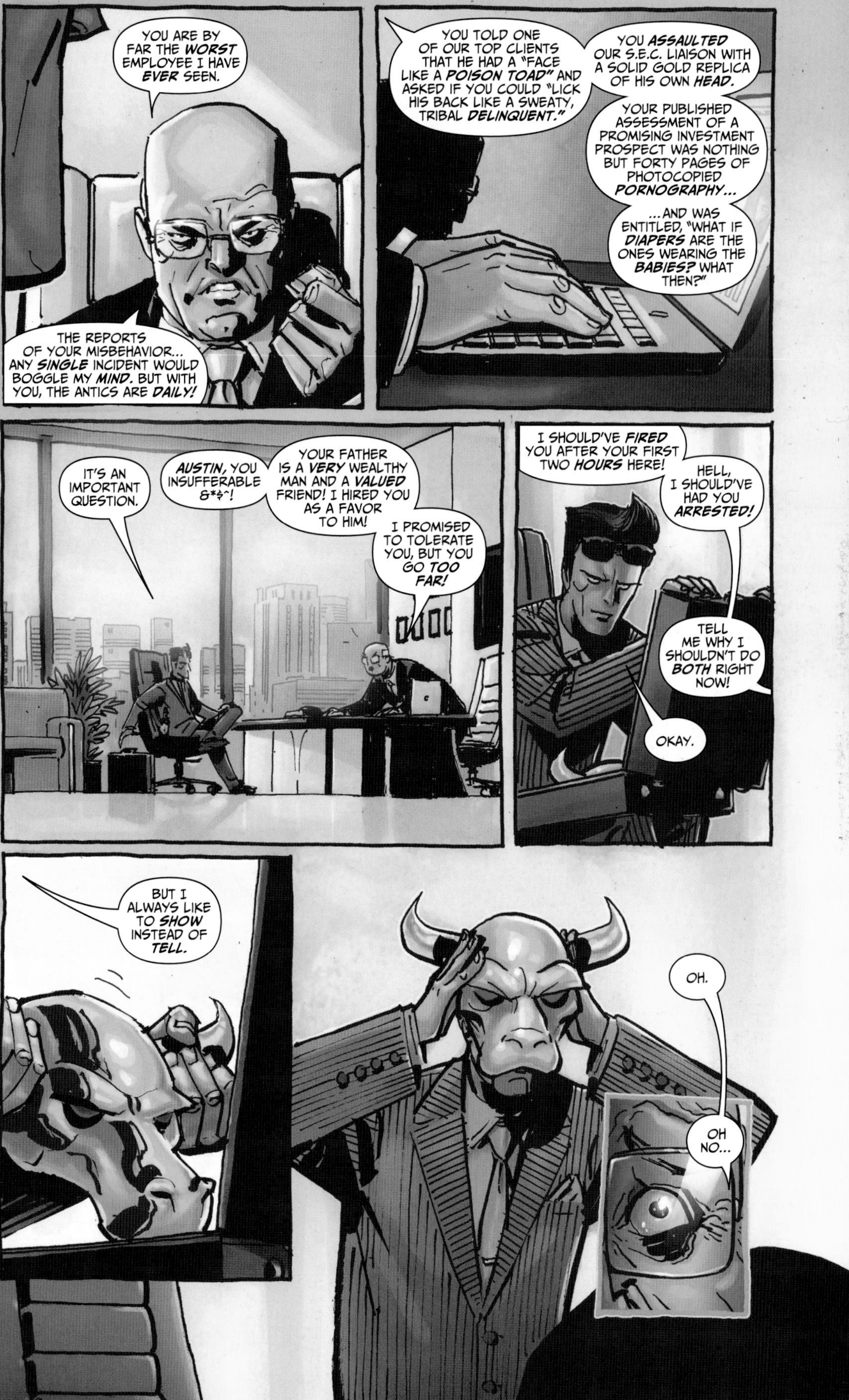
YOU ARE BY FAR THE WORST EMPLOYEE I HAVE EVER SEEN.
THE REPORTS OF YOUR MISBEHAVIOR... ANY SINGLE INCIDENT WOULD BOGGLE MY MIND. BUT WITH YOU, THE ANTICS ARE DAILY!
YOU TOLD ONE OF OUR TOP CLIENTS THAT HE HAD A "FACE LIKE A POISON TOAD" AND ASKED IF YOU COULD "LICK HIS BACK LIKE A SWEATY, TRIBAL DELINQUENT."
YOU ASSAULTED OUR S.E.C. LIAISON WITH A SOLID GOLD REPLICA OF HIS OWN HEAD.
YOUR PUBLISHED ASSESSMENT OF A PROMISING INVESTMENT PROSPECT WAS NOTHING BUT FORTY PAGES OF PHOTOCOPIED PORNOGRAPHY...
...AND WAS ENTITLED, "WHAT IF DIAPERS ARE THE ONES WEARING THE BABIES? WHAT THEN?"
IT'S AN IMPORTANT QUESTION.
AUSTIN, YOU INSUFFERABLE &*$^!
YOUR FATHER IS A VERY WEALTHY MAN AND A VALUED FRIEND! I HIRED YOU AS A FAVOR TO HIM!
I PROMISED TO TOLERATE YOU, BUT YOU GO TOO FAR!
I SHOULD'VE FIRED YOU AFTER YOUR FIRST TWO HOURS HERE!
HELL, I SHOULD'VE HAD YOU ARRESTED!
TELL ME WHY I SHOULDN'T DO BOTH RIGHT NOW!
OKAY.
BUT I ALWAYS LIKE TO SHOW INSTEAD OF TELL.
OH.
OH NO...

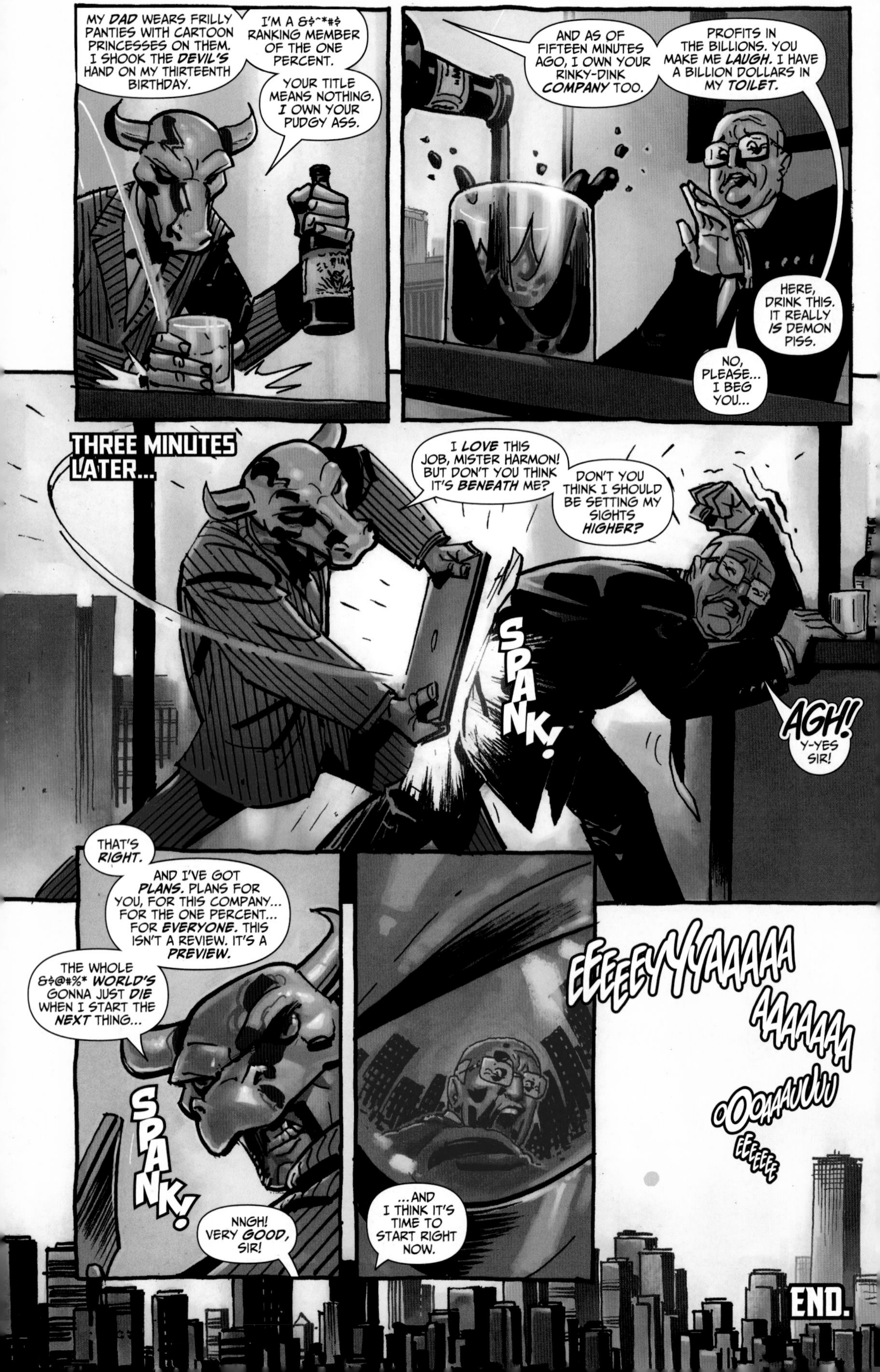

MY DAD WEARS FRILLY PANTIES WITH CARTOON PRINCESSES ON THEM. I SHOOK THE DEVIL'S HAND ON MY THIRTEENTH BIRTHDAY.
I'M A &$^*#$ RANKING MEMBER OF THE ONE PERCENT.
YOUR TITLE MEANS NOTHING. I OWN YOUR PUDGY ASS.
AND AS OF FIFTEEN MINUTES AGO, I OWN YOUR RINKY-DINK COMPANY TOO.
PROFITS IN THE BILLIONS. YOU MAKE ME LAUGH. I HAVE A BILLION DOLLARS IN MY TOILET.
HERE, DRINK THIS. IT REALLY IS DEMON PISS.
NO, PLEASE... I BEG YOU...
THREE MINUTES LATER...
I LOVE THIS JOB, MISTER HARMON! BUT DON'T YOU THINK IT'S BENEATH ME?
DON'T YOU THINK I SHOULD BE SETTING MY SIGHTS HIGHER?
SPANK!
AGH! Y-YES SIR!
THAT'S RIGHT.
AND I'VE GOT PLANS. PLANS FOR YOU, FOR THIS COMPANY... FOR THE ONE PERCENT... FOR EVERYONE. THIS ISN'T A REVIEW. IT'S A PREVIEW.
THE WHOLE &$@#%* WORLD'S GONNA JUST DIE WHEN I START THE NEXT THING...
SPANK!
NNGH! VERY GOOD, SIR!
...AND I THINK IT'S TIME TO START RIGHT NOW.
EEEEEYYYAAAAA AAAAAAA OOOAAAUUUU EEEEEE
END.

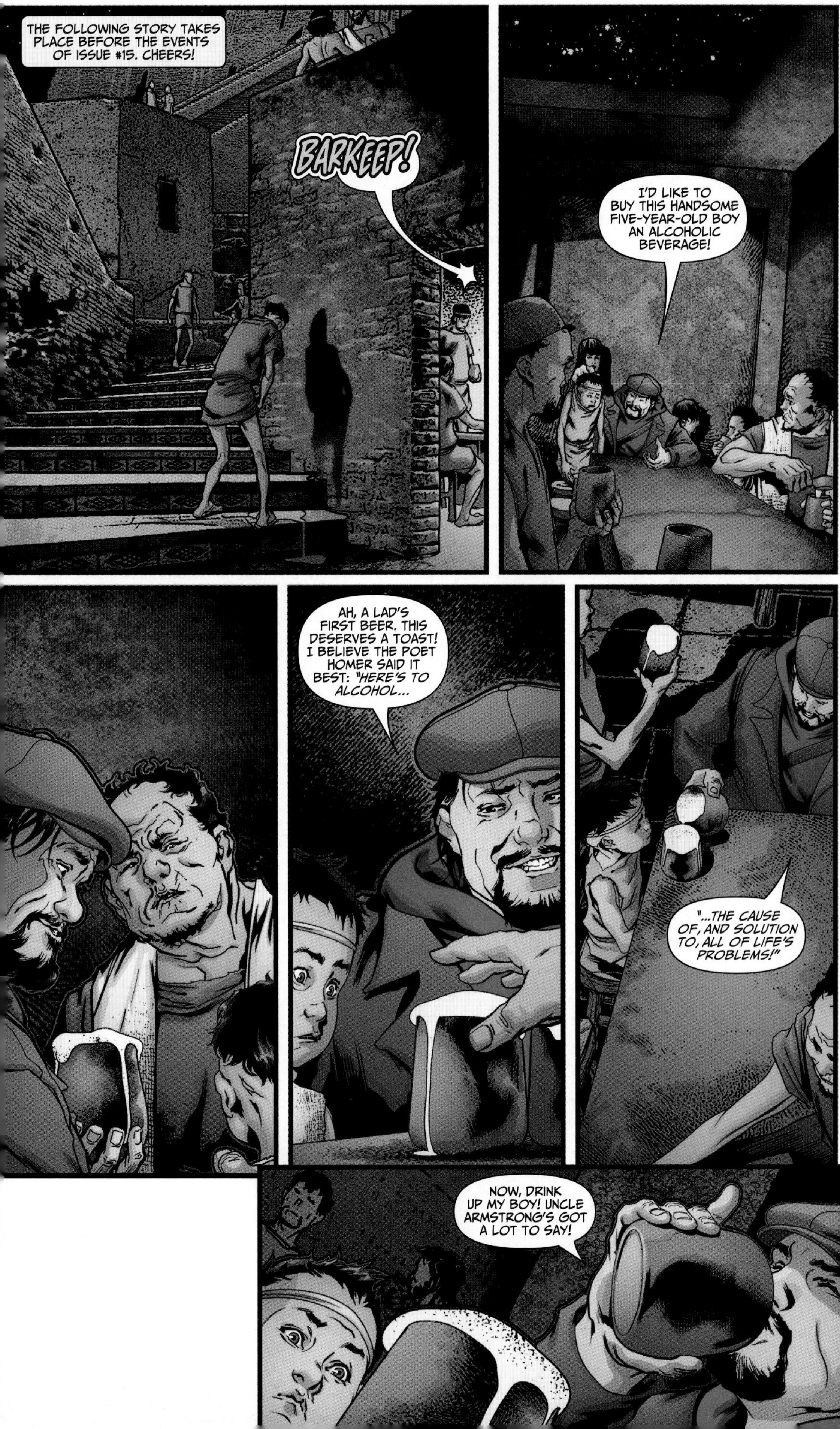
THE FOLLOWING STORY TAKES PLACE BEFORE THE EVENTS OF ISSUE #15. CHEERS!
BARKEEP!
I'D LIKE TO BUY THIS HANDSOME FIVE-YEAR-OLD BOY AN ALCOHOLIC BEVERAGE!
AH, A LAD'S FIRST BEER. THIS DESERVES A TOAST! I BELIEVE THE POET HOMER SAID IT BEST: "HERE'S TO ALCOHOL...
"...THE CAUSE OF, AND SOLUTION TO, ALL OF LIFE'S PROBLEMS!"
NOW, DRINK UP MY BOY! UNCLE ARMSTRONG'S GOT A LOT TO SAY!

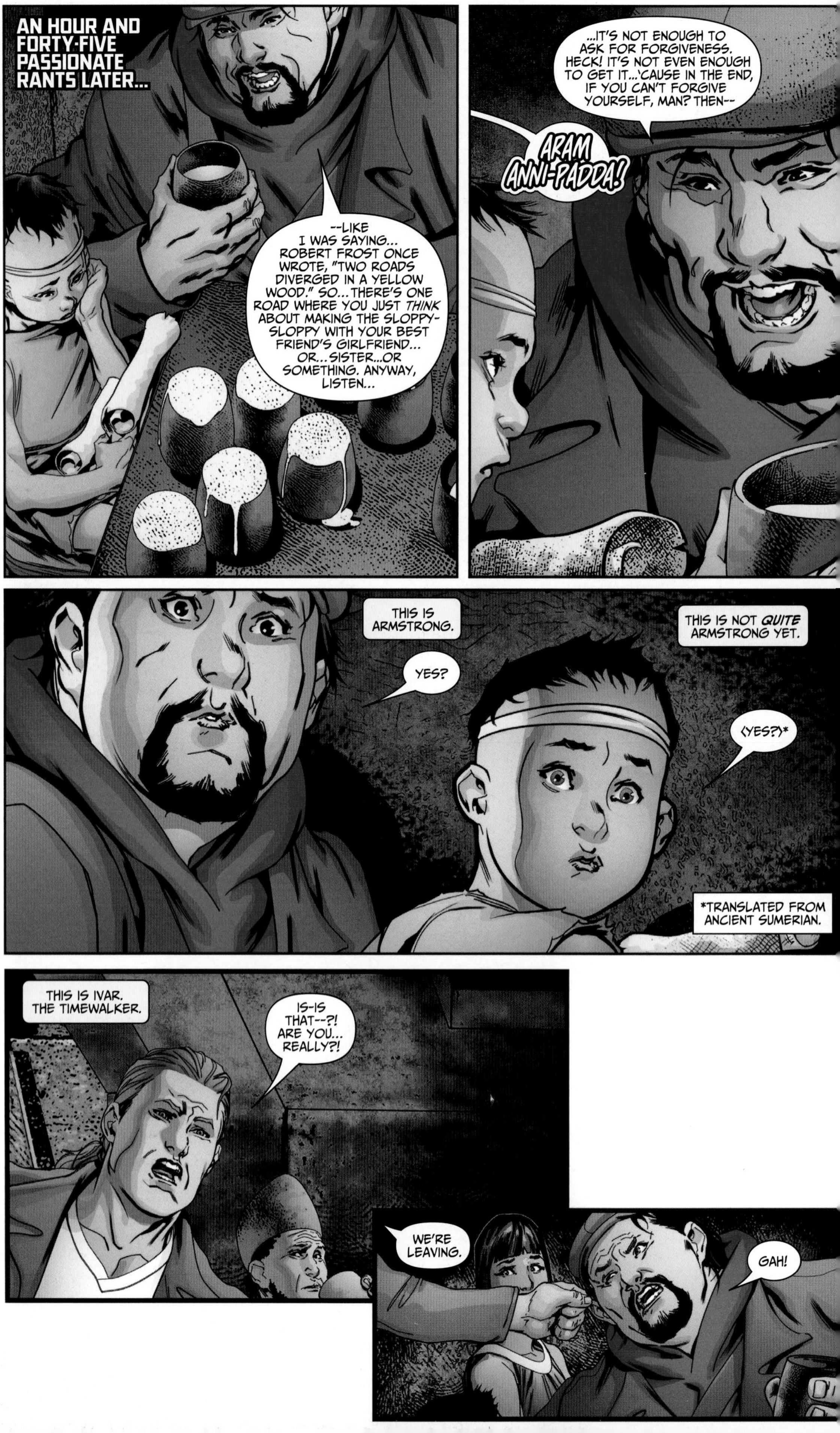
AN HOUR AND FORTY-FIVE PASSIONATE RANTS LATER...
--LIKE I WAS SAYING... ROBERT FROST ONCE WROTE, "TWO ROADS DIVERGED IN A YELLOW WOOD." SO... THERE'S ONE ROAD WHERE YOU JUST THINK ABOUT MAKING THE SLOPPY-SLOPPY WITH YOUR BEST FRIEND'S GIRLFRIEND... OR... SISTER...OR SOMETHING. ANYWAY, LISTEN...
...IT'S NOT ENOUGH TO ASK FOR FORGIVENESS. HECK! IT'S NOT EVEN ENOUGH TO GET IT...'CAUSE IN THE END, IF YOU CAN'T FORGIVE YOURSELF, MAN? THEN--
ARAM ANNI-PADDA!
THIS IS ARMSTRONG.
YES?
THIS IS NOT QUITE ARMSTRONG YET.
‹YES?›*
*TRANSLATED FROM ANCIENT SUMERIAN.
THIS IS IVAR. THE TIMEWALKER.
IS-IS THAT--?! ARE YOU... REALLY?!
WE'RE LEAVING.
GAH!

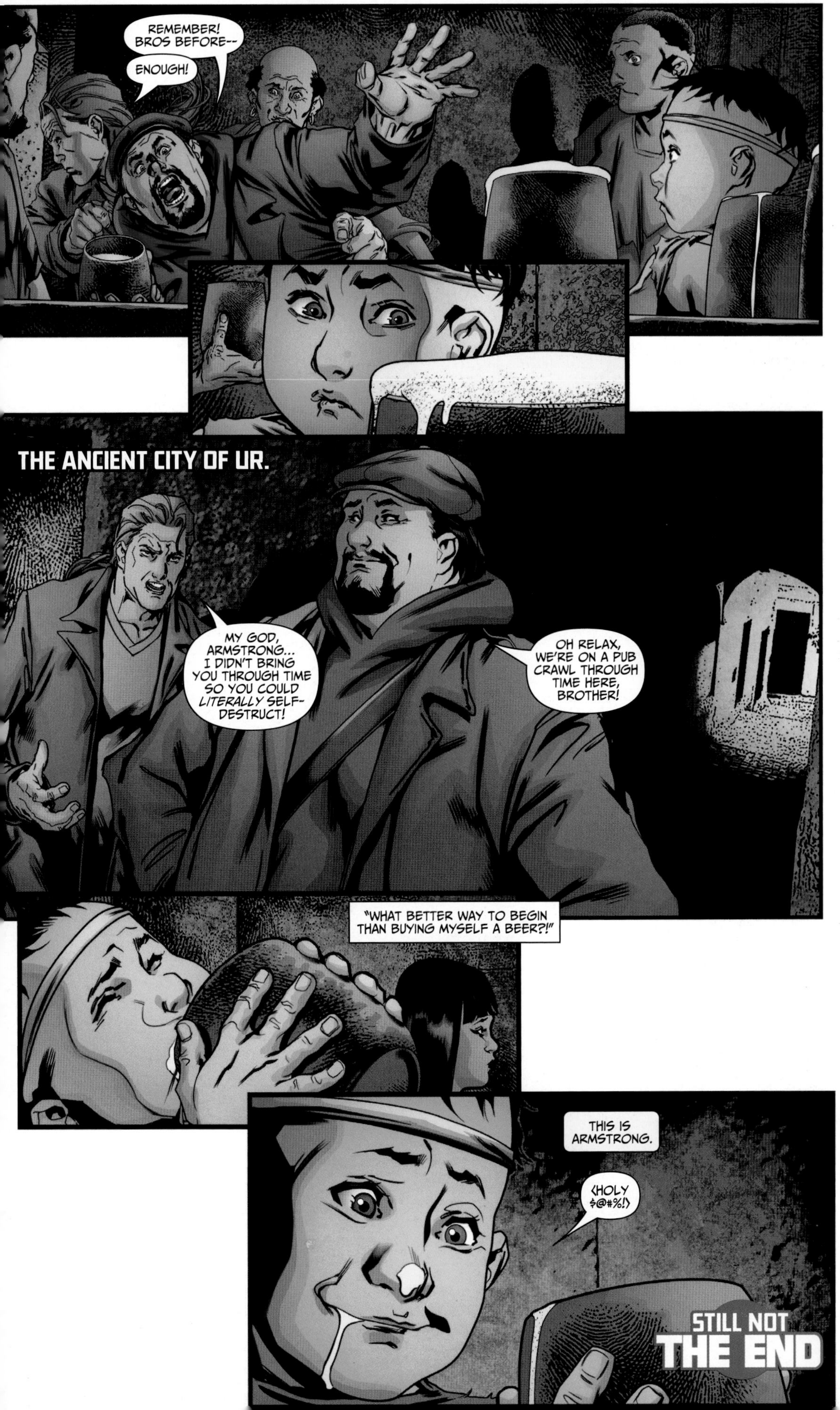
REMEMBER! BROS BEFORE--
ENOUGH!
THE ANCIENT CITY OF UR.
MY GOD, ARMSTRONG... I DIDN'T BRING YOU THROUGH TIME SO YOU COULD LITERALLY SELF-DESTRUCT!
OH RELAX, WE'RE ON A PUB CRAWL THROUGH TIME HERE, BROTHER!
"WHAT BETTER WAY TO BEGIN THAN BUYING MYSELF A BEER?!"
THIS IS ARMSTRONG.
‹HOLY $@#%!›
STILL NOT THE END

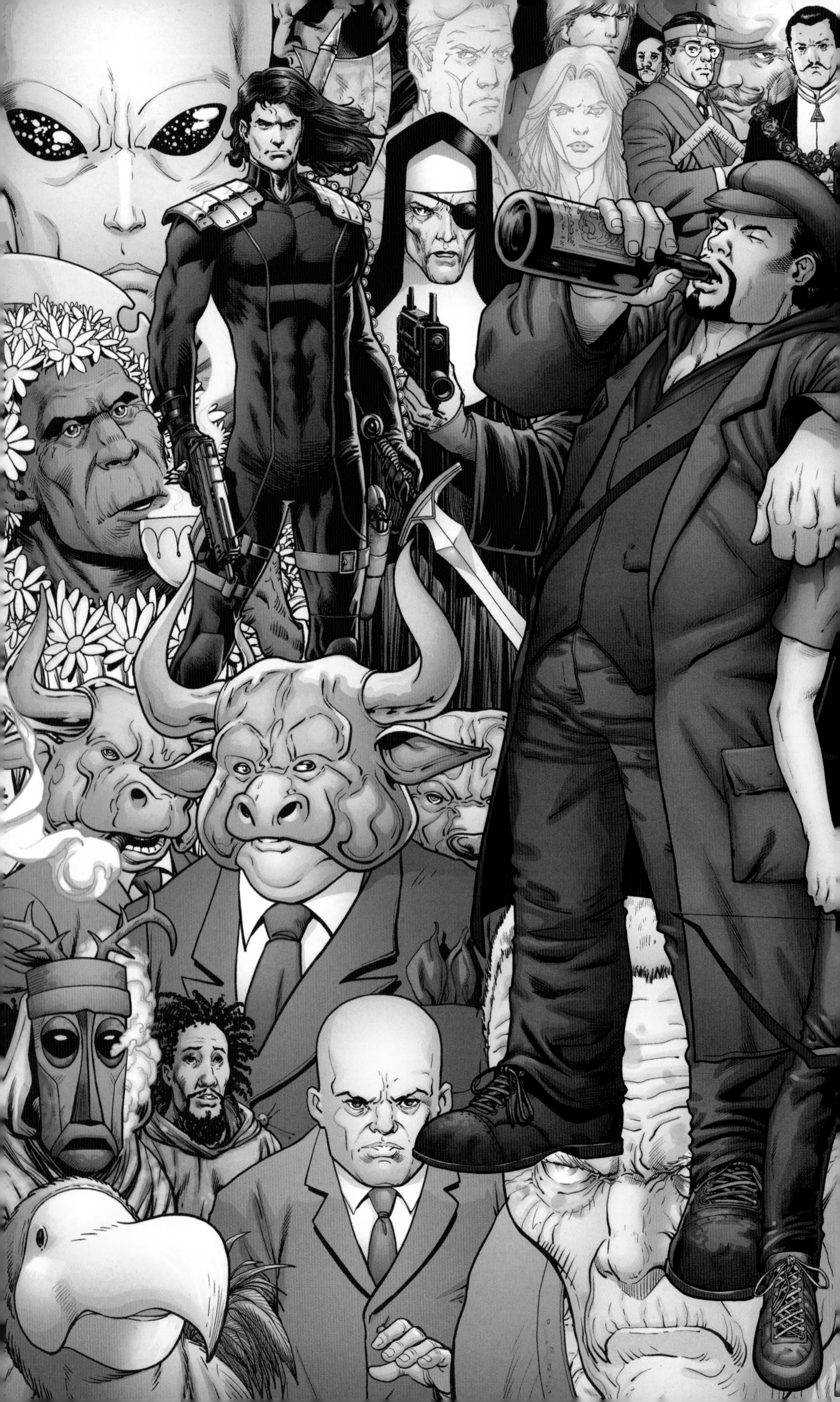

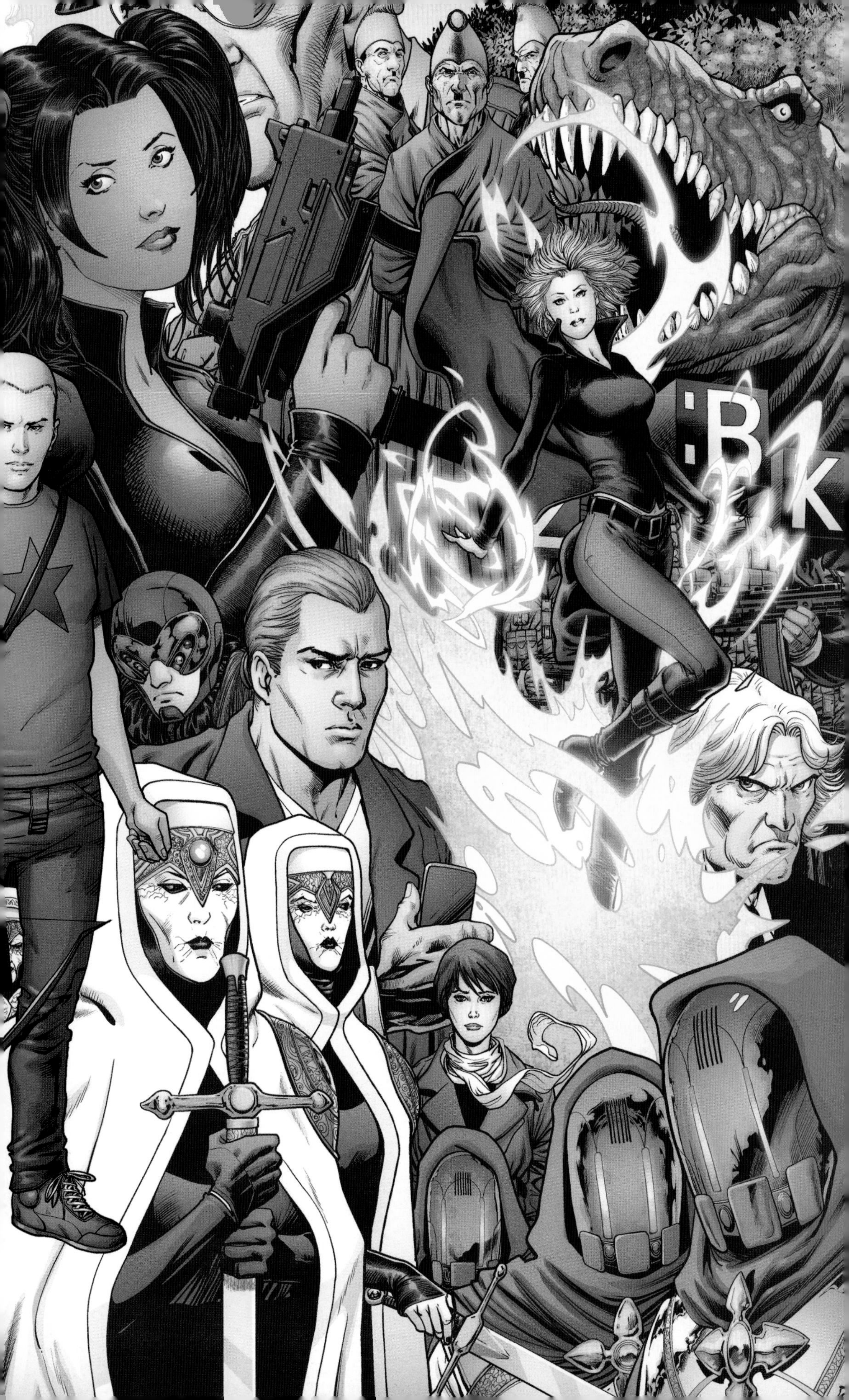

B
K

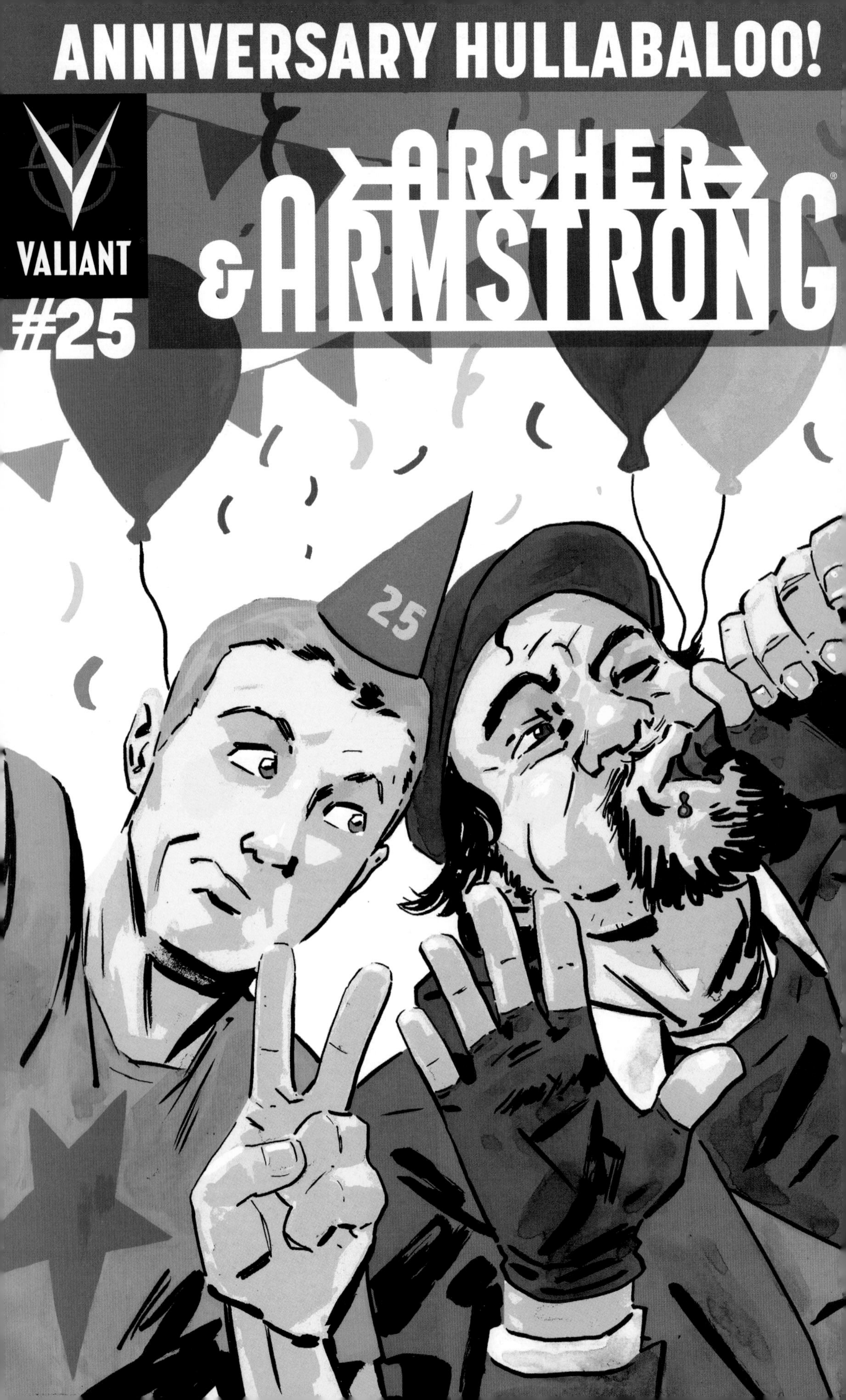
ANNIVERSARY HULLABALOO!
VALIANT
#25
ARCHER & ARMSTRONG
25

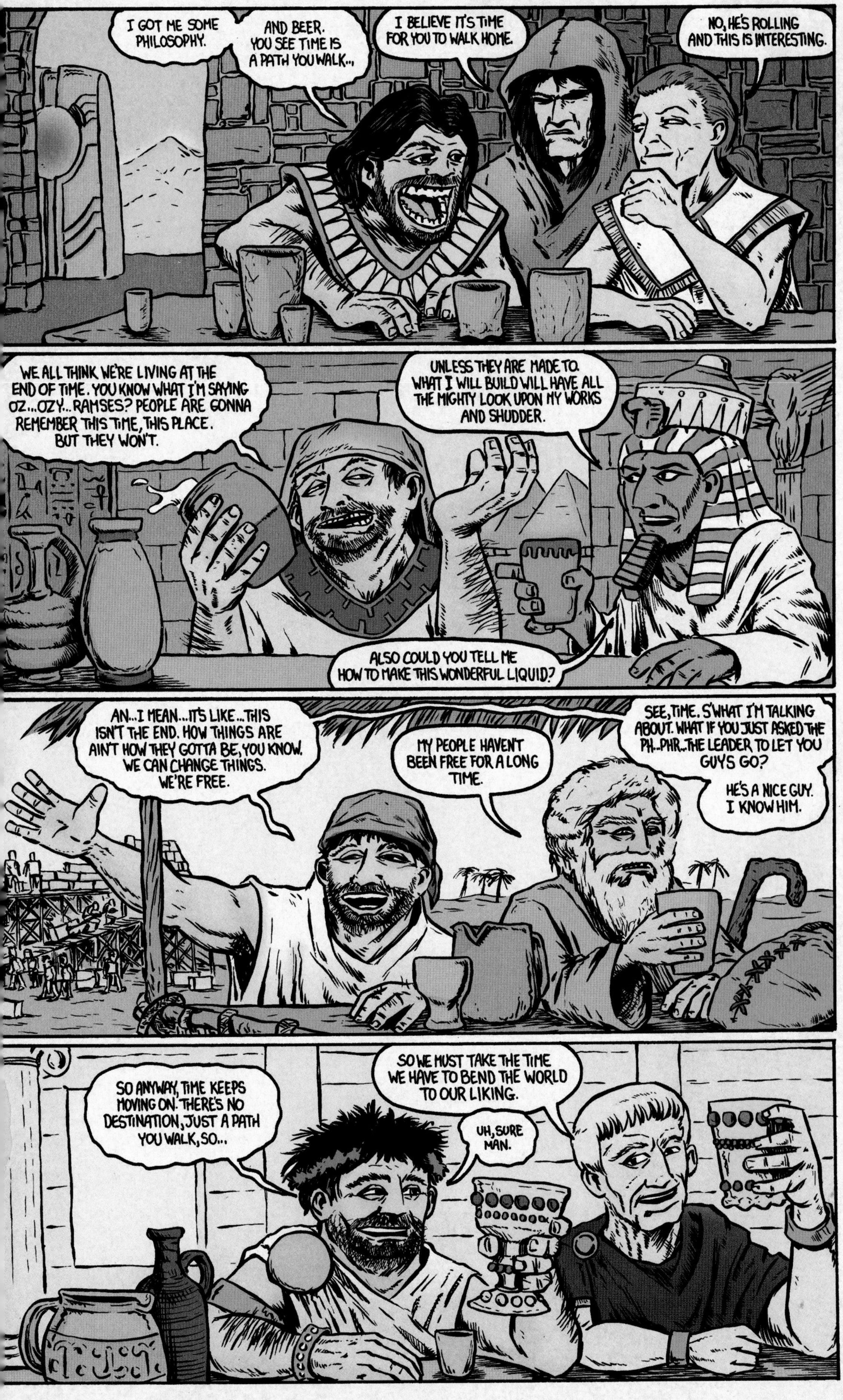
I GOT ME SOME PHILOSOPHY.
AND BEER. YOU SEE TIME IS A PATH YOU WALK...,
I BELIEVE IT'S TIME FOR YOU TO WALK HOME.
NO, HE'S ROLLING AND THIS IS INTERESTING.
WE ALL THINK WE'RE LIVING AT THE END OF TIME. YOU KNOW WHAT I'M SAYING OZ...OZY...RAMSES? PEOPLE ARE GONNA REMEMBER THIS TIME, THIS PLACE. BUT THEY WON'T.
UNLESS THEY ARE MADE TO. WHAT I WILL BUILD WILL HAVE ALL THE MIGHTY LOOK UPON MY WORKS AND SHUDDER.
ALSO COULD YOU TELL ME HOW TO MAKE THIS WONDERFUL LIQUID?
AN...I MEAN...IT'S LIKE...THIS ISN'T THE END. HOW THINGS ARE AIN'T HOW THEY GOTTA BE, YOU KNOW. WE CAN CHANGE THINGS. WE'RE FREE.
MY PEOPLE HAVEN'T BEEN FREE FOR A LONG TIME.
SEE, TIME. S'WHAT I'M TALKING ABOUT. WHAT IF YOU JUST ASKED THE PH...PHR...THE LEADER TO LET YOU GUYS GO?
HE'S A NICE GUY. I KNOW HIM.
SO ANYWAY, TIME KEEPS MOVING ON. THERE'S NO DESTINATION, JUST A PATH YOU WALK, SO...
SO WE MUST TAKE THE TIME WE HAVE TO BEND THE WORLD TO OUR LIKING.
UH, SURE MAN.

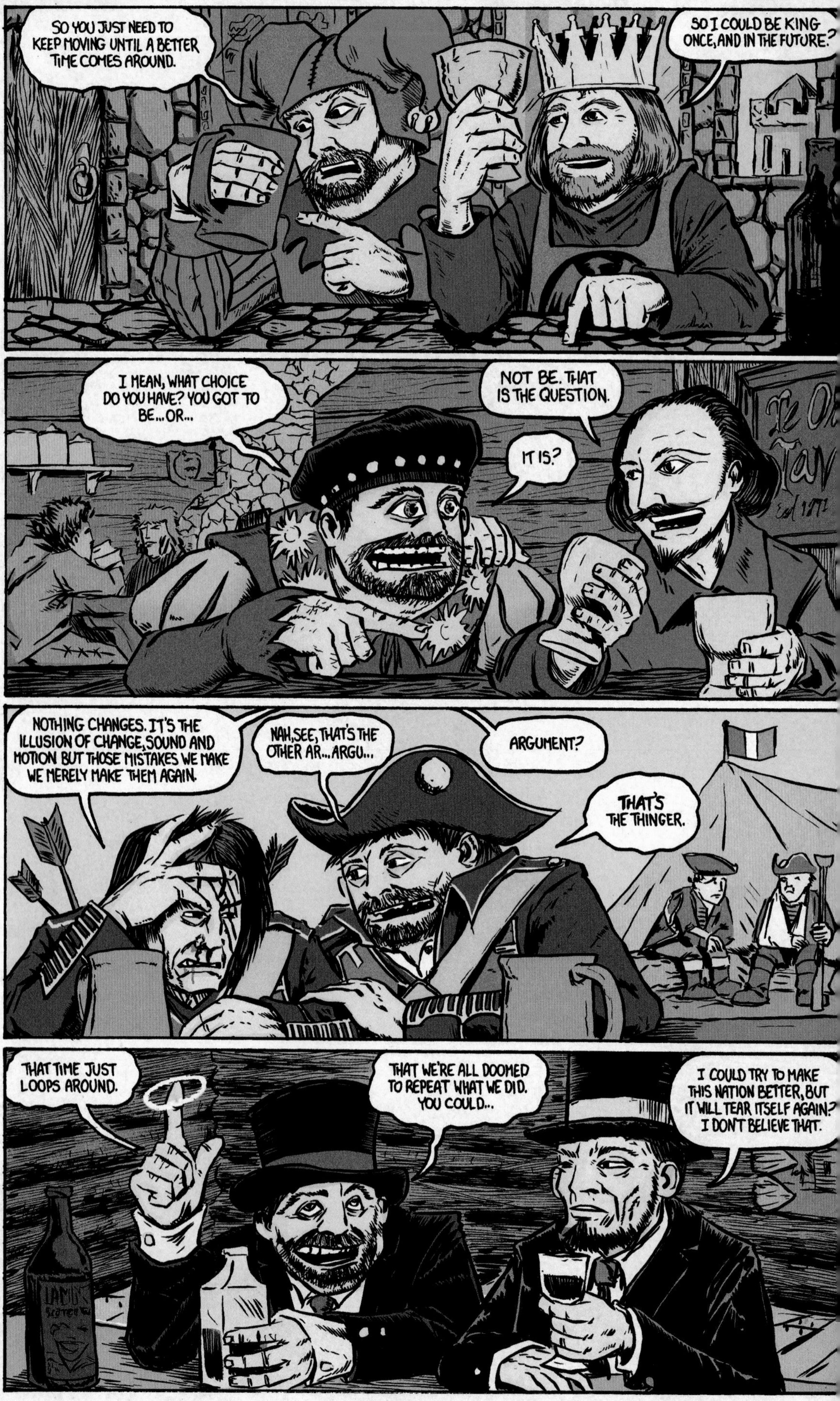

SO YOU JUST NEED TO KEEP MOVING UNTIL A BETTER TIME COMES AROUND.
SO I COULD BE KING ONCE, AND IN THE FUTURE?
I MEAN, WHAT CHOICE DO YOU HAVE? YOU GOT TO BE...OR...
NOT BE. THAT IS THE QUESTION.
IT IS?
NOTHING CHANGES. IT'S THE ILLUSION OF CHANGE, SOUND AND MOTION BUT THOSE MISTAKES WE MAKE WE MERELY MAKE THEM AGAIN.
NAH, SEE, THAT'S THE OTHER AR...ARGU...
ARGUMENT?
THAT'S THE THINGER.
THAT TIME JUST LOOPS AROUND.
THAT WE'RE ALL DOOMED TO REPEAT WHAT WE DID. YOU COULD...
I COULD TRY TO MAKE THIS NATION BETTER, BUT IT WILL TEAR ITSELF AGAIN? I DON'T BELIEVE THAT.

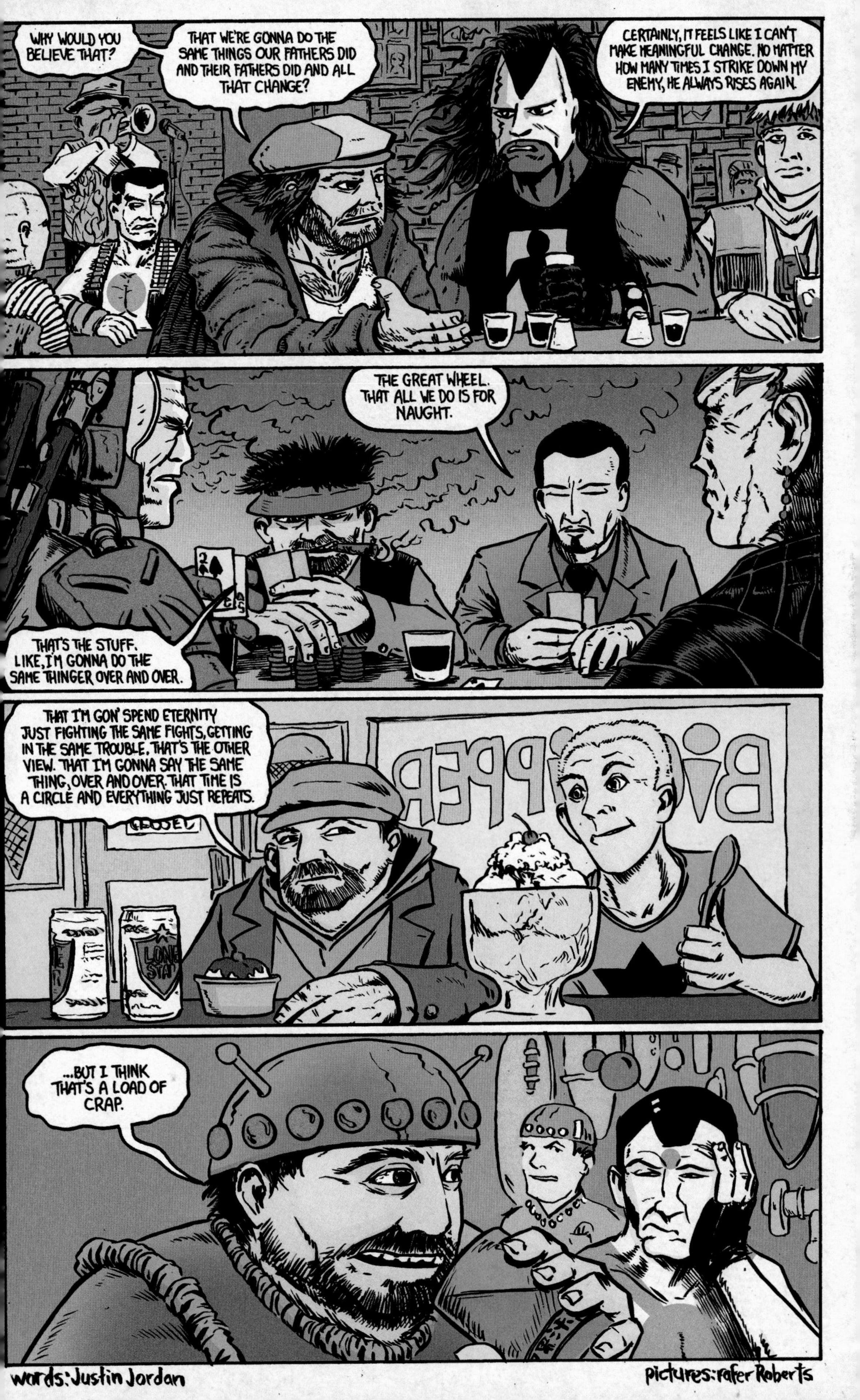
WHY WOULD YOU BELIEVE THAT?
THAT WE'RE GONNA DO THE SAME THINGS OUR FATHERS DID AND THEIR FATHERS DID AND ALL THAT CHANGE?
CERTAINLY, IT FEELS LIKE I CAN'T MAKE MEANINGFUL CHANGE. NO MATTER HOW MANY TIMES I STRIKE DOWN MY ENEMY, HE ALWAYS RISES AGAIN.
THE GREAT WHEEL. THAT ALL WE DO IS FOR NAUGHT.
THAT'S THE STUFF. LIKE, I'M GONNA DO THE SAME THINGER OVER AND OVER.
THAT I'M GON' SPEND ETERNITY JUST FIGHTING THE SAME FIGHTS, GETTING IN THE SAME TROUBLE. THAT'S THE OTHER VIEW. THAT I'M GONNA SAY THE SAME THING, OVER AND OVER. THAT TIME IS A CIRCLE AND EVERYTHING JUST REPEATS.
...BUT I THINK THAT'S A LOAD OF CRAP.
words: Justin Jordan
pictures: rafer Roberts

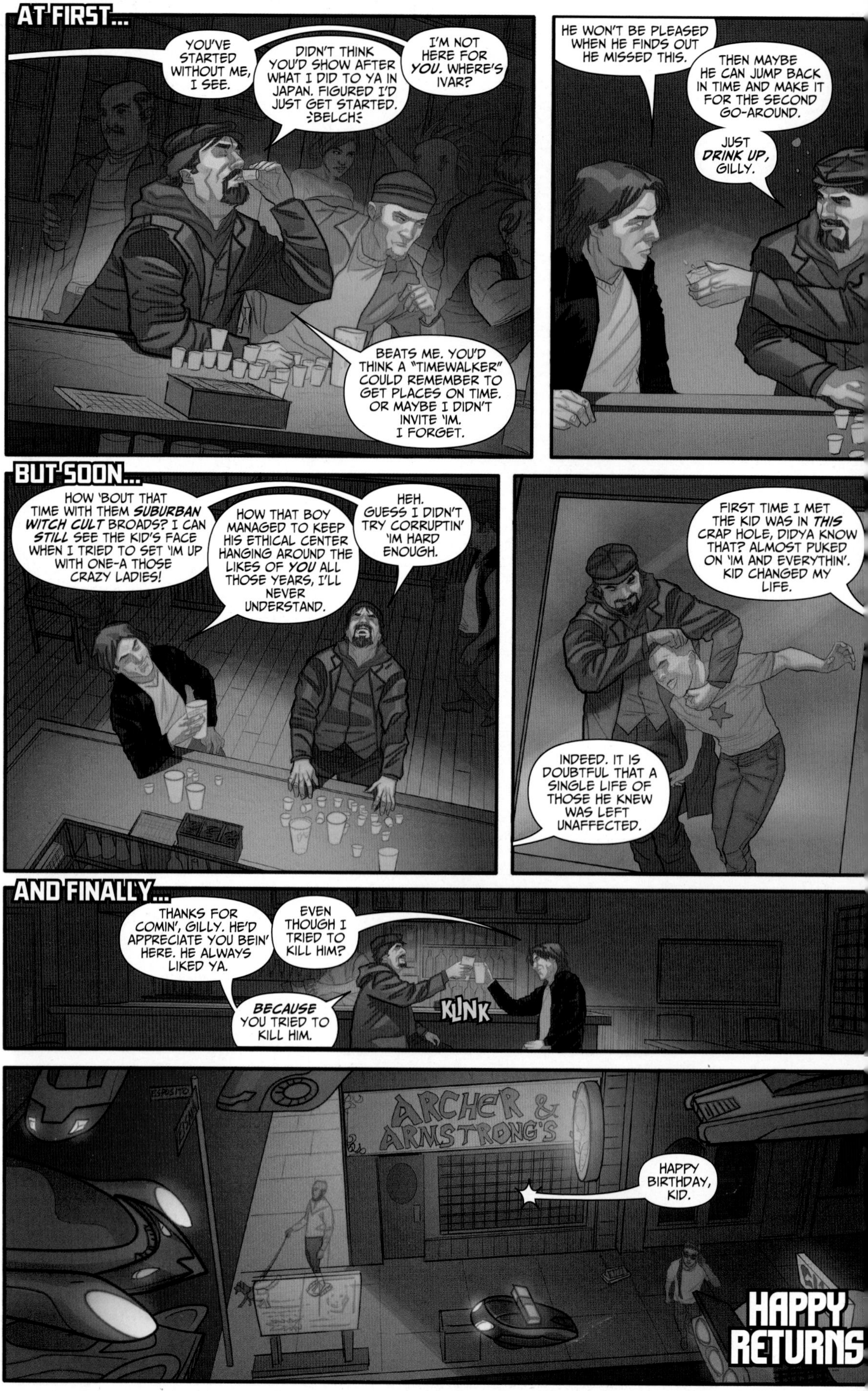
AT FIRST...
YOU'VE STARTED WITHOUT ME, I SEE.
DIDN'T THINK YOU'D SHOW AFTER WHAT I DID TO YA IN JAPAN. FIGURED I'D JUST GET STARTED. *BELCH*
I'M NOT HERE FOR YOU. WHERE'S IVAR?
BEATS ME. YOU'D THINK A "TIMEWALKER" COULD REMEMBER TO GET PLACES ON TIME. OR MAYBE I DIDN'T INVITE 'IM. I FORGET.
HE WON'T BE PLEASED WHEN HE FINDS OUT HE MISSED THIS.
THEN MAYBE HE CAN JUMP BACK IN TIME AND MAKE IT FOR THE SECOND GO-AROUND.
JUST DRINK UP, GILLY.
BUT SOON...
HOW 'BOUT THAT TIME WITH THEM SUBURBAN WITCH CULT BROADS? I CAN STILL SEE THE KID'S FACE WHEN I TRIED TO SET 'IM UP WITH ONE-A THOSE CRAZY LADIES!
HOW THAT BOY MANAGED TO KEEP HIS ETHICAL CENTER HANGING AROUND THE LIKES OF YOU ALL THOSE YEARS, I'LL NEVER UNDERSTAND.
HEH. GUESS I DIDN'T TRY CORRUPTIN' 'IM HARD ENOUGH.
FIRST TIME I MET THE KID WAS IN THIS CRAP HOLE, DIDYA KNOW THAT? ALMOST PUKED ON 'IM AND EVERYTHIN'. KID CHANGED MY LIFE.
INDEED. IT IS DOUBTFUL THAT A SINGLE LIFE OF THOSE HE KNEW WAS LEFT UNAFFECTED.
AND FINALLY...
THANKS FOR COMIN', GILLY. HE'D APPRECIATE YOU BEIN' HERE. HE ALWAYS LIKED YA.
EVEN THOUGH I TRIED TO KILL HIM?
BECAUSE YOU TRIED TO KILL HIM.
KLINK
ARCHER & ARMSTRONG'S
HAPPY BIRTHDAY, KID.
HAPPY RETURNS

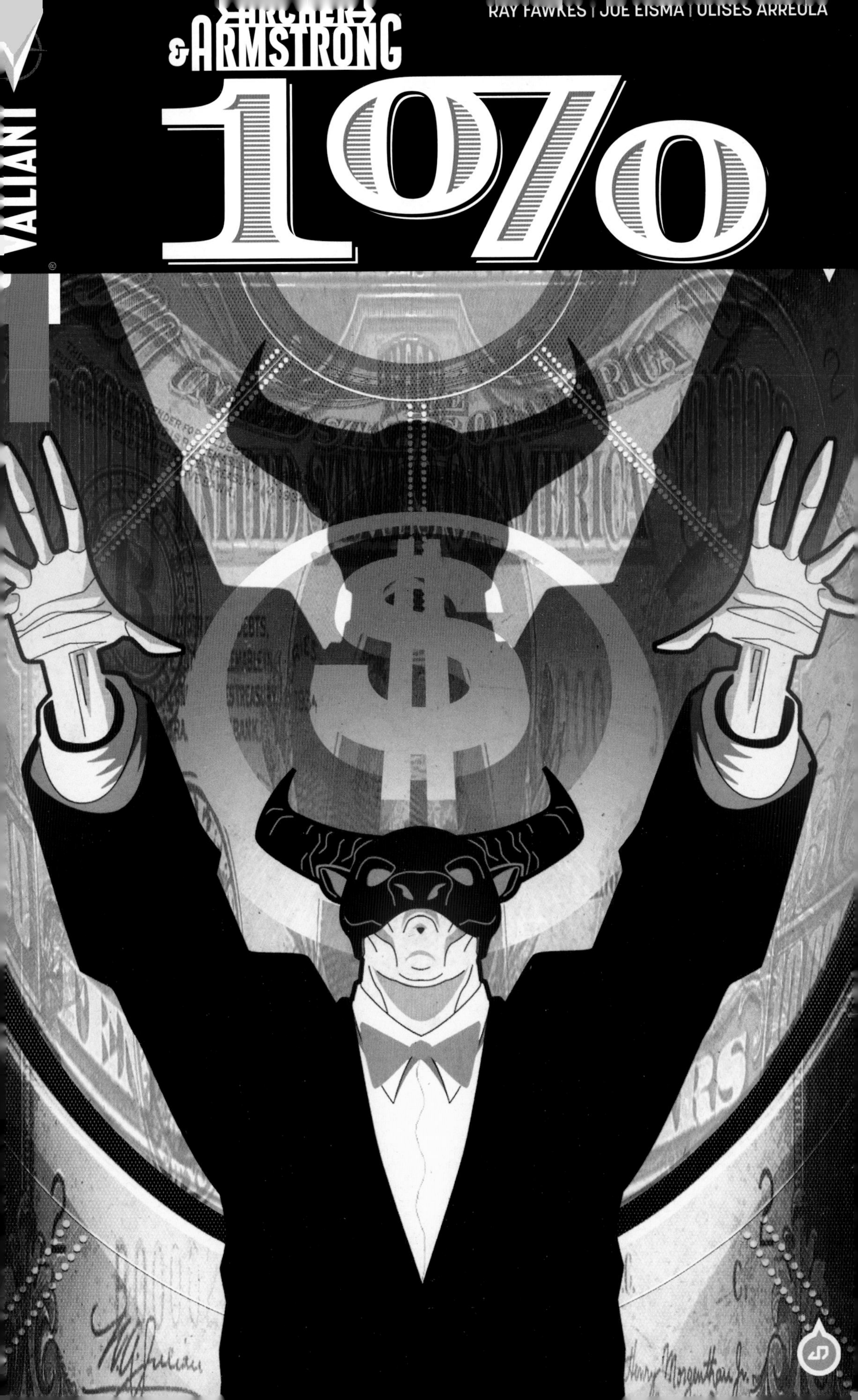

RAY FAWKES | JOE EISMA | ULISES ARREOLA
ARCHER & ARMSTRONG
1%
VALIANT

VALIANT

1%

ARCHER & ARMSTRONG

Welcome to the One Percent, old sport! If you are reading this funny book, you have taken an interest in joining us among the world's wealthy elite. But before initiation can begin, a little bit about us...

For centuries, our sinister sect has secretly skewed the financial markets of the world, buying and selling the livelihoods of hard-working citizens just like you, loyal comic reader! Now this affluent lifestyle of the ultra-wealthy does not come without cost. Weekly sacrifices to Mammon (praise Mammon) and constant interference from those conspiracy-busting do-gooders Archer & Armstrong take their toll, and even our plush, prosperous, and formally flush fraternity has fallen on hard times.

Luckily for us, a NEW crop of children of the One Percent is always just around the corner! So sit back and enjoy a fascinatir look into the life and times of the next generation of the One Percent!

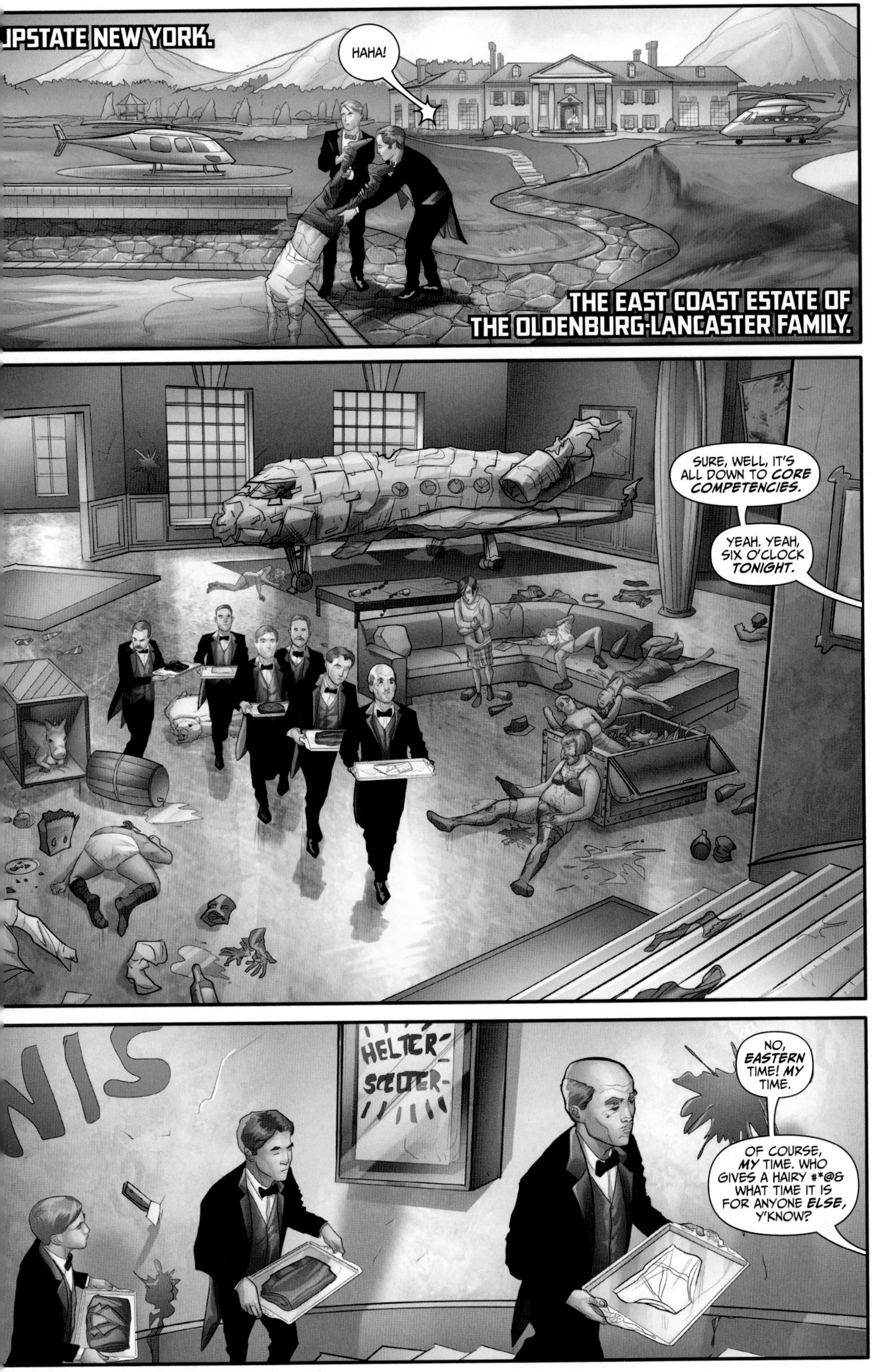
UPSTATE NEW YORK.
HAHA!
THE EAST COAST ESTATE OF THE OLDENBURG-LANCASTER FAMILY.
SURE, WELL, IT'S ALL DOWN TO *CORE COMPETENCIES.*
YEAH. YEAH, SIX O'CLOCK *TONIGHT.*
HELTER-
SKELTER-
NO, *EASTERN* TIME! *MY* TIME.
OF COURSE, *MY* TIME. WHO GIVES A HAIRY #*@& WHAT TIME IT IS FOR ANYONE *ELSE,* Y'KNOW?

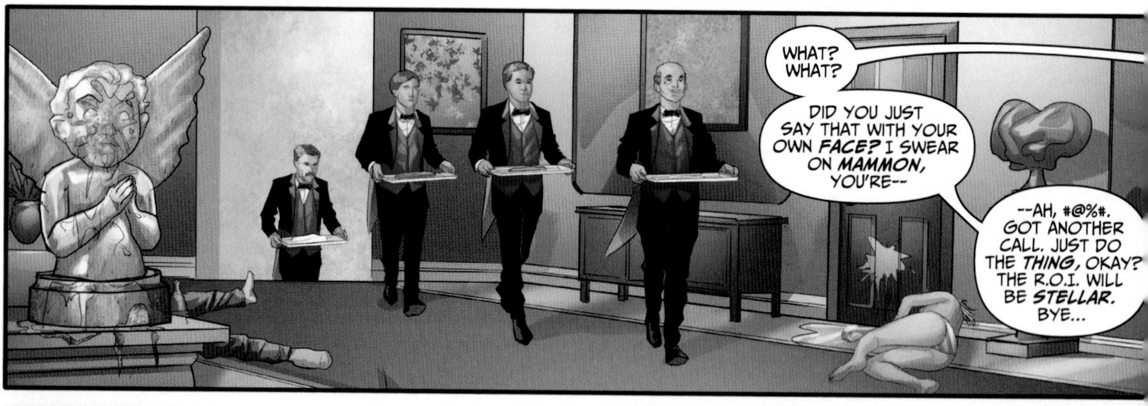
WHAT? WHAT?
DID YOU JUST SAY THAT WITH YOUR OWN FACE? I SWEAR ON MAMMON, YOU'RE--
--AH, #@%#. GOT ANOTHER CALL. JUST DO THE THING, OKAY? THE R.O.I. WILL BE STELLAR. BYE...

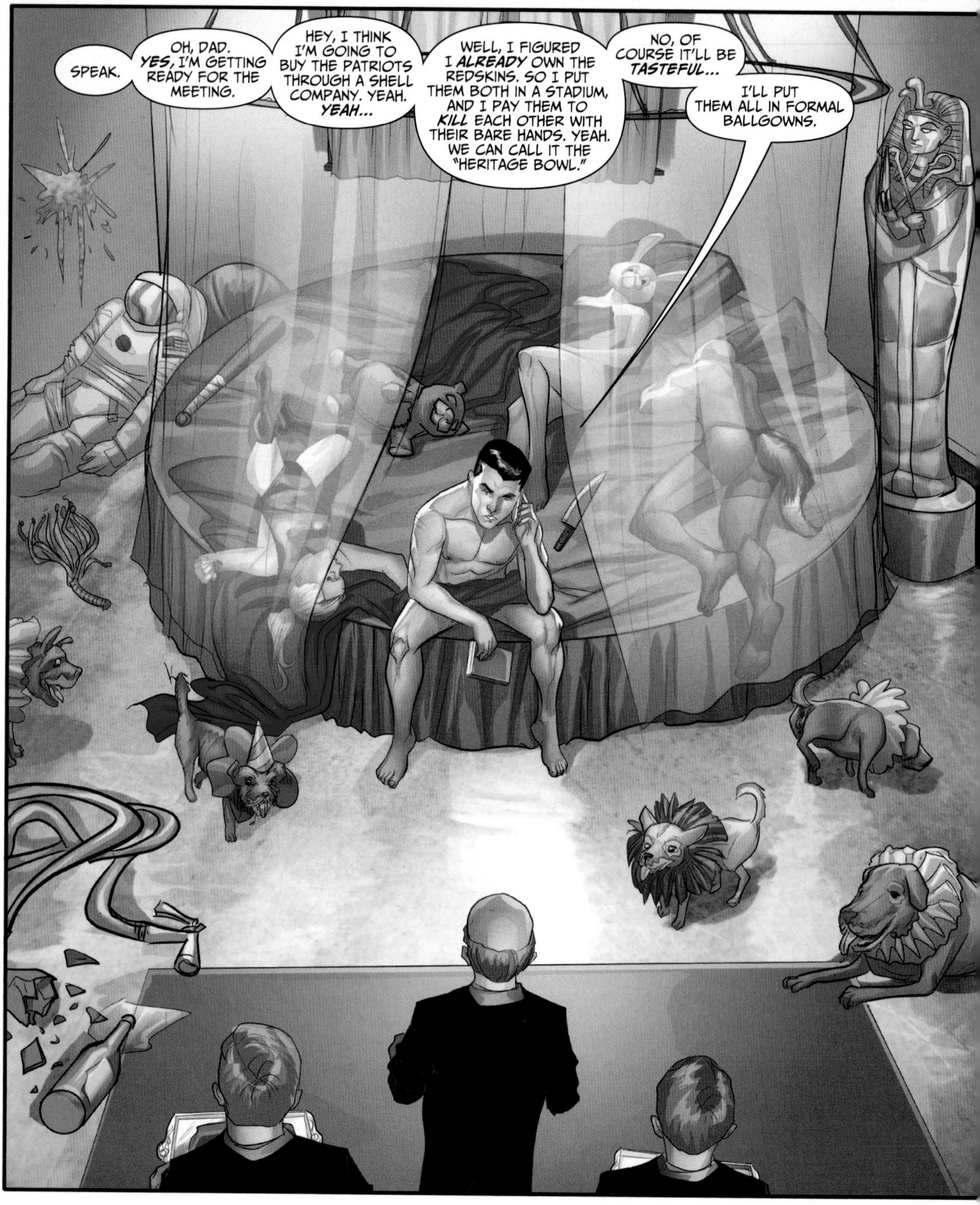
SPEAK.
OH, DAD. YES, I'M GETTING READY FOR THE MEETING.
HEY, I THINK I'M GOING TO BUY THE PATRIOTS THROUGH A SHELL COMPANY. YEAH. YEAH...
WELL, I FIGURED I ALREADY OWN THE REDSKINS. SO I PUT THEM BOTH IN A STADIUM, AND I PAY THEM TO KILL EACH OTHER WITH THEIR BARE HANDS. YEAH. WE CAN CALL IT THE "HERITAGE BOWL."
NO, OF COURSE IT'LL BE TASTEFUL...
I'LL PUT THEM ALL IN FORMAL BALLGOWNS.

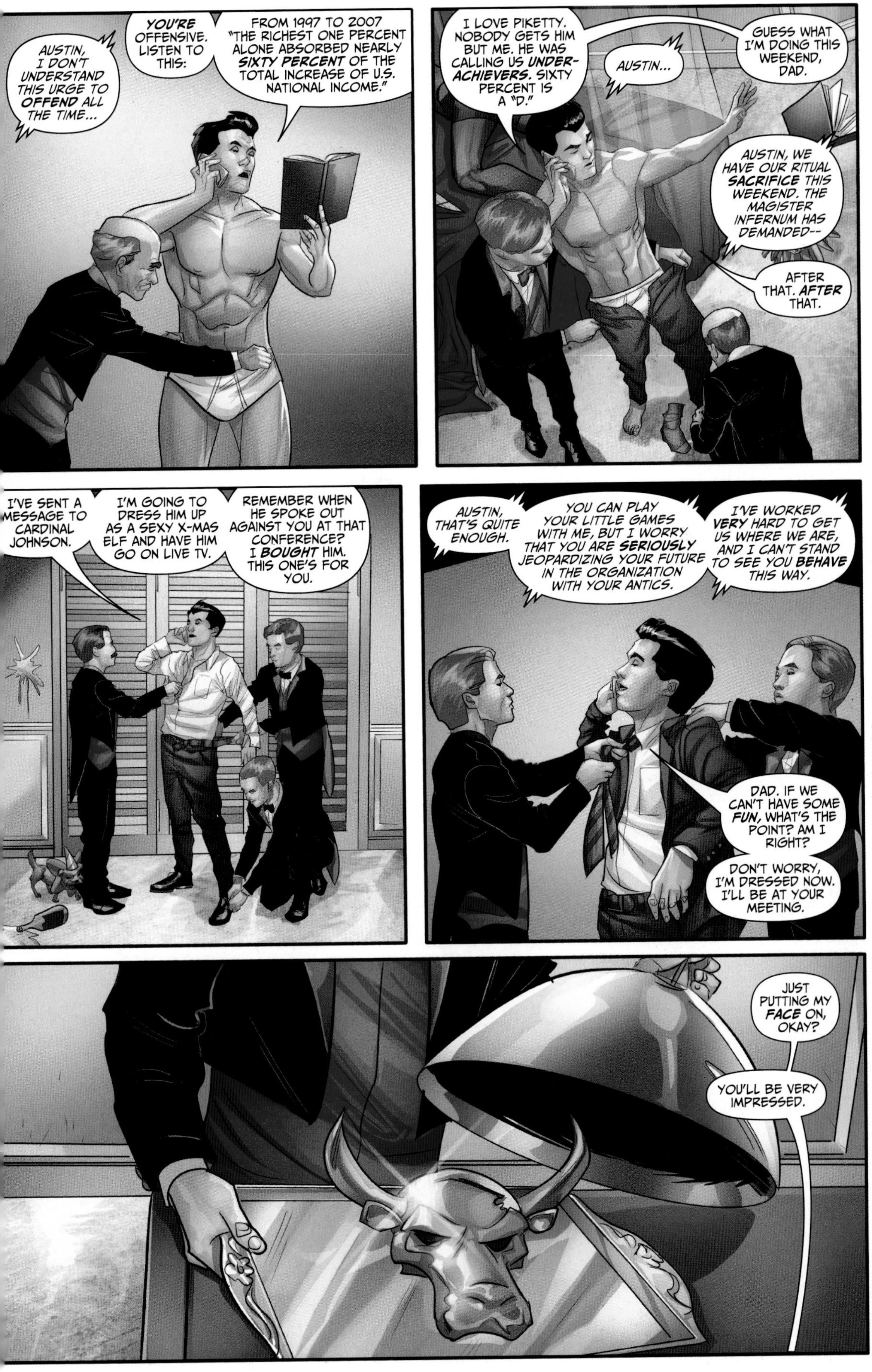
AUSTIN, I DON'T UNDERSTAND THIS URGE TO OFFEND ALL THE TIME...
YOU'RE OFFENSIVE. LISTEN TO THIS:
FROM 1997 TO 2007 "THE RICHEST ONE PERCENT ALONE ABSORBED NEARLY SIXTY PERCENT OF THE TOTAL INCREASE OF U.S. NATIONAL INCOME."
I LOVE PIKETTY. NOBODY GETS HIM BUT ME. HE WAS CALLING US UNDER-ACHIEVERS. SIXTY PERCENT IS A "D."
AUSTIN...
GUESS WHAT I'M DOING THIS WEEKEND, DAD.
AUSTIN, WE HAVE OUR RITUAL SACRIFICE THIS WEEKEND. THE MAGISTER INFERNUM HAS DEMANDED--
AFTER THAT. AFTER THAT.
I'VE SENT A MESSAGE TO CARDINAL JOHNSON.
I'M GOING TO DRESS HIM UP AS A SEXY X-MAS ELF AND HAVE HIM GO ON LIVE TV.
REMEMBER WHEN HE SPOKE OUT AGAINST YOU AT THAT CONFERENCE? I BOUGHT HIM. THIS ONE'S FOR YOU.
AUSTIN, THAT'S QUITE ENOUGH.
YOU CAN PLAY YOUR LITTLE GAMES WITH ME, BUT I WORRY THAT YOU ARE SERIOUSLY JEOPARDIZING YOUR FUTURE IN THE ORGANIZATION WITH YOUR ANTICS.
I'VE WORKED VERY HARD TO GET US WHERE WE ARE, AND I CAN'T STAND TO SEE YOU BEHAVE THIS WAY.
DAD. IF WE CAN'T HAVE SOME FUN, WHAT'S THE POINT? AM I RIGHT?
DON'T WORRY, I'M DRESSED NOW. I'LL BE AT YOUR MEETING.
JUST PUTTING MY FACE ON, OKAY?
YOU'LL BE VERY IMPRESSED.

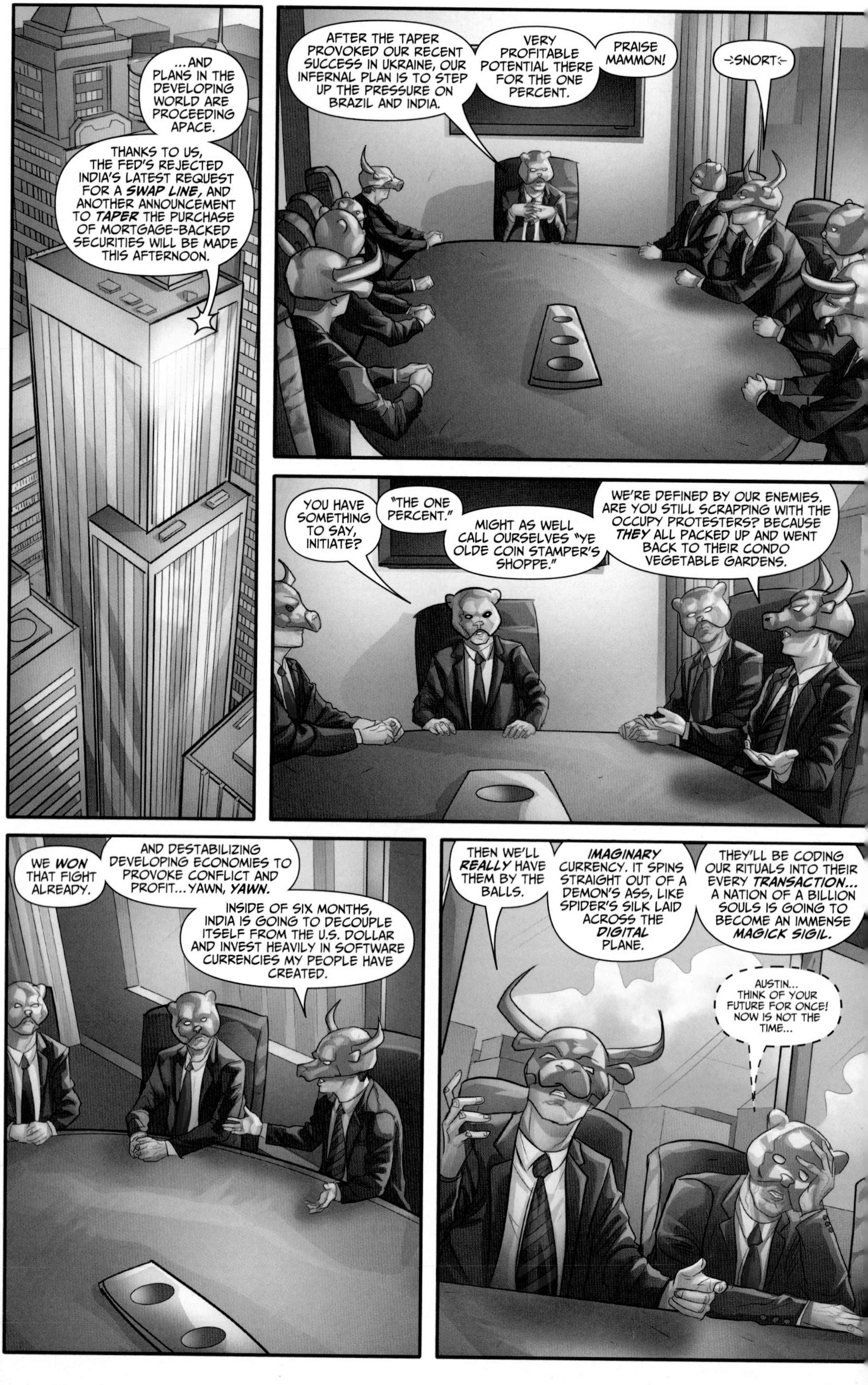
...AND PLANS IN THE DEVELOPING WORLD ARE PROCEEDING APACE.
THANKS TO US, THE FED'S REJECTED INDIA'S LATEST REQUEST FOR A *SWAP LINE,* AND ANOTHER ANNOUNCEMENT TO *TAPER* THE PURCHASE OF MORTGAGE-BACKED SECURITIES WILL BE MADE THIS AFTERNOON.
AFTER THE TAPER PROVOKED OUR RECENT SUCCESS IN UKRAINE, OUR INFERNAL PLAN IS TO STEP UP THE PRESSURE ON BRAZIL AND INDIA.
VERY PROFITABLE POTENTIAL THERE FOR THE ONE PERCENT.
PRAISE MAMMON!
SNORT
YOU HAVE SOMETHING TO SAY, INITIATE?
"THE ONE PERCENT."
MIGHT AS WELL CALL OURSELVES "YE OLDE COIN STAMPER'S SHOPPE."
WE'RE DEFINED BY OUR ENEMIES. ARE YOU STILL SCRAPPING WITH THE OCCUPY PROTESTERS? BECAUSE *THEY* ALL PACKED UP AND WENT BACK TO THEIR CONDO VEGETABLE GARDENS.
WE *WON* THAT FIGHT ALREADY.
AND DESTABILIZING DEVELOPING ECONOMIES TO PROVOKE CONFLICT AND PROFIT... YAWN, *YAWN.*
INSIDE OF SIX MONTHS, INDIA IS GOING TO DECOUPLE ITSELF FROM THE U.S. DOLLAR AND INVEST HEAVILY IN SOFTWARE CURRENCIES MY PEOPLE HAVE CREATED.
THEN WE'LL *REALLY* HAVE THEM BY THE BALLS.
IMAGINARY CURRENCY. IT SPINS STRAIGHT OUT OF A DEMON'S ASS, LIKE SPIDER'S SILK LAID ACROSS THE *DIGITAL* PLANE.
THEY'LL BE CODING OUR RITUALS INTO THEIR EVERY *TRANSACTION...* A NATION OF A BILLION SOULS IS GOING TO BECOME AN IMMENSE *MAGICK SIGIL.*
AUSTIN... THINK OF YOUR FUTURE FOR ONCE! NOW IS NOT THE TIME...

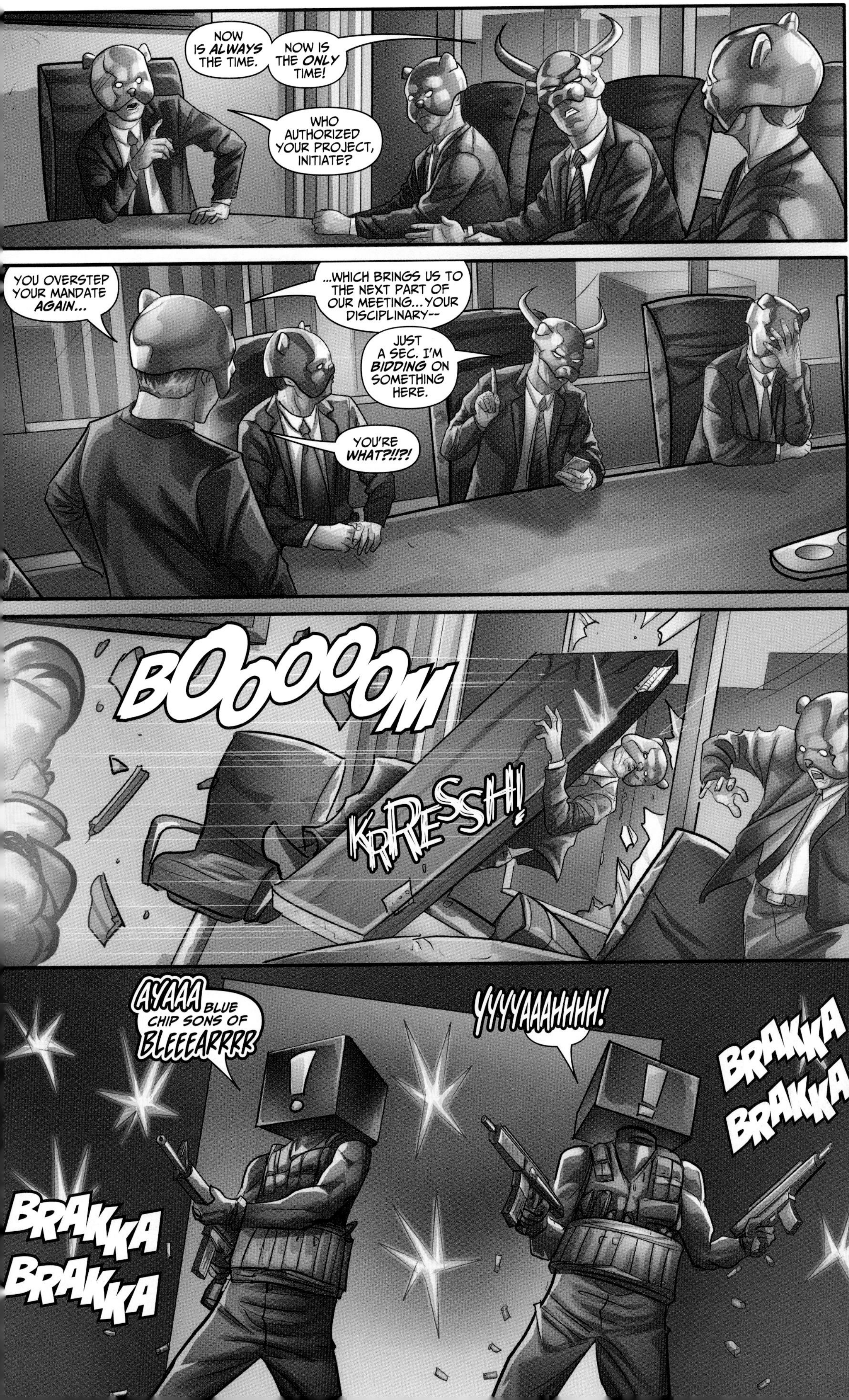
NOW IS ALWAYS THE TIME.
NOW IS THE ONLY TIME!
WHO AUTHORIZED YOUR PROJECT, INITIATE?
YOU OVERSTEP YOUR MANDATE AGAIN...
...WHICH BRINGS US TO THE NEXT PART OF OUR MEETING...YOUR DISCIPLINARY--
JUST A SEC. I'M BIDDING ON SOMETHING HERE.
YOU'RE WHAT?!!?!
BOOOOOOM
KRRESSH!
AYAAA BLUE CHIP SONS OF BLEEEARRRR
YYYYAAAHHHH!
BRAKKA BRAKKA
BRAKKA BRAKKA

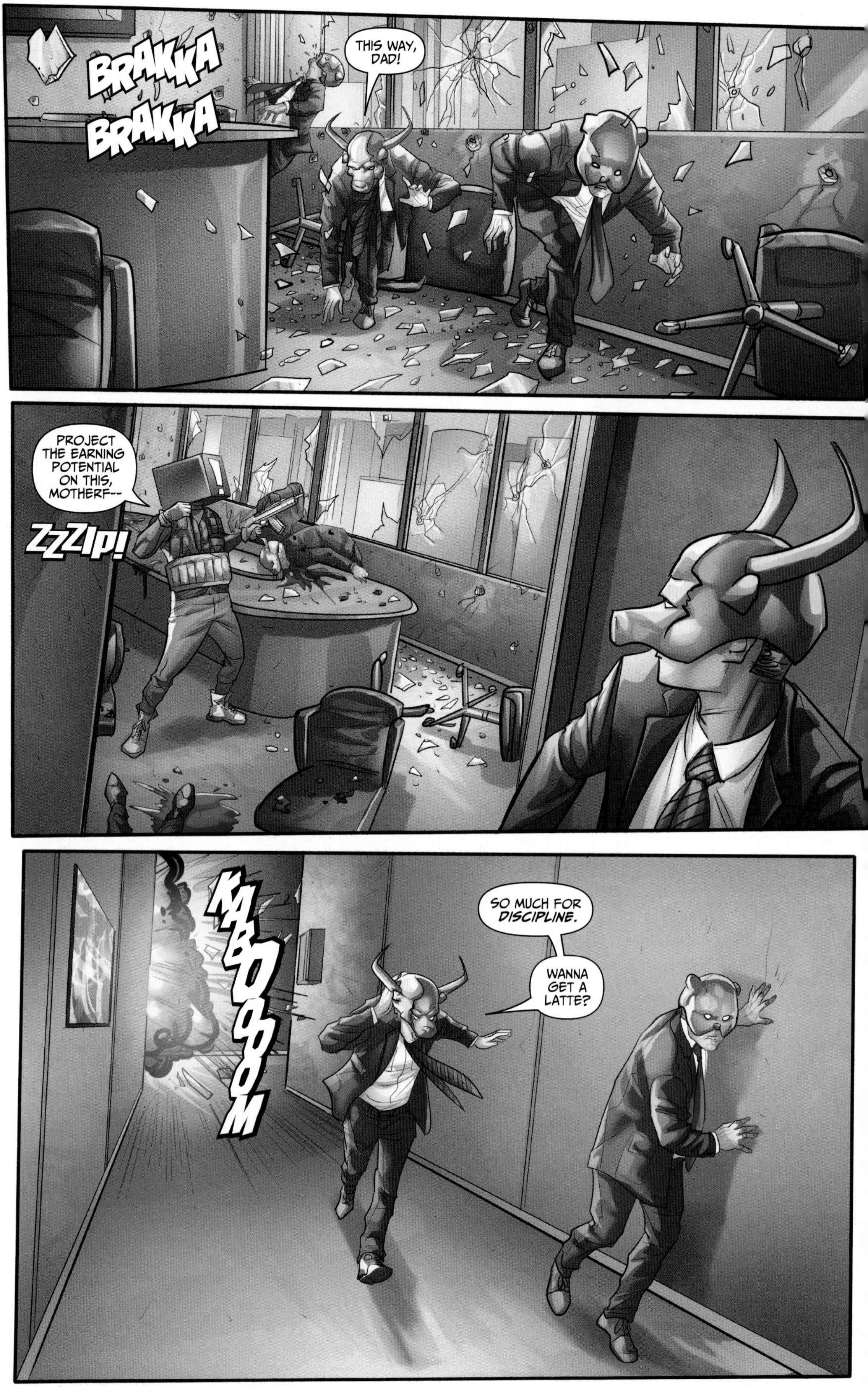
BRAKKA
BRAKKA
THIS WAY, DAD!
PROJECT THE EARNING POTENTIAL ON THIS, MOTHERF--
ZZZIP!
KABOOOOM
SO MUCH FOR *DISCIPLINE.*
WANNA GET A LATTE?

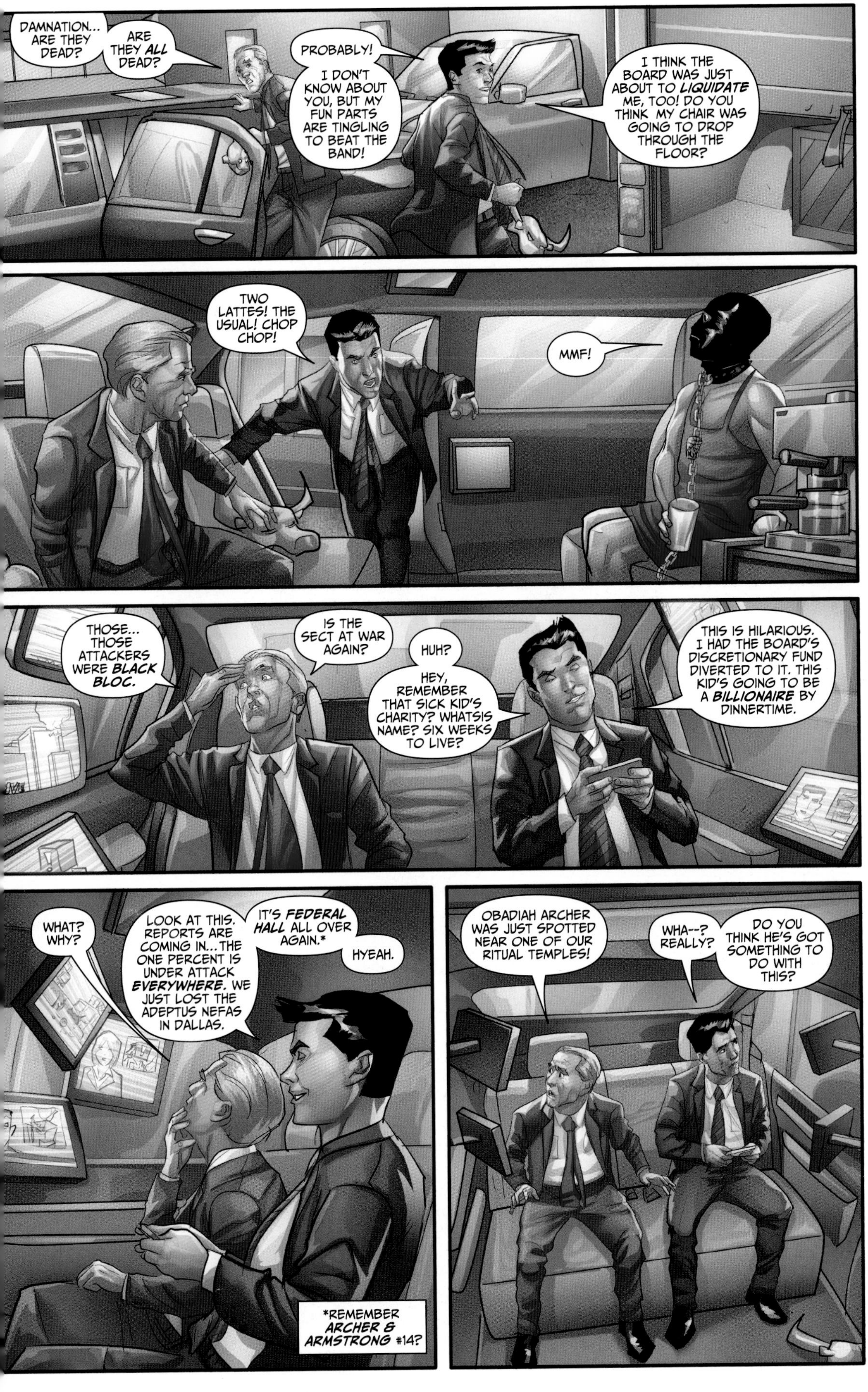

DAMNATION... ARE THEY DEAD?
ARE THEY ALL DEAD?
PROBABLY!
I DON'T KNOW ABOUT YOU, BUT MY FUN PARTS ARE TINGLING TO BEAT THE BAND!
I THINK THE BOARD WAS JUST ABOUT TO LIQUIDATE ME, TOO! DO YOU THINK MY CHAIR WAS GOING TO DROP THROUGH THE FLOOR?
TWO LATTES! THE USUAL! CHOP CHOP!
MMF!
THOSE... THOSE ATTACKERS WERE BLACK BLOC.
IS THE SECT AT WAR AGAIN?
HUH?
HEY, REMEMBER THAT SICK KID'S CHARITY? WHATSIS NAME? SIX WEEKS TO LIVE?
THIS IS HILARIOUS. I HAD THE BOARD'S DISCRETIONARY FUND DIVERTED TO IT. THIS KID'S GOING TO BE A BILLIONAIRE BY DINNERTIME.
WHAT? WHY?
LOOK AT THIS. REPORTS ARE COMING IN... THE ONE PERCENT IS UNDER ATTACK EVERYWHERE. WE JUST LOST THE ADEPTUS NEFAS IN DALLAS.
IT'S FEDERAL HALL ALL OVER AGAIN.*
HYEAH.
*REMEMBER ARCHER & ARMSTRONG #14?
OBADIAH ARCHER WAS JUST SPOTTED NEAR ONE OF OUR RITUAL TEMPLES!
WHA--? REALLY?
DO YOU THINK HE'S GOT SOMETHING TO DO WITH THIS?

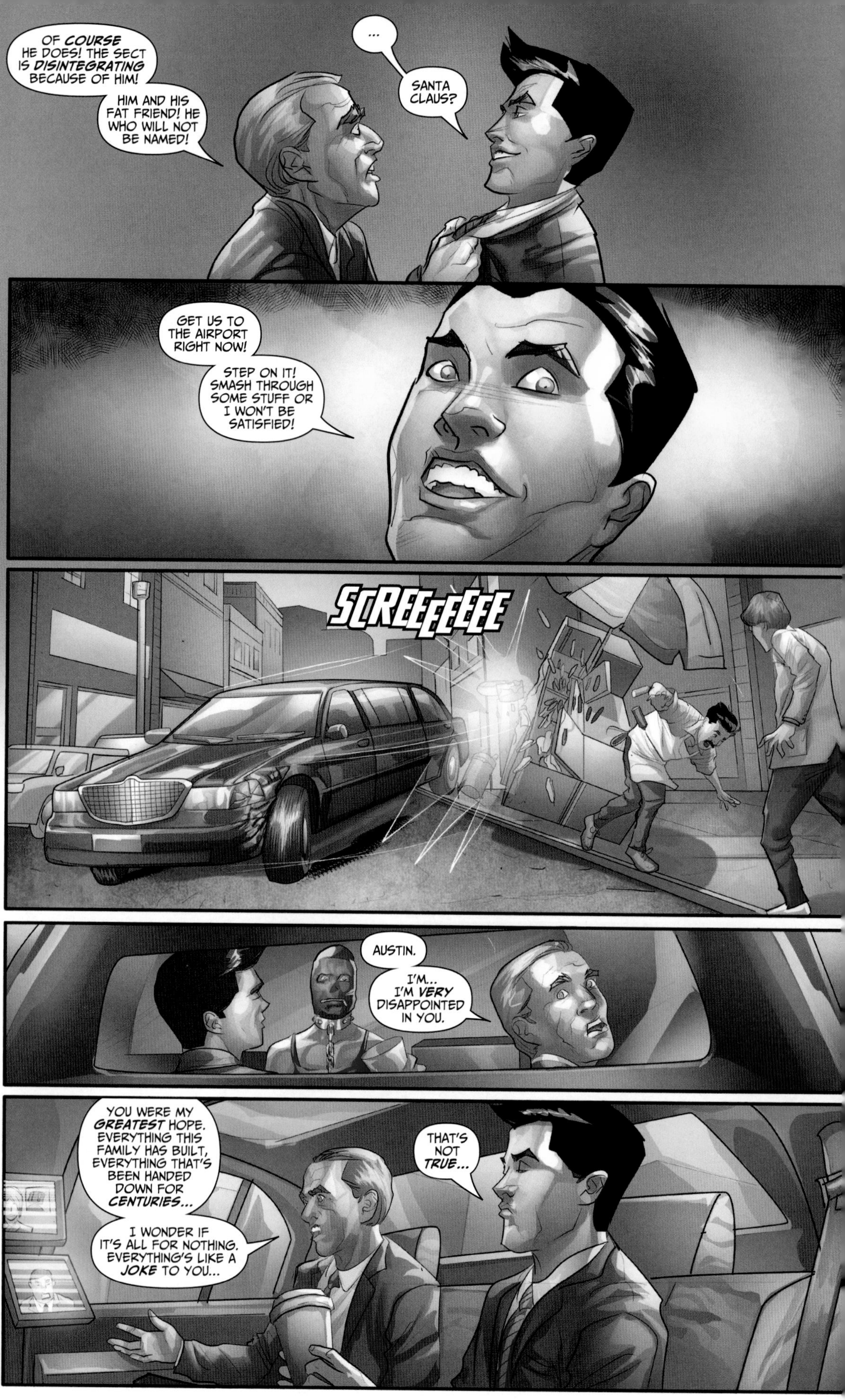
OF COURSE HE DOES! THE SECT IS DISINTEGRATING BECAUSE OF HIM!
HIM AND HIS FAT FRIEND! HE WHO WILL NOT BE NAMED!
...
SANTA CLAUS?
GET US TO THE AIRPORT RIGHT NOW!
STEP ON IT! SMASH THROUGH SOME STUFF OR I WON'T BE SATISFIED!
SCREEEEEEE
AUSTIN.
I'M... I'M VERY DISAPPOINTED IN YOU.
YOU WERE MY GREATEST HOPE. EVERYTHING THIS FAMILY HAS BUILT, EVERYTHING THAT'S BEEN HANDED DOWN FOR CENTURIES...
THAT'S NOT TRUE...
I WONDER IF IT'S ALL FOR NOTHING. EVERYTHING'S LIKE A JOKE TO YOU...

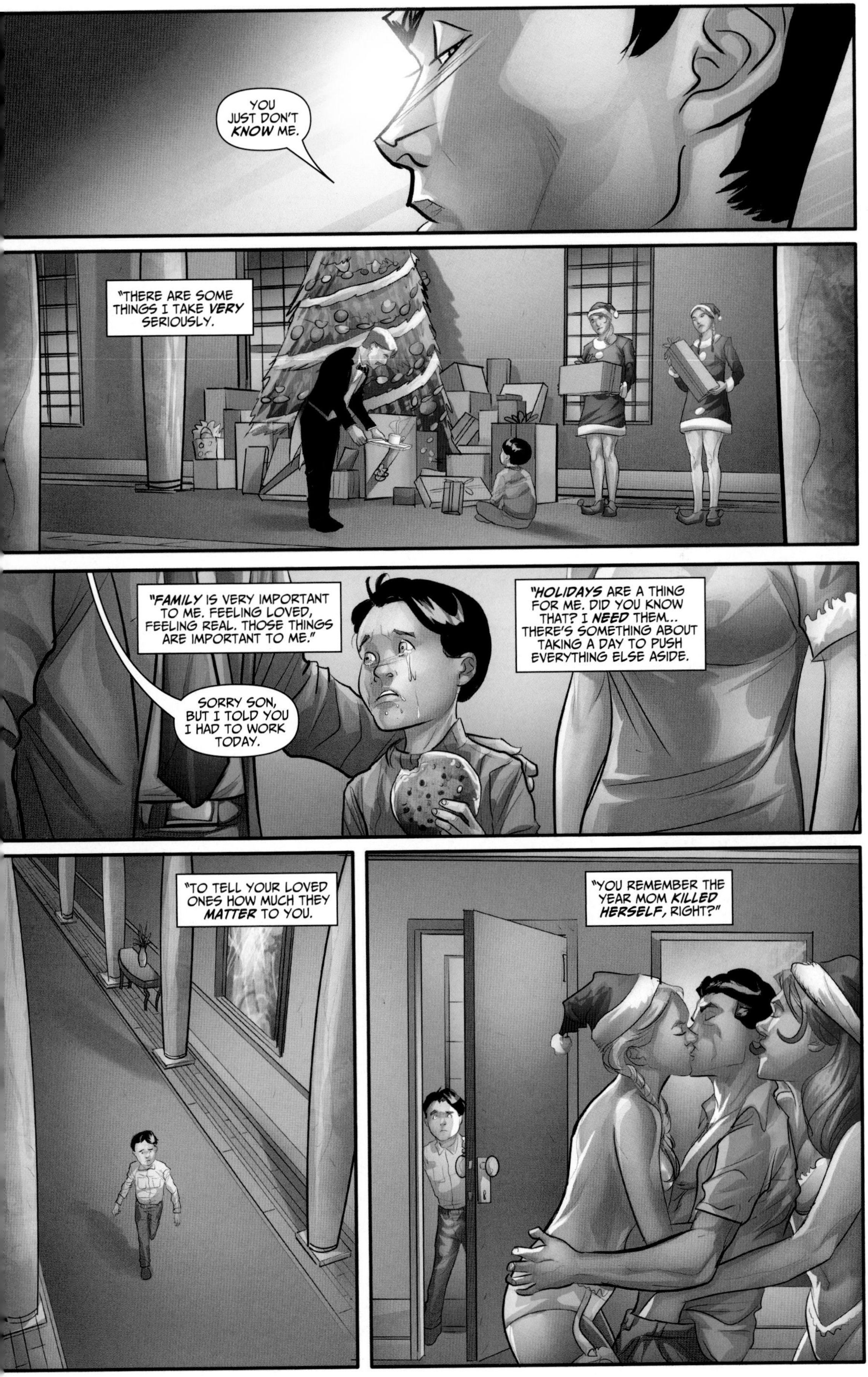
YOU JUST DON'T KNOW ME.
"THERE ARE SOME THINGS I TAKE VERY SERIOUSLY.
"FAMILY IS VERY IMPORTANT TO ME. FEELING LOVED, FEELING REAL. THOSE THINGS ARE IMPORTANT TO ME."
SORRY SON, BUT I TOLD YOU I HAD TO WORK TODAY.
"HOLIDAYS ARE A THING FOR ME. DID YOU KNOW THAT? I NEED THEM... THERE'S SOMETHING ABOUT TAKING A DAY TO PUSH EVERYTHING ELSE ASIDE.
"TO TELL YOUR LOVED ONES HOW MUCH THEY MATTER TO YOU.
"YOU REMEMBER THE YEAR MOM KILLED HERSELF, RIGHT?"

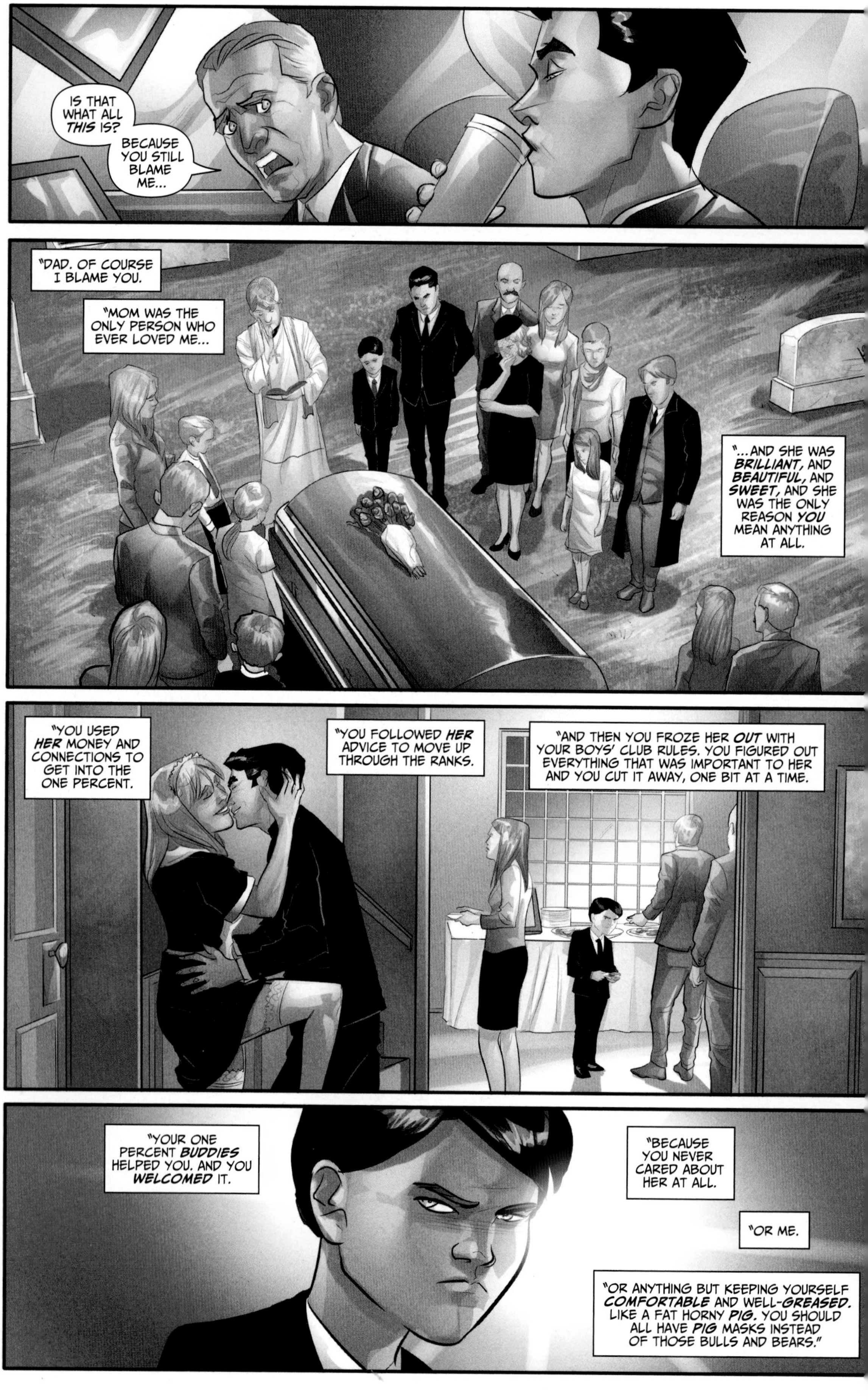
IS THAT WHAT ALL THIS IS?
BECAUSE YOU STILL BLAME ME...
"DAD. OF COURSE I BLAME YOU.
"MOM WAS THE ONLY PERSON WHO EVER LOVED ME...
"...AND SHE WAS BRILLIANT, AND BEAUTIFUL, AND SWEET, AND SHE WAS THE ONLY REASON YOU MEAN ANYTHING AT ALL.
"YOU USED HER MONEY AND CONNECTIONS TO GET INTO THE ONE PERCENT.
"YOU FOLLOWED HER ADVICE TO MOVE UP THROUGH THE RANKS.
"AND THEN YOU FROZE HER OUT WITH YOUR BOYS' CLUB RULES. YOU FIGURED OUT EVERYTHING THAT WAS IMPORTANT TO HER AND YOU CUT IT AWAY, ONE BIT AT A TIME.
"YOUR ONE PERCENT BUDDIES HELPED YOU. AND YOU WELCOMED IT.
"BECAUSE YOU NEVER CARED ABOUT HER AT ALL.
"OR ME.
"OR ANYTHING BUT KEEPING YOURSELF COMFORTABLE AND WELL-GREASED. LIKE A FAT HORNY PIG. YOU SHOULD ALL HAVE PIG MASKS INSTEAD OF THOSE BULLS AND BEARS."

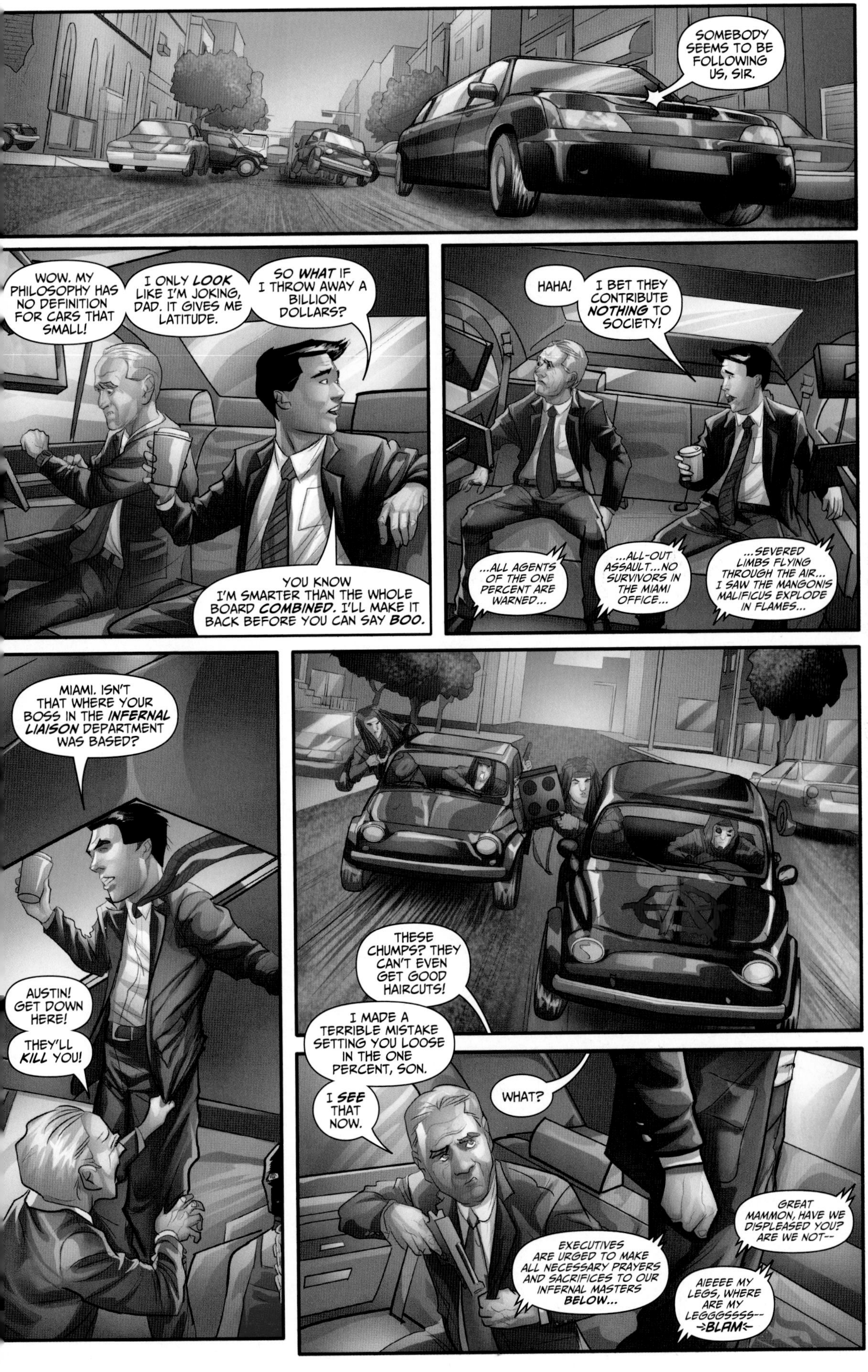

SOMEBODY SEEMS TO BE FOLLOWING US, SIR.
WOW. MY PHILOSOPHY HAS NO DEFINITION FOR CARS THAT SMALL!
I ONLY LOOK LIKE I'M JOKING, DAD. IT GIVES ME LATITUDE.
SO WHAT IF I THROW AWAY A BILLION DOLLARS?
YOU KNOW I'M SMARTER THAN THE WHOLE BOARD COMBINED. I'LL MAKE IT BACK BEFORE YOU CAN SAY BOO.
HAHA!
I BET THEY CONTRIBUTE NOTHING TO SOCIETY!
...ALL AGENTS OF THE ONE PERCENT ARE WARNED...
...ALL-OUT ASSAULT...NO SURVIVORS IN THE MIAMI OFFICE...
...SEVERED LIMBS FLYING THROUGH THE AIR... I SAW THE MANGONIS MALIFICUS EXPLODE IN FLAMES...
MIAMI. ISN'T THAT WHERE YOUR BOSS IN THE INFERNAL LIAISON DEPARTMENT WAS BASED?
AUSTIN! GET DOWN HERE!
THEY'LL KILL YOU!
THESE CHUMPS? THEY CAN'T EVEN GET GOOD HAIRCUTS!
I MADE A TERRIBLE MISTAKE SETTING YOU LOOSE IN THE ONE PERCENT, SON.
I SEE THAT NOW.
WHAT?
EXECUTIVES ARE URGED TO MAKE ALL NECESSARY PRAYERS AND SACRIFICES TO OUR INFERNAL MASTERS BELOW...
GREAT MAMMON, HAVE WE DISPLEASED YOU? ARE WE NOT--
AIEEEE MY LEGS, WHERE ARE MY LEGGGSSSS--
BLAM

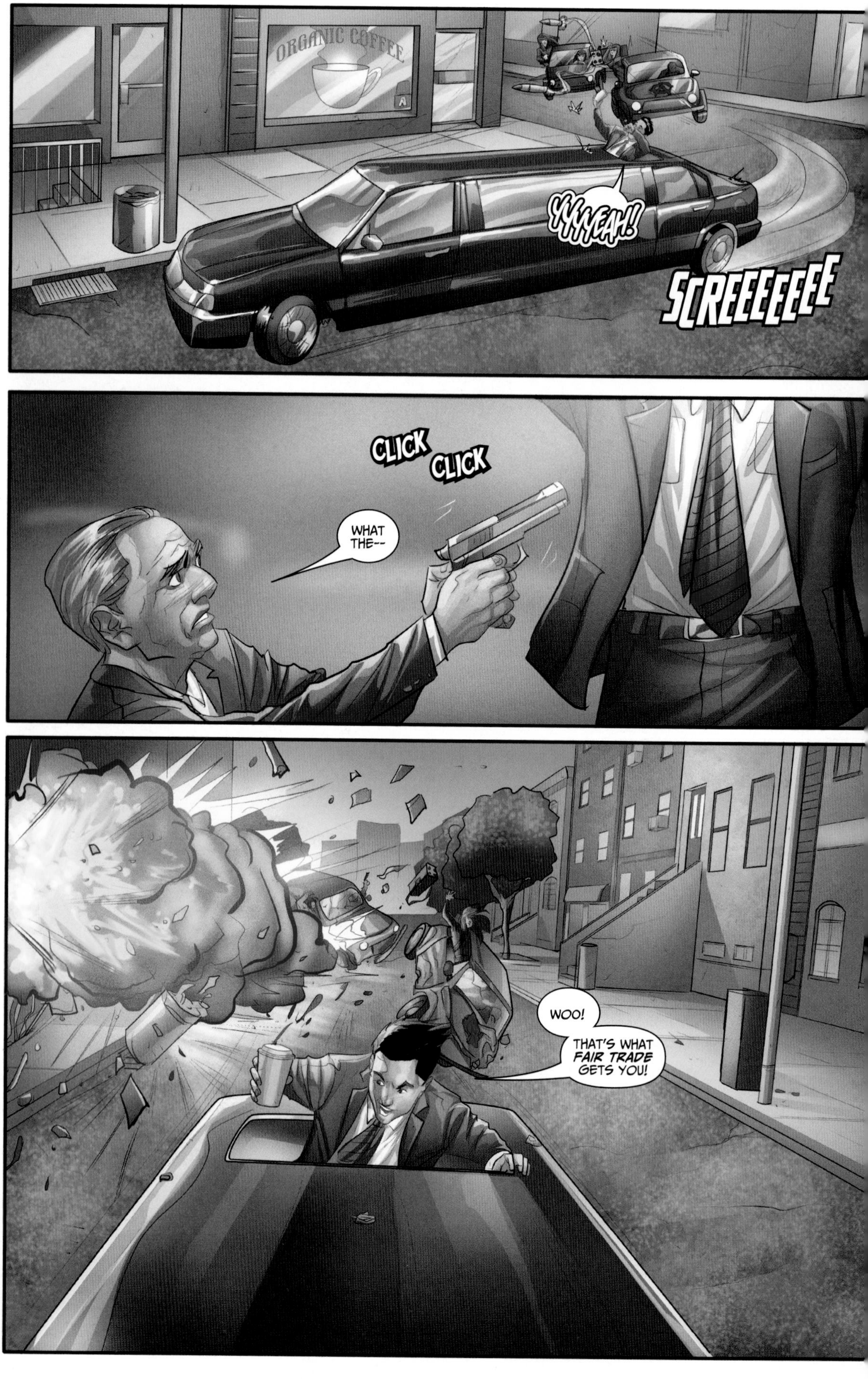
ORGANIC COFFEE
YYYYEAH!
SCREEEEEEE
CLICK
CLICK
WHAT THE--
WOO!
THAT'S WHAT *FAIR TRADE* GETS YOU!

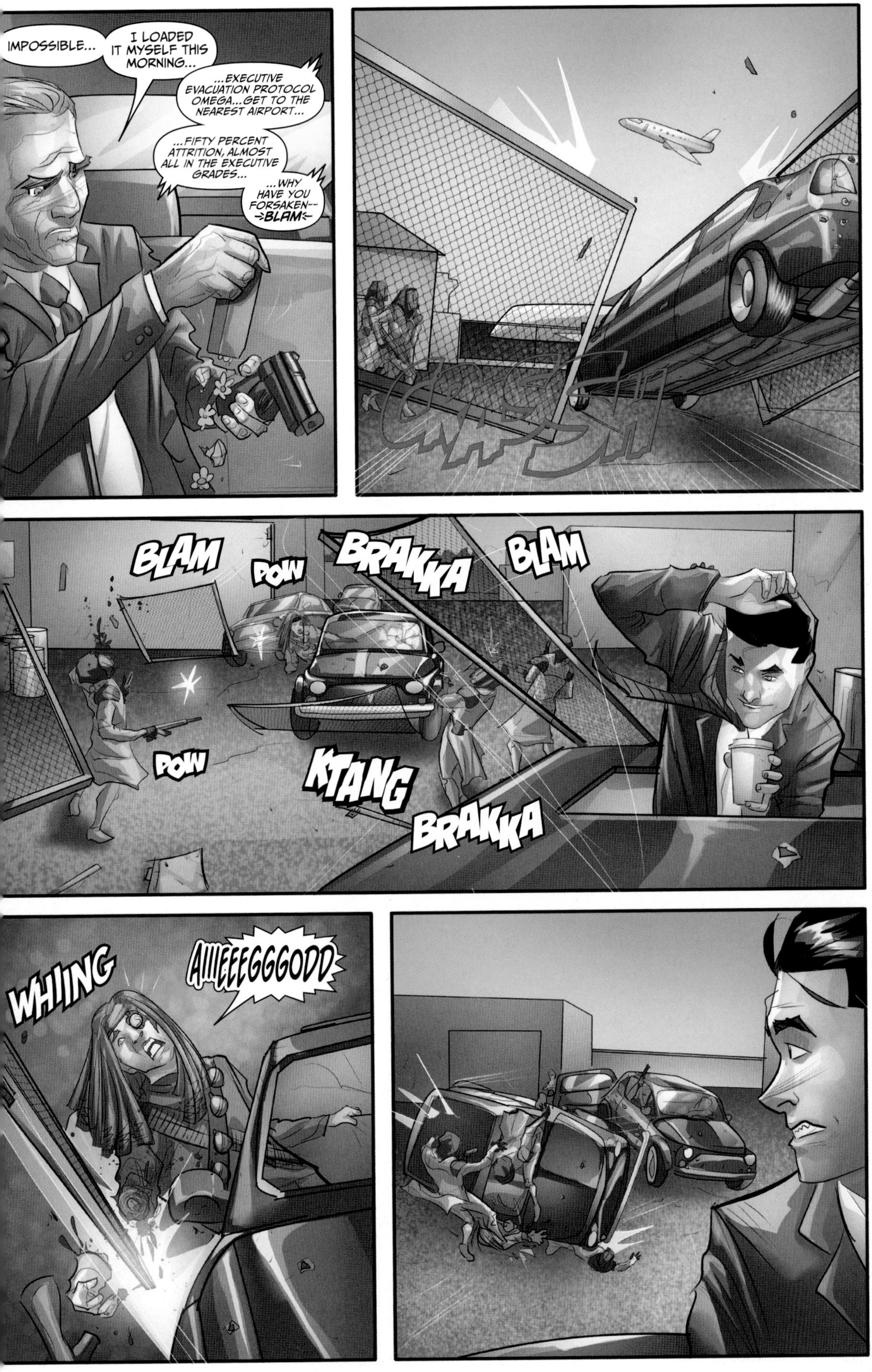
IMPOSSIBLE...
I LOADED IT MYSELF THIS MORNING...
...EXECUTIVE EVACUATION PROTOCOL OMEGA...GET TO THE NEAREST AIRPORT...
...FIFTY PERCENT ATTRITION, ALMOST ALL IN THE EXECUTIVE GRADES...
...WHY HAVE YOU FORSAKEN-- BLAM
CRASH
BLAM
POW
BRAKKA
BLAM
POW
KTANG
BRAKKA
WHIING
AIIIEEEGGGODD

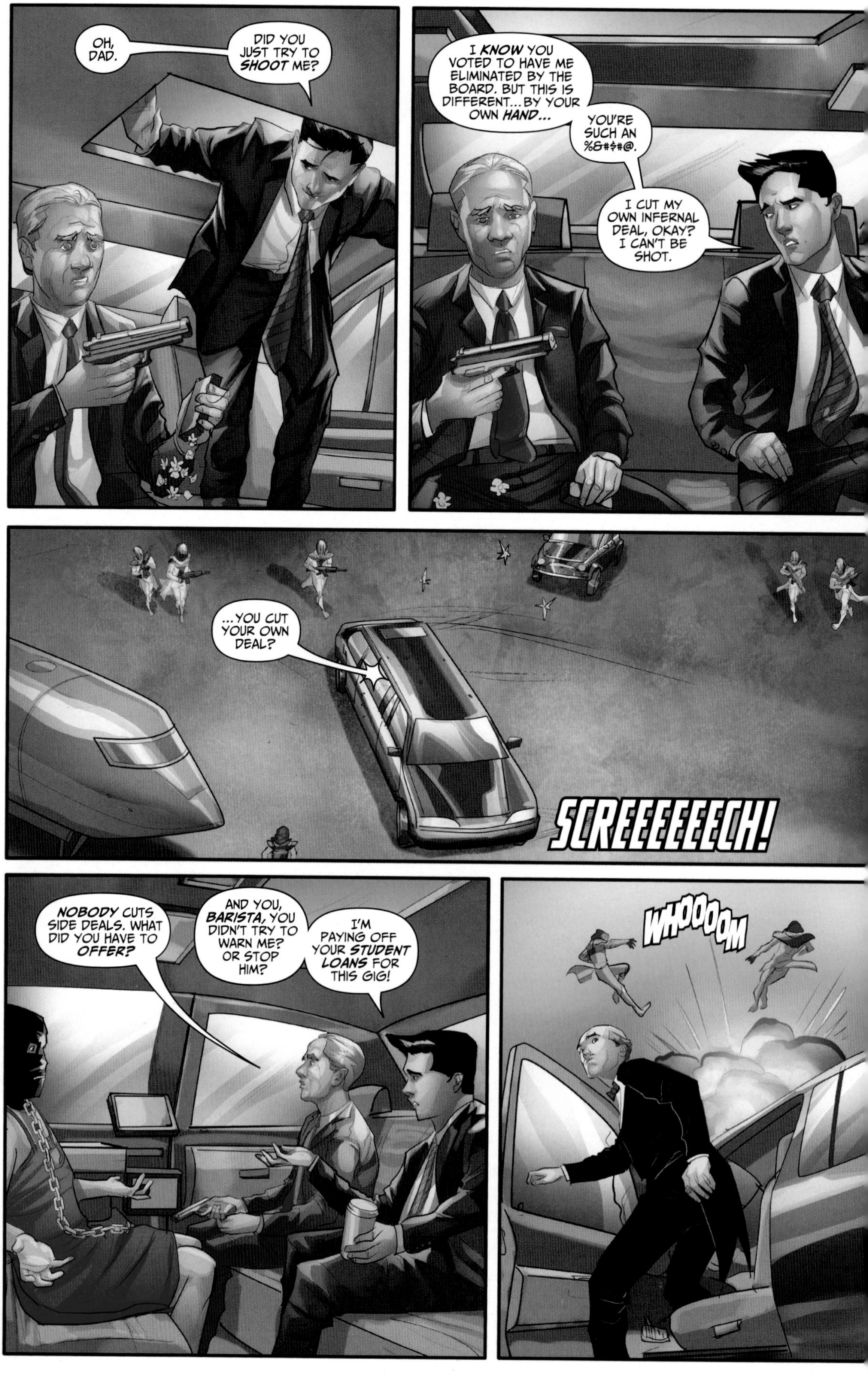
OH, DAD.
DID YOU JUST TRY TO SHOOT ME?
I KNOW YOU VOTED TO HAVE ME ELIMINATED BY THE BOARD. BUT THIS IS DIFFERENT... BY YOUR OWN HAND...
YOU'RE SUCH AN %&#$#@.
I CUT MY OWN INFERNAL DEAL, OKAY? I CAN'T BE SHOT.
...YOU CUT YOUR OWN DEAL?
SCREEEEEEECH!
NOBODY CUTS SIDE DEALS. WHAT DID YOU HAVE TO OFFER?
AND YOU, BARISTA, YOU DIDN'T TRY TO WARN ME? OR STOP HIM?
I'M PAYING OFF YOUR STUDENT LOANS FOR THIS GIG!
WHOOOOM

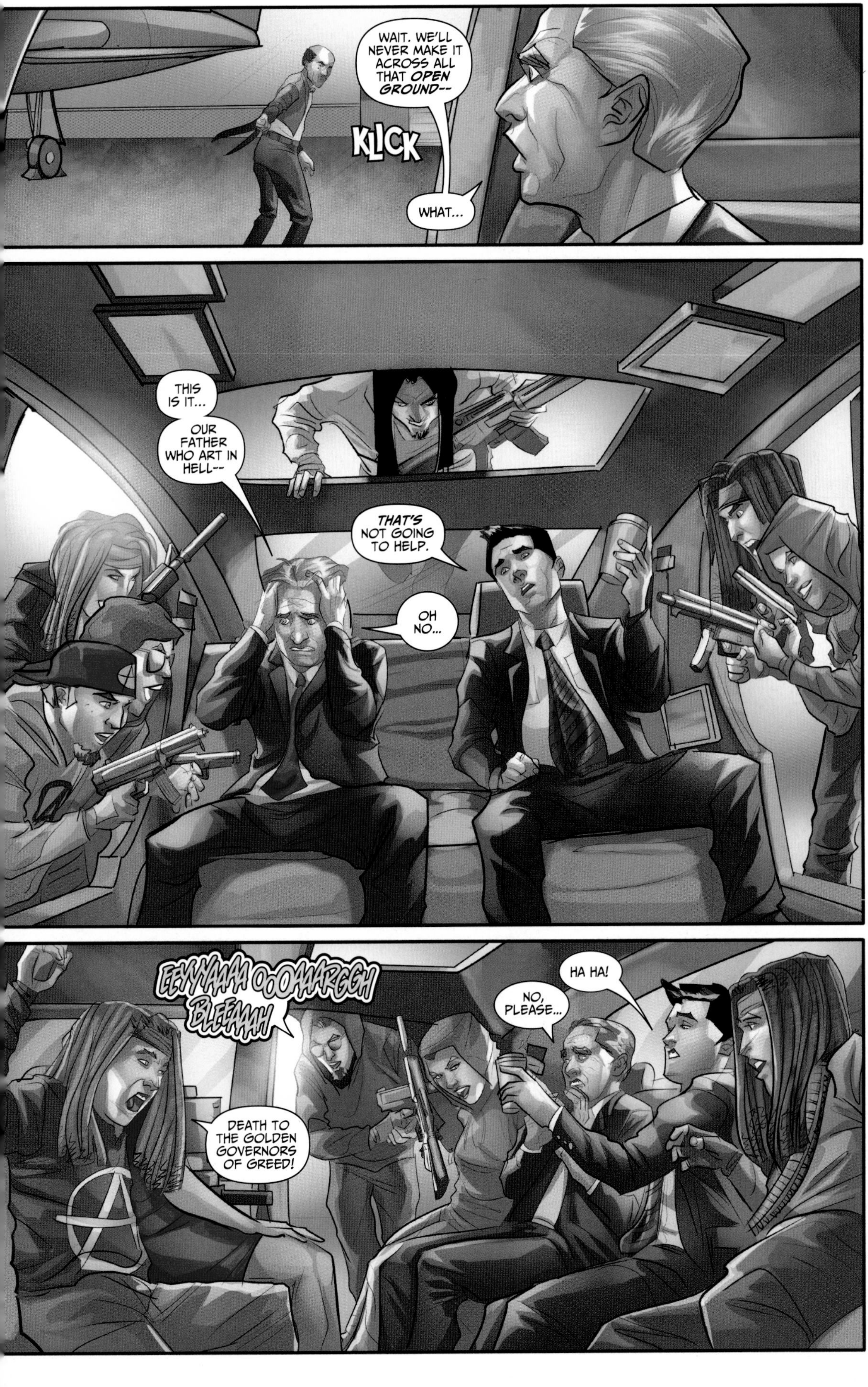
WAIT. WE'LL NEVER MAKE IT ACROSS ALL THAT *OPEN GROUND*--
KLICK
WHAT...
THIS IS IT...
OUR FATHER WHO ART IN HELL--
THAT'S NOT GOING TO HELP.
OH NO...
EEYYYAAAA OoOAAARGGH BLEEAAAH
DEATH TO THE GOLDEN GOVERNORS OF GREED!
NO, PLEASE...
HA HA!

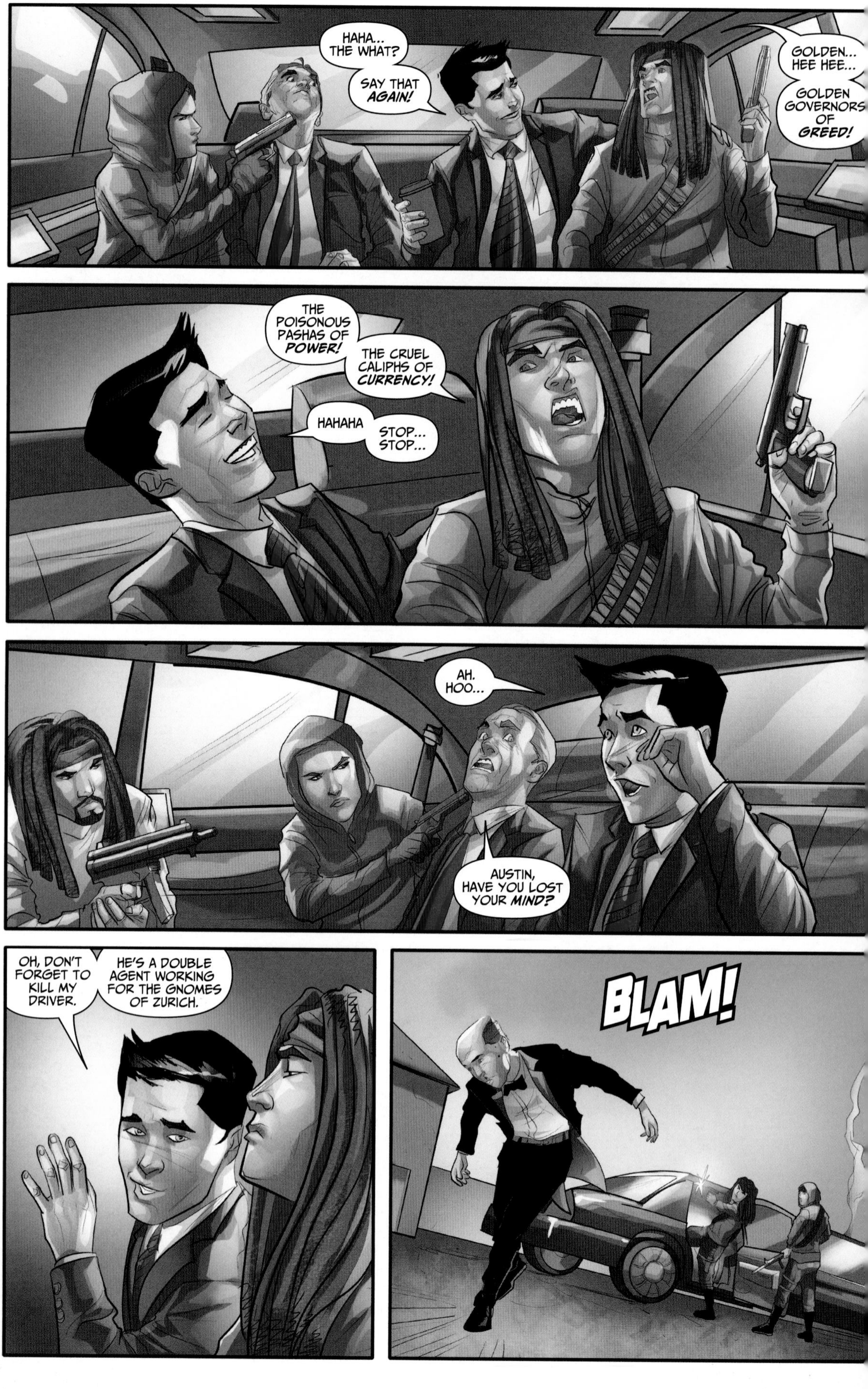
HAHA... THE WHAT?
SAY THAT AGAIN!
GOLDEN... HEE HEE...
GOLDEN GOVERNORS OF GREED!
THE POISONOUS PASHAS OF POWER!
THE CRUEL CALIPHS OF CURRENCY!
HAHAHA
STOP... STOP...
AH. HOO...
AUSTIN, HAVE YOU LOST YOUR MIND?
OH, DON'T FORGET TO KILL MY DRIVER.
HE'S A DOUBLE AGENT WORKING FOR THE GNOMES OF ZURICH.
BLAM!

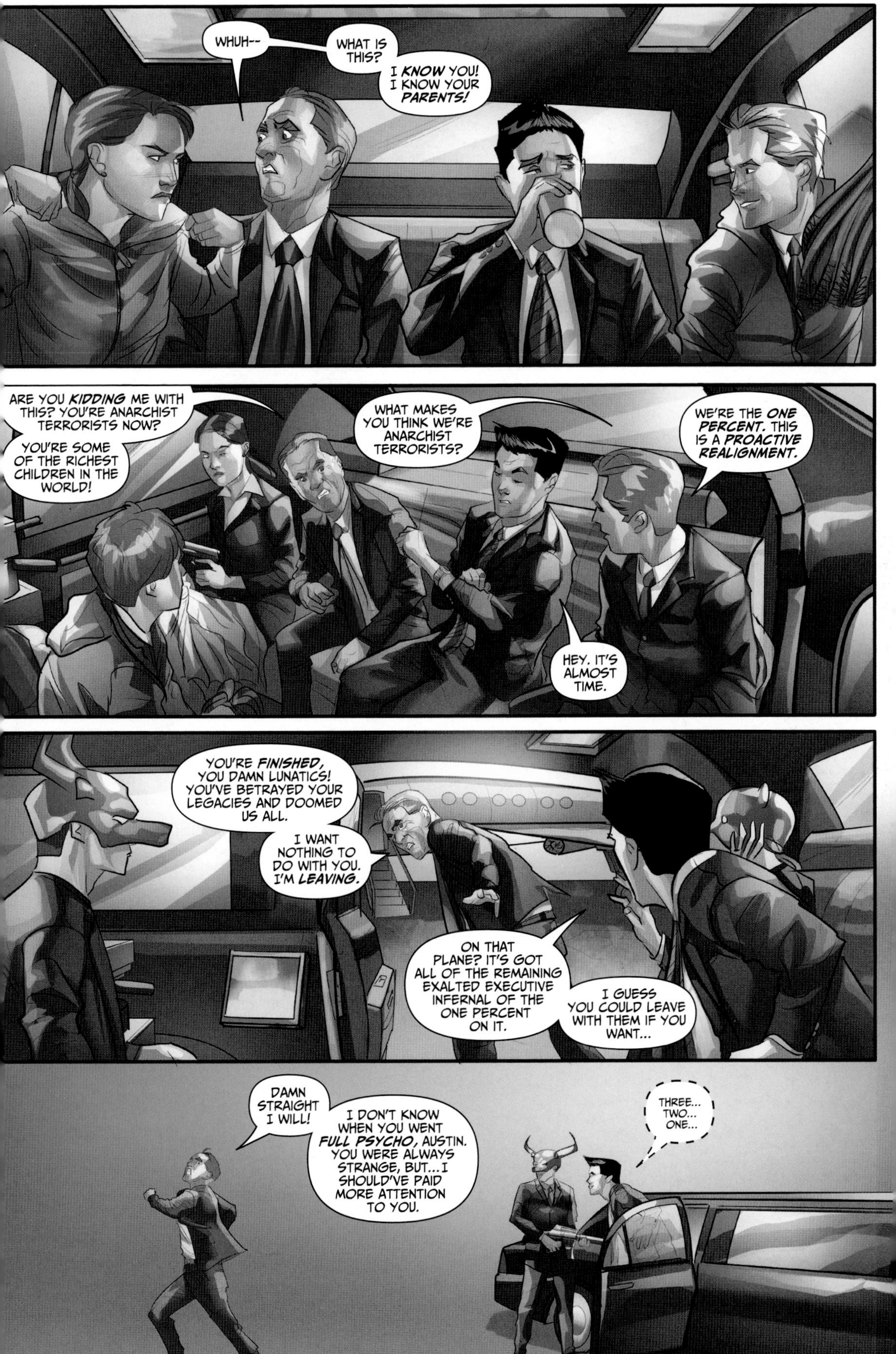
WHUH--
WHAT IS THIS?
I *KNOW* YOU! I KNOW YOUR *PARENTS!*
ARE YOU *KIDDING* ME WITH THIS? YOU'RE ANARCHIST TERRORISTS NOW?
YOU'RE SOME OF THE RICHEST CHILDREN IN THE WORLD!
WHAT MAKES YOU THINK WE'RE ANARCHIST TERRORISTS?
WE'RE THE *ONE PERCENT.* THIS IS A *PROACTIVE REALIGNMENT.*
HEY. IT'S ALMOST TIME.
YOU'RE *FINISHED,* YOU DAMN LUNATICS! YOU'VE BETRAYED YOUR LEGACIES AND DOOMED US ALL.
I WANT NOTHING TO DO WITH YOU. I'M *LEAVING.*
ON THAT PLANE? IT'S GOT ALL OF THE REMAINING EXALTED EXECUTIVE INFERNAL OF THE ONE PERCENT ON IT.
I GUESS YOU COULD LEAVE WITH THEM IF YOU WANT...
DAMN STRAIGHT I WILL!
I DON'T KNOW WHEN YOU WENT *FULL PSYCHO,* AUSTIN. YOU WERE ALWAYS STRANGE, BUT...I SHOULD'VE PAID MORE ATTENTION TO YOU.
THREE... TWO... ONE...

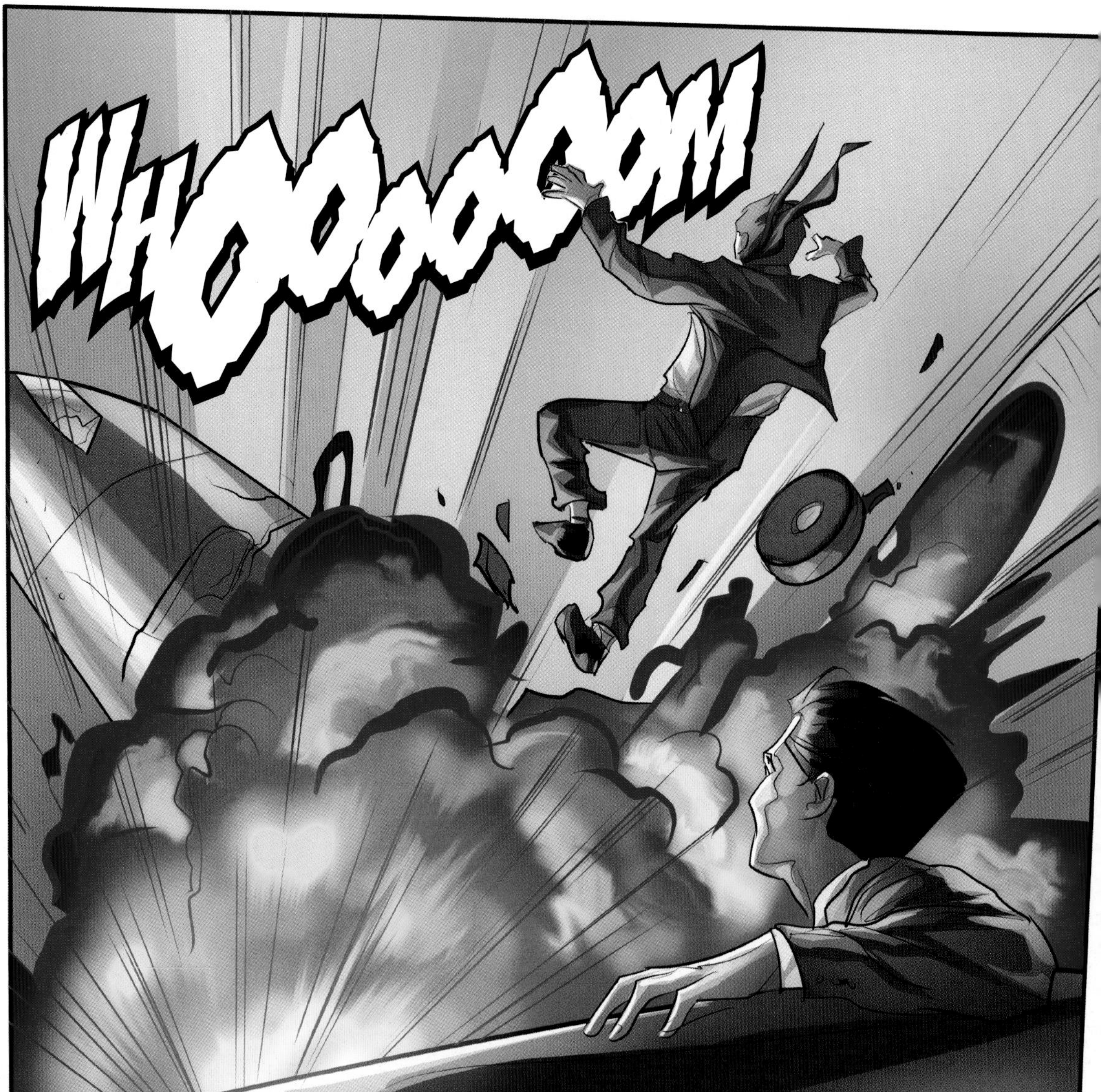
WHOOOOOOM

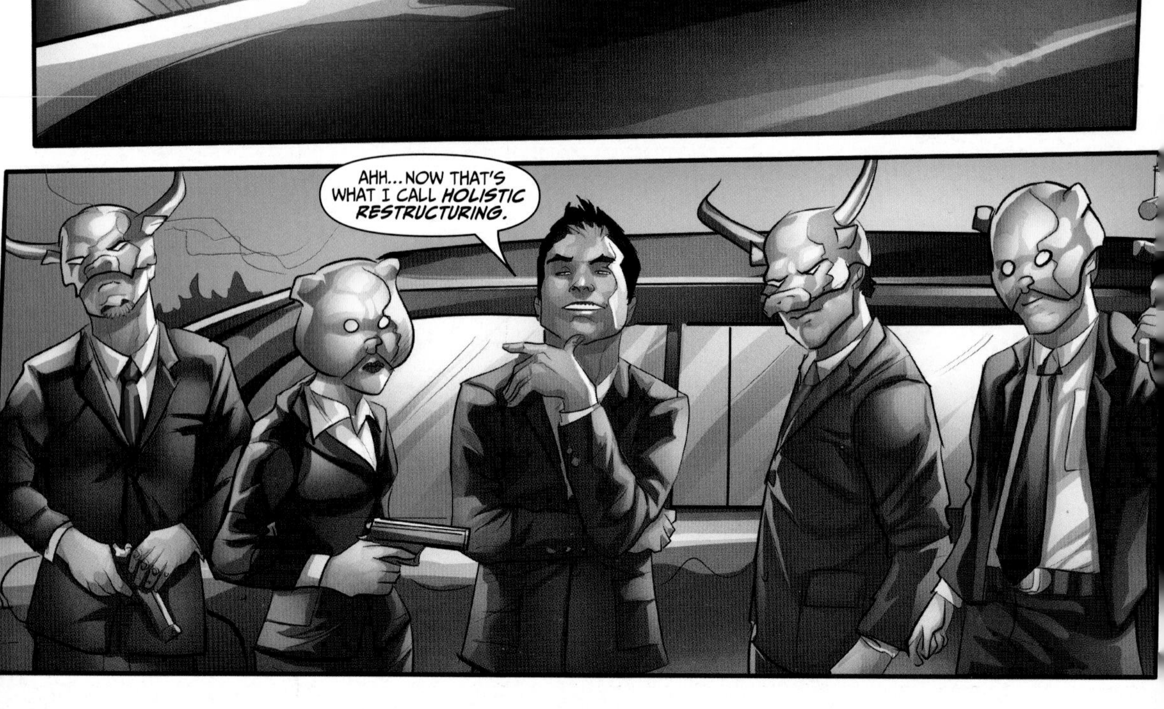
AHH...NOW THAT'S WHAT I CALL HOLISTIC RESTRUCTURING.

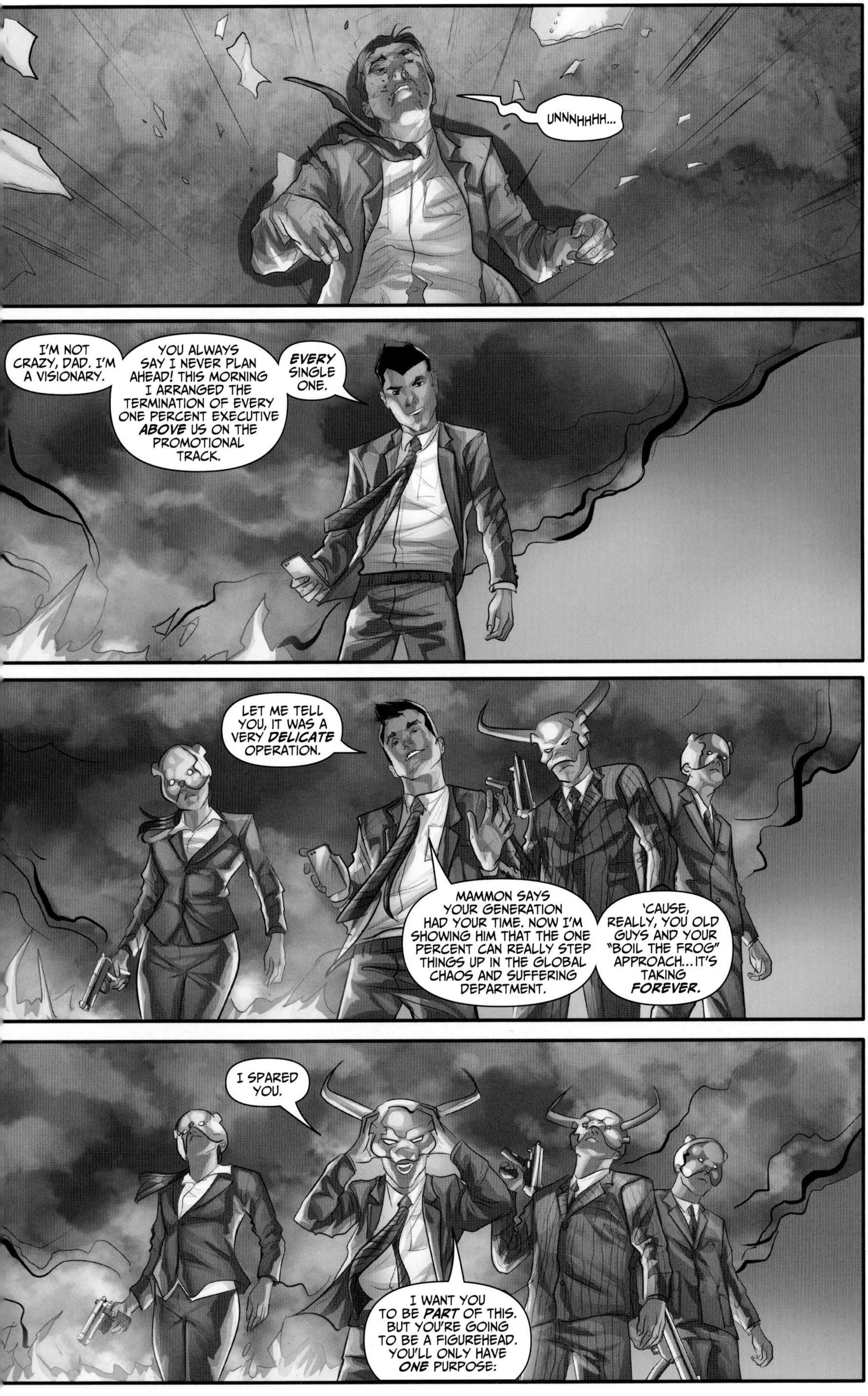

UNNNHHHH...
I'M NOT CRAZY, DAD. I'M A VISIONARY.
YOU ALWAYS SAY I NEVER PLAN AHEAD! THIS MORNING I ARRANGED THE TERMINATION OF EVERY ONE PERCENT EXECUTIVE ABOVE US ON THE PROMOTIONAL TRACK.
EVERY SINGLE ONE.
LET ME TELL YOU, IT WAS A VERY DELICATE OPERATION.
MAMMON SAYS YOUR GENERATION HAD YOUR TIME. NOW I'M SHOWING HIM THAT THE ONE PERCENT CAN REALLY STEP THINGS UP IN THE GLOBAL CHAOS AND SUFFERING DEPARTMENT.
'CAUSE, REALLY, YOU OLD GUYS AND YOUR "BOIL THE FROG" APPROACH... IT'S TAKING FOREVER.
I SPARED YOU.
I WANT YOU TO BE PART OF THIS. BUT YOU'RE GOING TO BE A FIGUREHEAD. YOU'LL ONLY HAVE ONE PURPOSE:

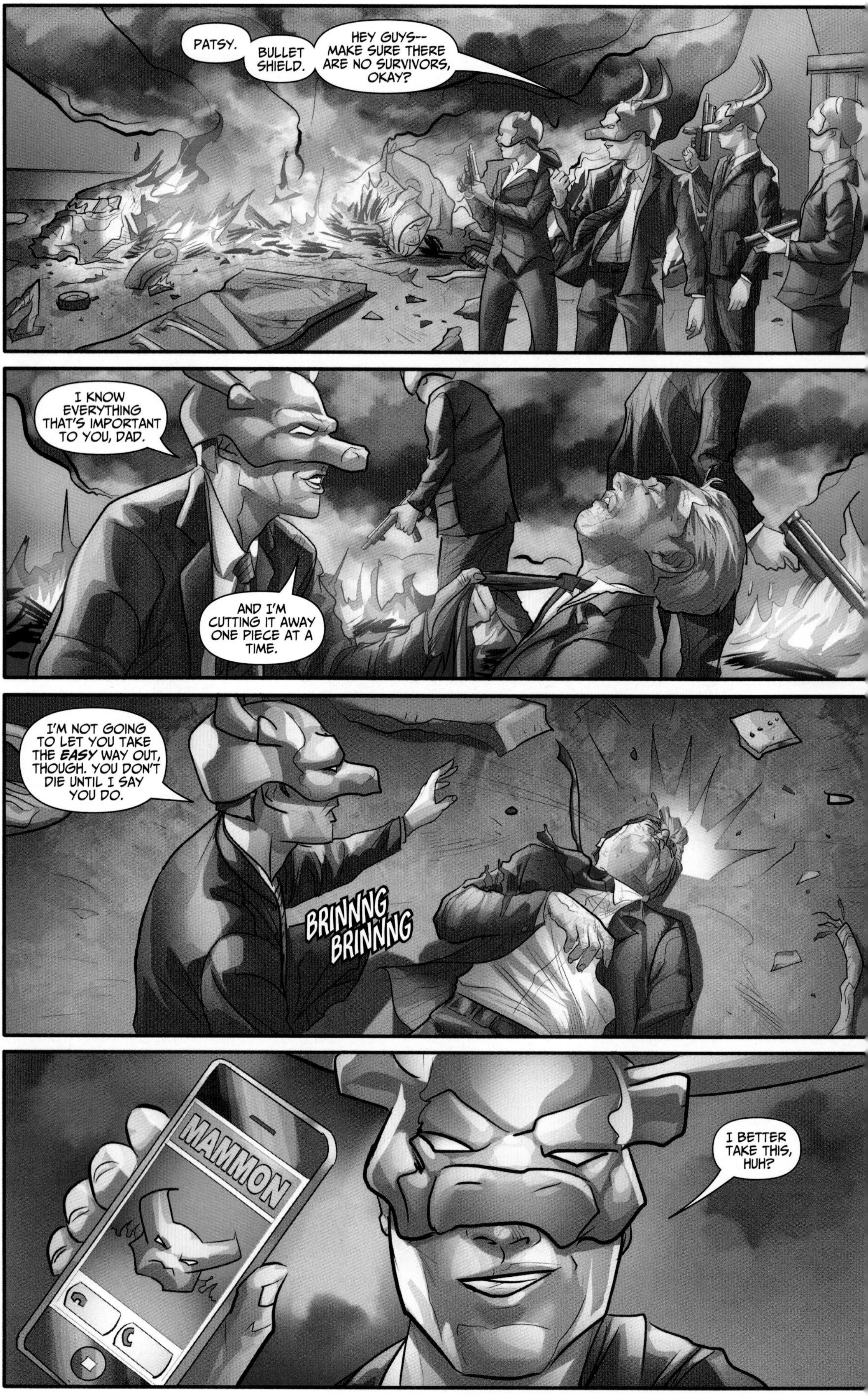
PATSY.
BULLET SHIELD.
HEY GUYS-- MAKE SURE THERE ARE NO SURVIVORS, OKAY?
I KNOW EVERYTHING THAT'S IMPORTANT TO YOU, DAD.
AND I'M CUTTING IT AWAY ONE PIECE AT A TIME.
I'M NOT GOING TO LET YOU TAKE THE EASY WAY OUT, THOUGH. YOU DON'T DIE UNTIL I SAY YOU DO.
BRINNNG BRINNNG
MAMMON
I BETTER TAKE THIS, HUH?

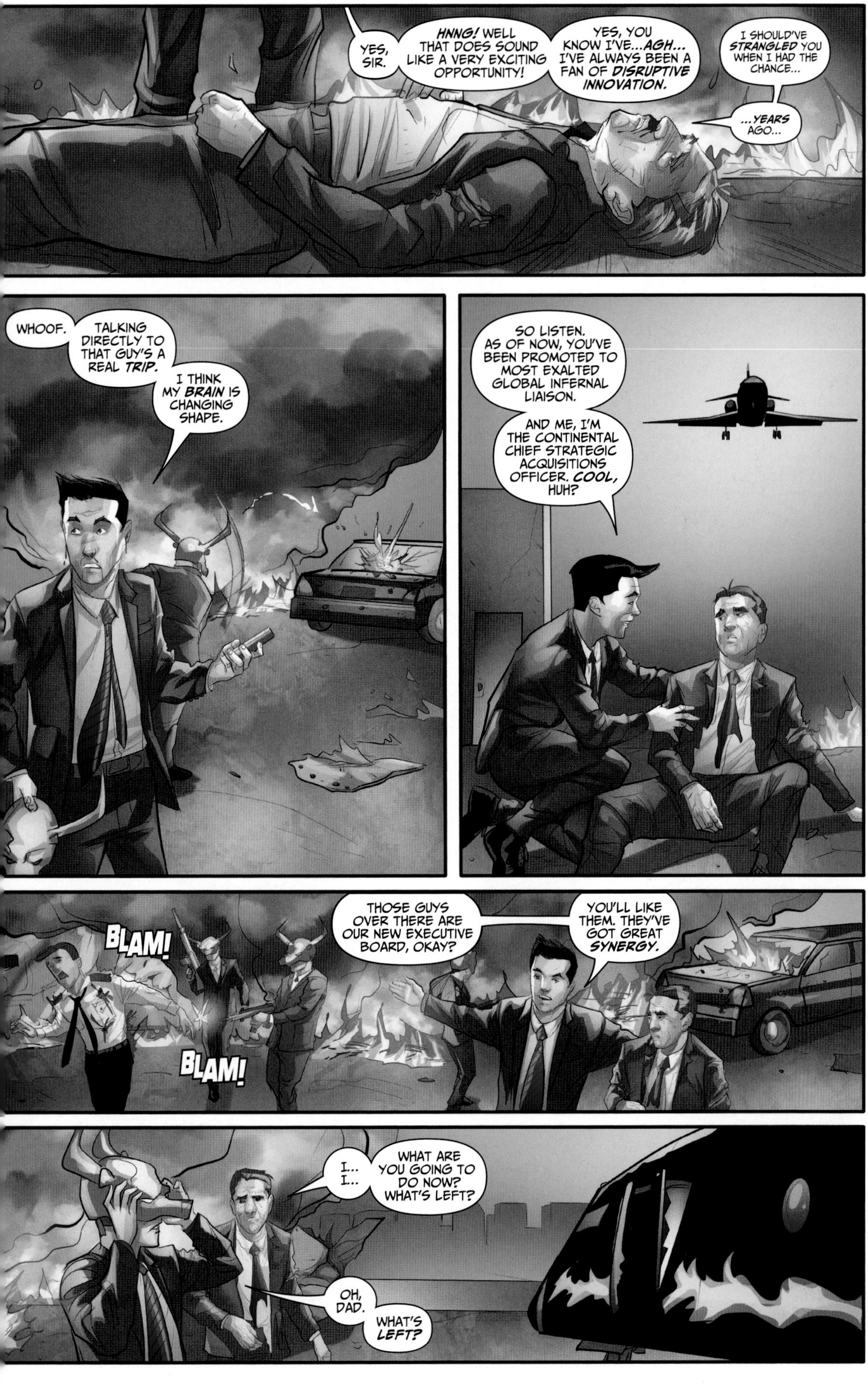
YES, SIR.
HNNG! WELL THAT DOES SOUND LIKE A VERY EXCITING OPPORTUNITY!
YES, YOU KNOW I'VE...AGH... I'VE ALWAYS BEEN A FAN OF DISRUPTIVE INNOVATION.
I SHOULD'VE STRANGLED YOU WHEN I HAD THE CHANCE...
...YEARS AGO...
WHOOF.
TALKING DIRECTLY TO THAT GUY'S A REAL TRIP.
I THINK MY BRAIN IS CHANGING SHAPE.
SO LISTEN. AS OF NOW, YOU'VE BEEN PROMOTED TO MOST EXALTED GLOBAL INFERNAL LIAISON.
AND ME, I'M THE CONTINENTAL CHIEF STRATEGIC ACQUISITIONS OFFICER. COOL, HUH?
BLAM!
BLAM!
THOSE GUYS OVER THERE ARE OUR NEW EXECUTIVE BOARD, OKAY?
YOU'LL LIKE THEM. THEY'VE GOT GREAT SYNERGY.
I... I...
WHAT ARE YOU GOING TO DO NOW? WHAT'S LEFT?
OH, DAD.
WHAT'S LEFT?

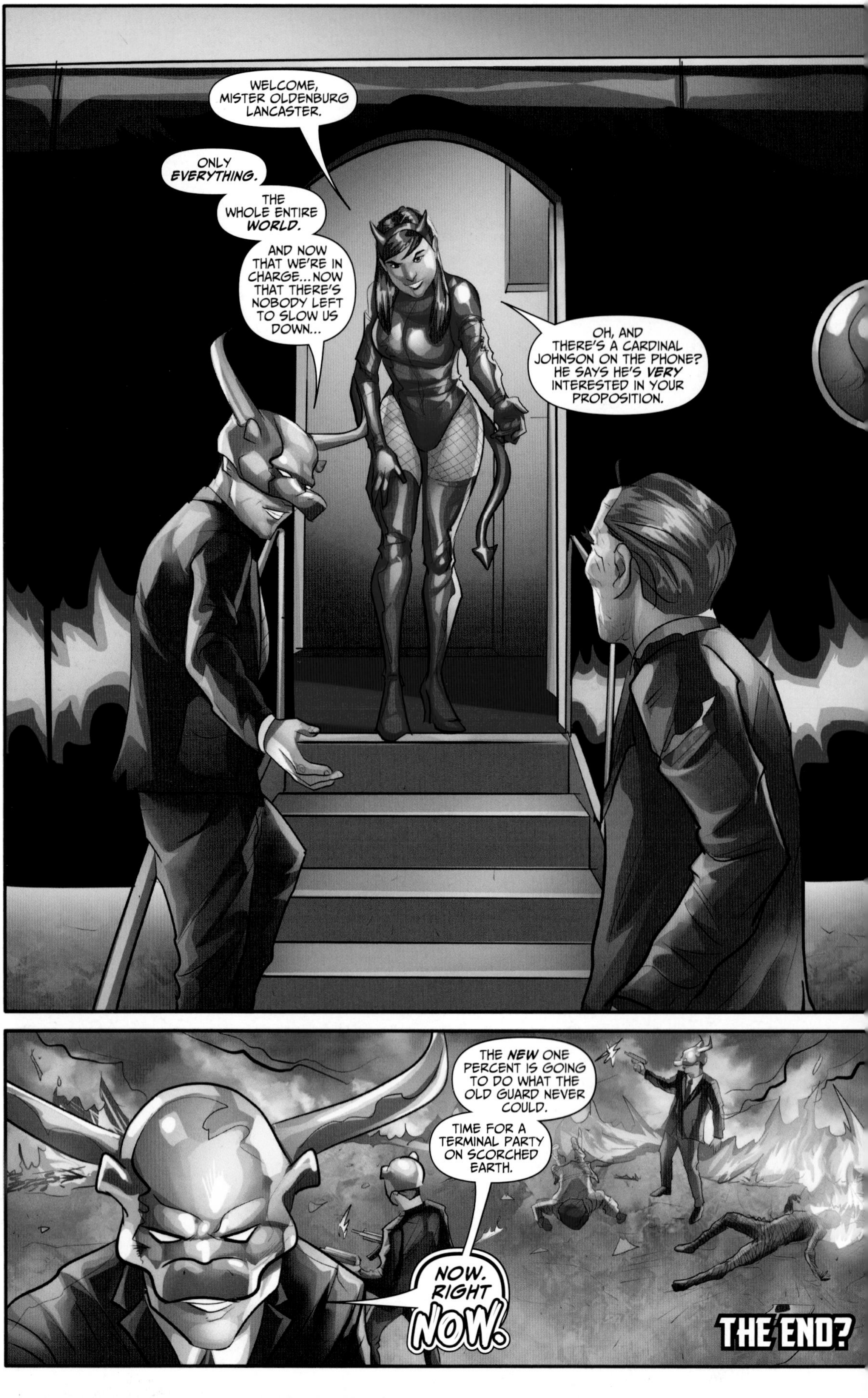
WELCOME, MISTER OLDENBURG LANCASTER.
ONLY EVERYTHING.
THE WHOLE ENTIRE WORLD.
AND NOW THAT WE'RE IN CHARGE...NOW THAT THERE'S NOBODY LEFT TO SLOW US DOWN...
OH, AND THERE'S A CARDINAL JOHNSON ON THE PHONE? HE SAYS HE'S VERY INTERESTED IN YOUR PROPOSITION.
THE NEW ONE PERCENT IS GOING TO DO WHAT THE OLD GUARD NEVER COULD.
TIME FOR A TERMINAL PARTY ON SCORCHED EARTH.
NOW. RIGHT NOW.
THE END?

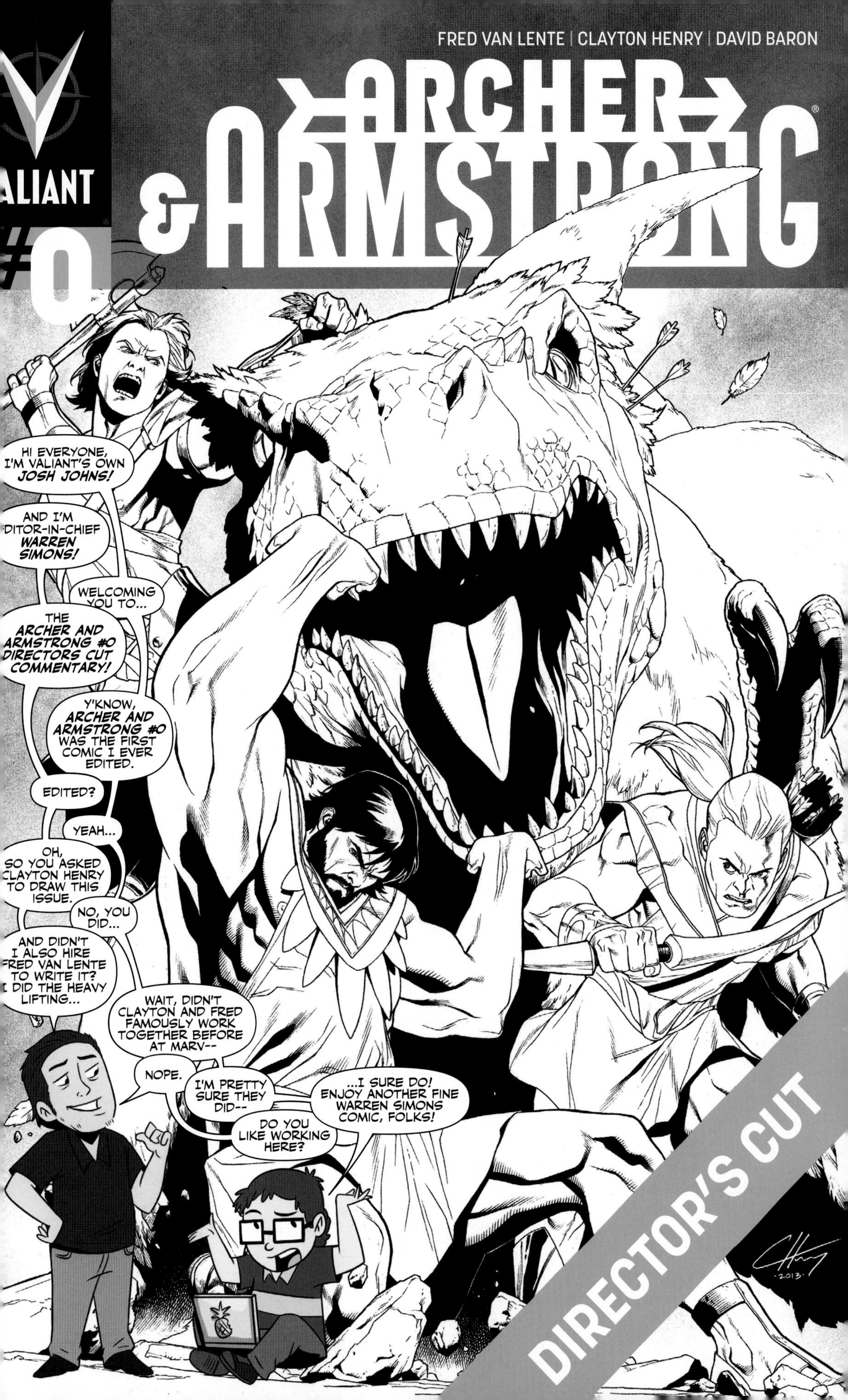
FRED VAN LENTE | CLAYTON HENRY | DAVID BARON
ARCHER & ARMSTRONG
VALIANT
#0
HI EVERYONE, I'M VALIANT'S OWN JOSH JOHNS!
AND I'M DITOR-IN-CHIEF WARREN SIMONS!
WELCOMING YOU TO...
THE ARCHER AND ARMSTRONG #0 DIRECTORS CUT COMMENTARY!
Y'KNOW, ARCHER AND ARMSTRONG #0 WAS THE FIRST COMIC I EVER EDITED.
EDITED?
YEAH...
OH, SO YOU ASKED CLAYTON HENRY TO DRAW THIS ISSUE.
NO, YOU DID...
AND DIDN'T I ALSO HIRE FRED VAN LENTE TO WRITE IT? I DID THE HEAVY LIFTING...
WAIT, DIDN'T CLAYTON AND FRED FAMOUSLY WORK TOGETHER BEFORE AT MARV--
NOPE.
I'M PRETTY SURE THEY DID--
DO YOU LIKE WORKING HERE?
...I SURE DO! ENJOY ANOTHER FINE WARREN SIMONS COMIC, FOLKS!
2013
DIRECTOR'S CUT

ARCHER & ARMSTRONG

OUR STORY SO FAR...

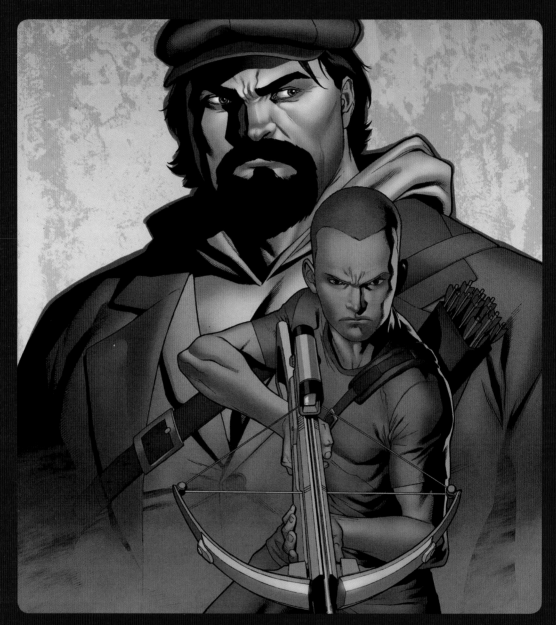

The immortal affectionately known around all the finest watering holes as Armstrong has had a busy year. Along with his naïve partner Archer, they have rescued the world by stopping the nefarious organization known as the Sect from acquiring a mystical "Boon" which grants immortality and doubles as a nasty WMD.

Soon after, they teamed up with the Geomancer and the Eternal Warrior to stop a cult from erasing existence altogether.

Good thing they went two for two.

Now our dysfunctional duo find themselves with some downtime on the Las Vegas strip...

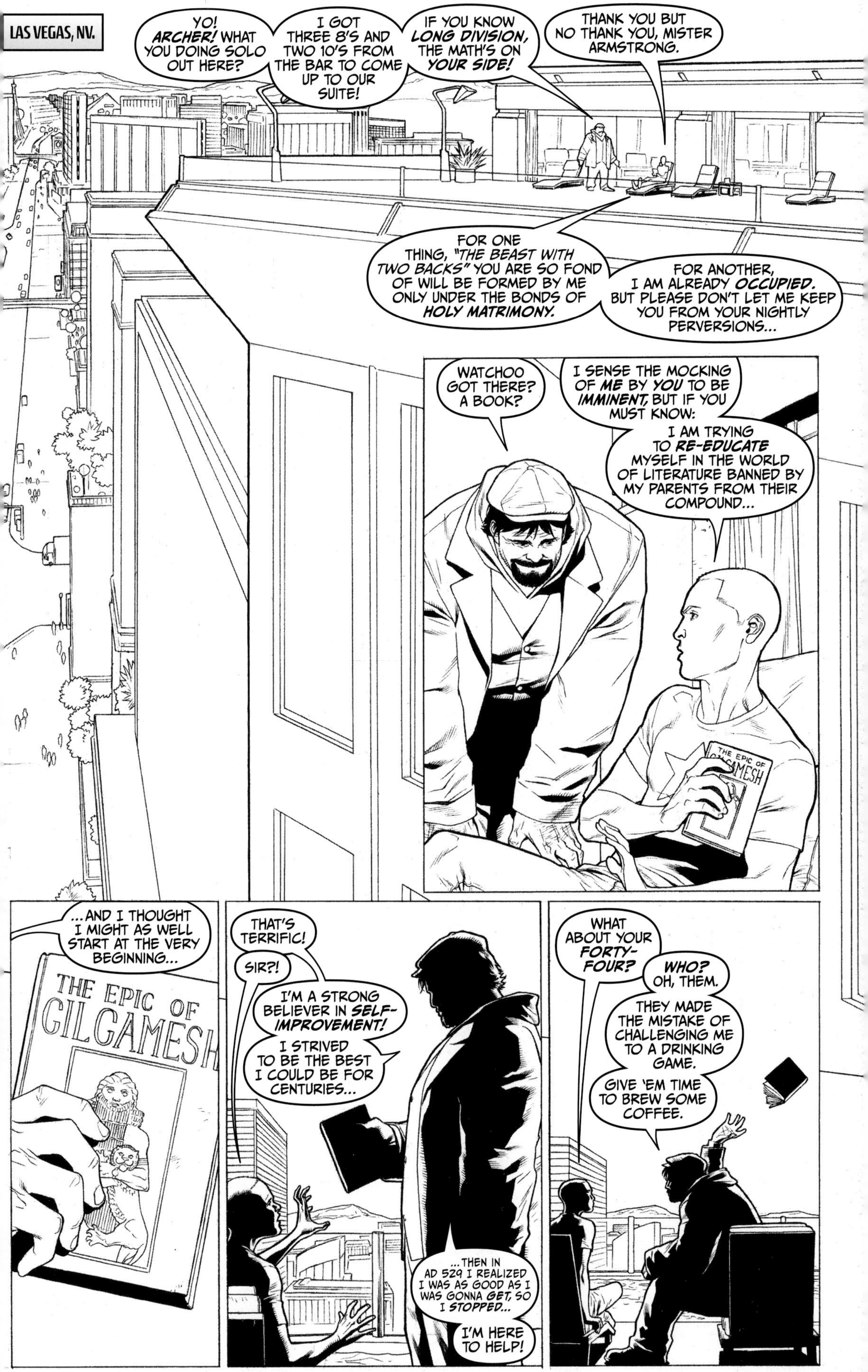
LAS VEGAS, NV.
YO! ARCHER! WHAT YOU DOING SOLO OUT HERE?
I GOT THREE 8'S AND TWO 10'S FROM THE BAR TO COME UP TO OUR SUITE!
IF YOU KNOW LONG DIVISION, THE MATH'S ON YOUR SIDE!
THANK YOU BUT NO THANK YOU, MISTER ARMSTRONG.
FOR ONE THING, "THE BEAST WITH TWO BACKS" YOU ARE SO FOND OF WILL BE FORMED BY ME ONLY UNDER THE BONDS OF HOLY MATRIMONY.
FOR ANOTHER, I AM ALREADY OCCUPIED. BUT PLEASE DON'T LET ME KEEP YOU FROM YOUR NIGHTLY PERVERSIONS...
WATCHOO GOT THERE? A BOOK?
I SENSE THE MOCKING OF ME BY YOU TO BE IMMINENT, BUT IF YOU MUST KNOW:
I AM TRYING TO RE-EDUCATE MYSELF IN THE WORLD OF LITERATURE BANNED BY MY PARENTS FROM THEIR COMPOUND...
THE EPIC OF GILGAMESH
...AND I THOUGHT I MIGHT AS WELL START AT THE VERY BEGINNING...
THE EPIC OF GILGAMESH
THAT'S TERRIFIC!
SIR?!
I'M A STRONG BELIEVER IN SELF-IMPROVEMENT!
I STRIVED TO BE THE BEST I COULD BE FOR CENTURIES...
...THEN IN AD 529 I REALIZED I WAS AS GOOD AS I WAS GONNA GET, SO I STOPPED...
I'M HERE TO HELP!
WHAT ABOUT YOUR FORTY-FOUR?
WHO? OH, THEM.
THEY MADE THE MISTAKE OF CHALLENGING ME TO A DRINKING GAME.
GIVE 'EM TIME TO BREW SOME COFFEE.

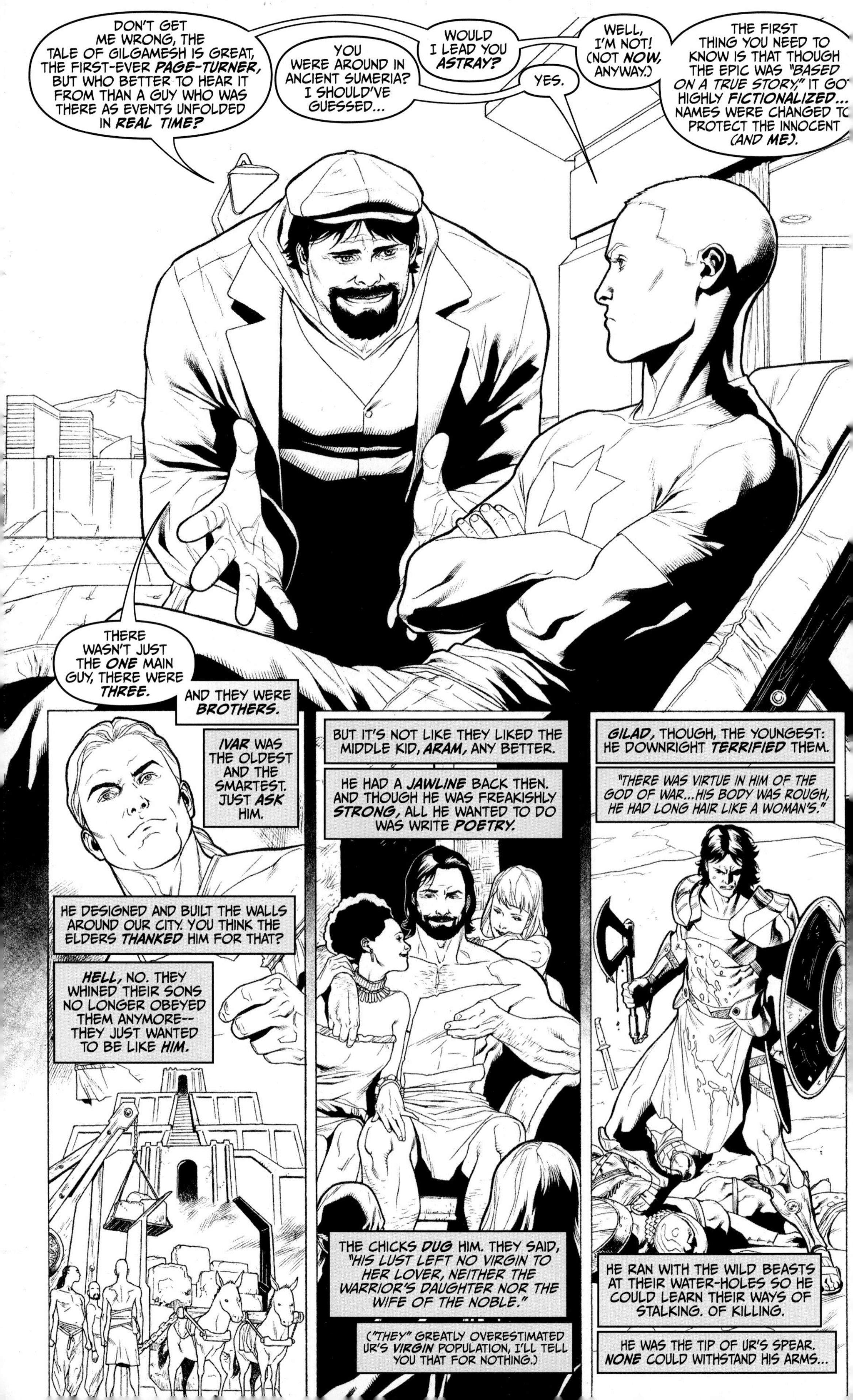
DON'T GET ME WRONG, THE TALE OF GILGAMESH IS GREAT, THE FIRST-EVER PAGE-TURNER, BUT WHO BETTER TO HEAR IT FROM THAN A GUY WHO WAS THERE AS EVENTS UNFOLDED IN REAL TIME?
YOU WERE AROUND IN ANCIENT SUMERIA? I SHOULD'VE GUESSED...
WOULD I LEAD YOU ASTRAY?
YES.
WELL, I'M NOT! (NOT NOW, ANYWAY.)
THE FIRST THING YOU NEED TO KNOW IS THAT THOUGH THE EPIC WAS "BASED ON A TRUE STORY," IT GOT HIGHLY FICTIONALIZED... NAMES WERE CHANGED TO PROTECT THE INNOCENT (AND ME).
THERE WASN'T JUST THE ONE MAIN GUY, THERE WERE THREE.
AND THEY WERE BROTHERS.
IVAR WAS THE OLDEST AND THE SMARTEST. JUST ASK HIM.
HE DESIGNED AND BUILT THE WALLS AROUND OUR CITY. YOU THINK THE ELDERS THANKED HIM FOR THAT?
HELL, NO. THEY WHINED THEIR SONS NO LONGER OBEYED THEM ANYMORE-- THEY JUST WANTED TO BE LIKE HIM.
BUT IT'S NOT LIKE THEY LIKED THE MIDDLE KID, ARAM, ANY BETTER.
HE HAD A JAWLINE BACK THEN. AND THOUGH HE WAS FREAKISHLY STRONG, ALL HE WANTED TO DO WAS WRITE POETRY.
THE CHICKS DUG HIM. THEY SAID, "HIS LUST LEFT NO VIRGIN TO HER LOVER, NEITHER THE WARRIOR'S DAUGHTER NOR THE WIFE OF THE NOBLE."
("THEY" GREATLY OVERESTIMATED UR'S VIRGIN POPULATION, I'LL TELL YOU THAT FOR NOTHING.)
GILAD, THOUGH, THE YOUNGEST: HE DOWNRIGHT TERRIFIED THEM.
"THERE WAS VIRTUE IN HIM OF THE GOD OF WAR...HIS BODY WAS ROUGH, HE HAD LONG HAIR LIKE A WOMAN'S."
HE RAN WITH THE WILD BEASTS AT THEIR WATER-HOLES SO HE COULD LEARN THEIR WAYS OF STALKING. OF KILLING.
HE WAS THE TIP OF UR'S SPEAR. NONE COULD WITHSTAND HIS ARMS...

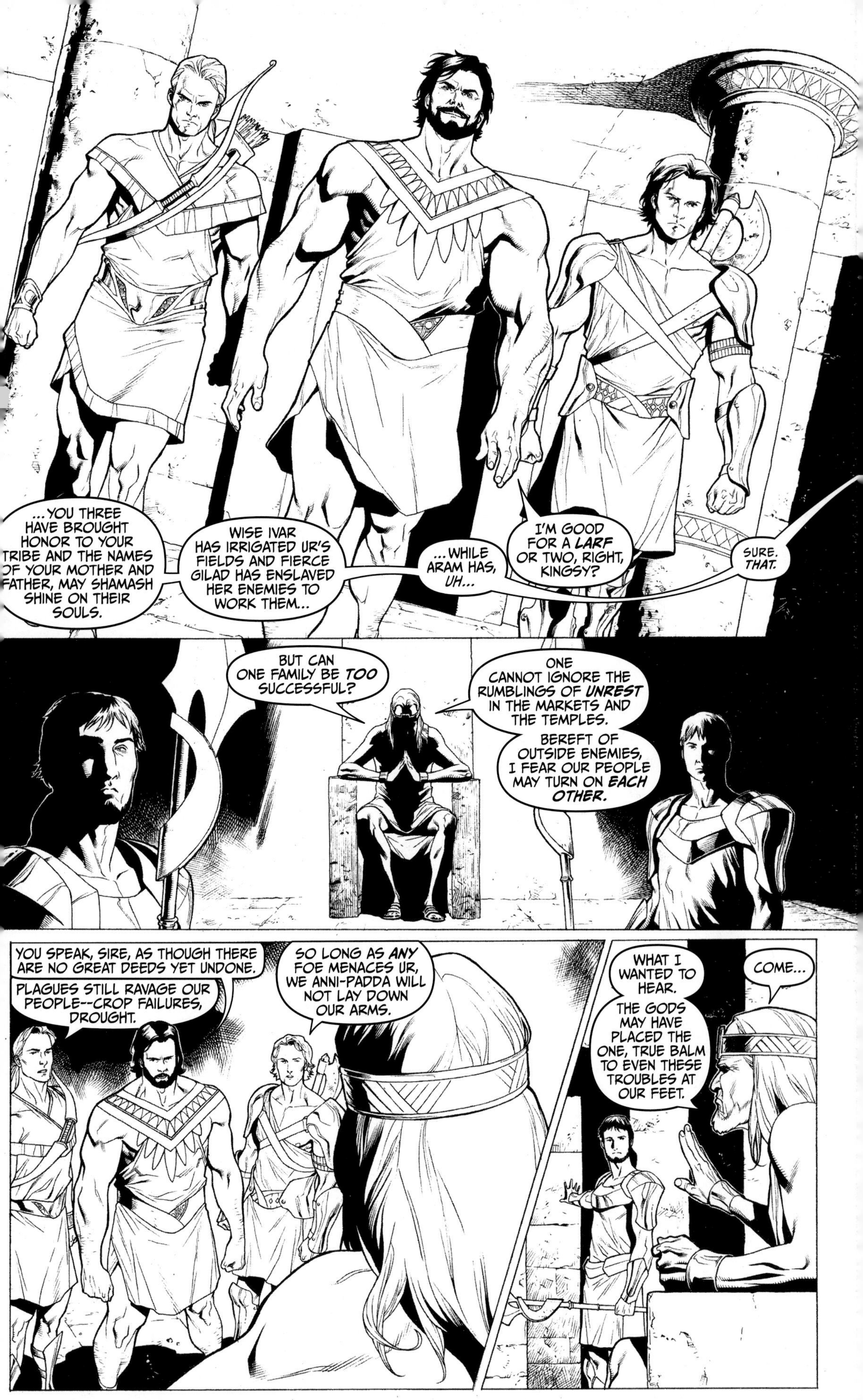
...YOU THREE HAVE BROUGHT HONOR TO YOUR TRIBE AND THE NAMES OF YOUR MOTHER AND FATHER, MAY SHAMASH SHINE ON THEIR SOULS.
WISE IVAR HAS IRRIGATED UR'S FIELDS AND FIERCE GILAD HAS ENSLAVED HER ENEMIES TO WORK THEM...
...WHILE ARAM HAS, UH...
I'M GOOD FOR A LARF OR TWO, RIGHT, KINGSY?
SURE. THAT.
BUT CAN ONE FAMILY BE TOO SUCCESSFUL?
ONE CANNOT IGNORE THE RUMBLINGS OF UNREST IN THE MARKETS AND THE TEMPLES.
BEREFT OF OUTSIDE ENEMIES, I FEAR OUR PEOPLE MAY TURN ON EACH OTHER.
YOU SPEAK, SIRE, AS THOUGH THERE ARE NO GREAT DEEDS YET UNDONE.
PLAGUES STILL RAVAGE OUR PEOPLE--CROP FAILURES, DROUGHT.
SO LONG AS ANY FOE MENACES UR, WE ANNI-PADDA WILL NOT LAY DOWN OUR ARMS.
WHAT I WANTED TO HEAR.
THE GODS MAY HAVE PLACED THE ONE, TRUE BALM TO EVEN THESE TROUBLES AT OUR FEET.
COME...

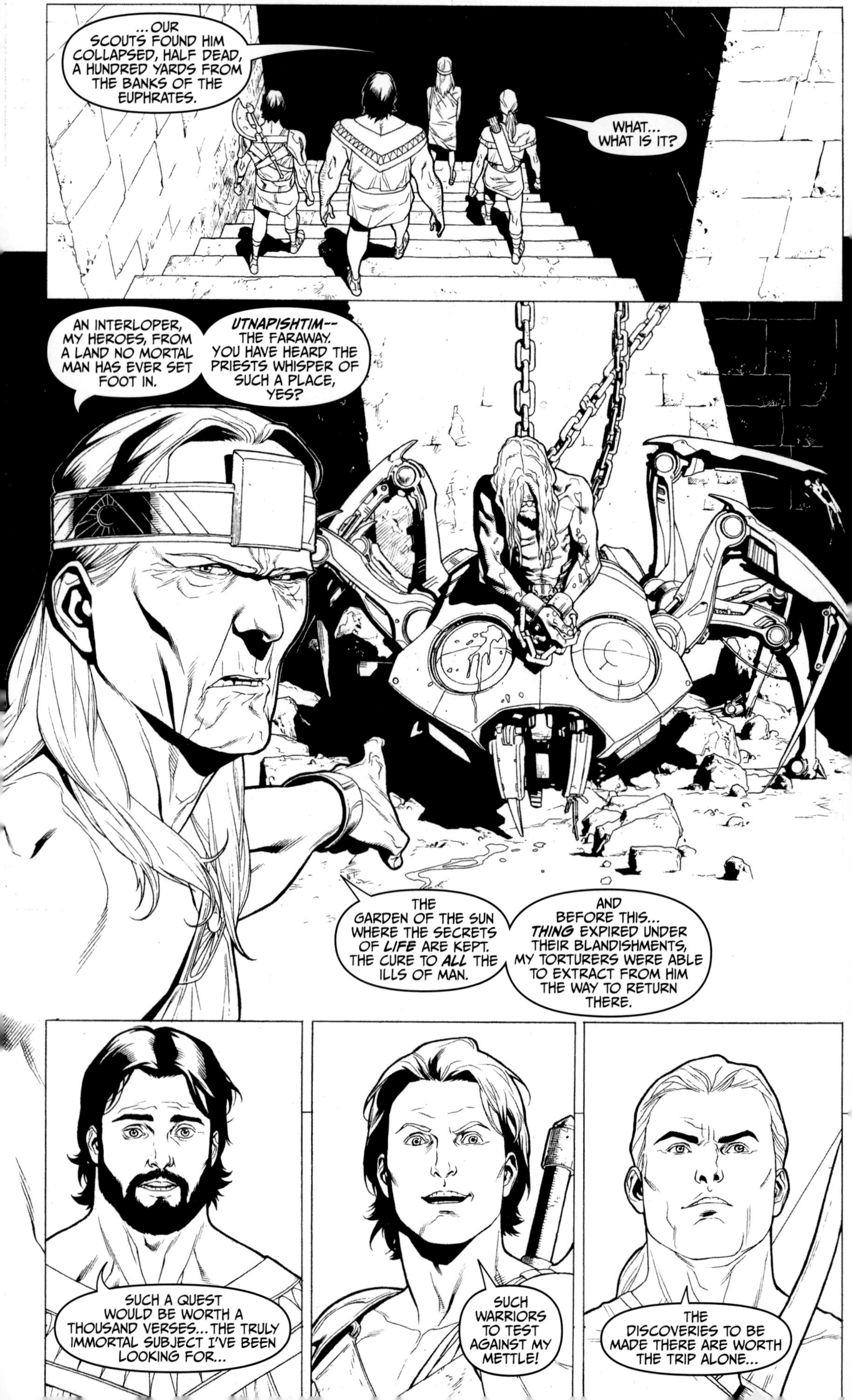
...OUR SCOUTS FOUND HIM COLLAPSED, HALF DEAD, A HUNDRED YARDS FROM THE BANKS OF THE EUPHRATES.
WHAT... WHAT IS IT?
AN INTERLOPER, MY HEROES, FROM A LAND NO MORTAL MAN HAS EVER SET FOOT IN.
UTNAPISHTIM-- THE FARAWAY. YOU HAVE HEARD THE PRIESTS WHISPER OF SUCH A PLACE, YES?
THE GARDEN OF THE SUN WHERE THE SECRETS OF *LIFE* ARE KEPT. THE CURE TO *ALL* THE ILLS OF MAN.
AND BEFORE THIS... *THING* EXPIRED UNDER THEIR BLANDISHMENTS, MY TORTURERS WERE ABLE TO EXTRACT FROM HIM THE WAY TO RETURN THERE.
SUCH A QUEST WOULD BE WORTH A THOUSAND VERSES... THE TRULY IMMORTAL SUBJECT I'VE BEEN LOOKING FOR...
SUCH WARRIORS TO TEST AGAINST MY METTLE!
THE DISCOVERIES TO BE MADE THERE ARE WORTH THE TRIP ALONE...

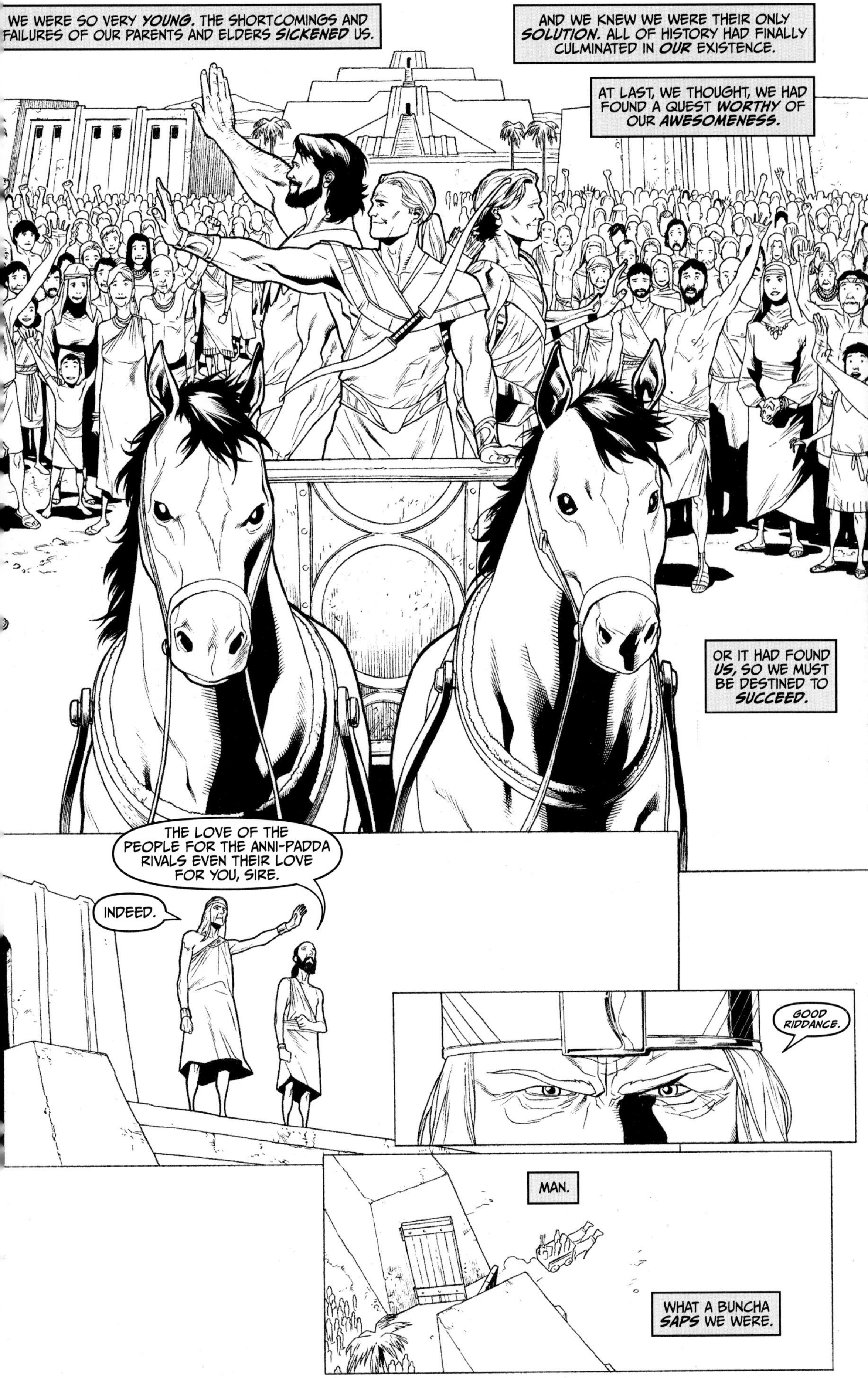
WE WERE SO VERY YOUNG. THE SHORTCOMINGS AND FAILURES OF OUR PARENTS AND ELDERS SICKENED US.
AND WE KNEW WE WERE THEIR ONLY SOLUTION. ALL OF HISTORY HAD FINALLY CULMINATED IN OUR EXISTENCE.
AT LAST, WE THOUGHT, WE HAD FOUND A QUEST WORTHY OF OUR AWESOMENESS.
OR IT HAD FOUND US, SO WE MUST BE DESTINED TO SUCCEED.
THE LOVE OF THE PEOPLE FOR THE ANNI-PADDA RIVALS EVEN THEIR LOVE FOR YOU, SIRE.
INDEED.
GOOD RIDDANCE.
MAN.
WHAT A BUNCHA SAPS WE WERE.

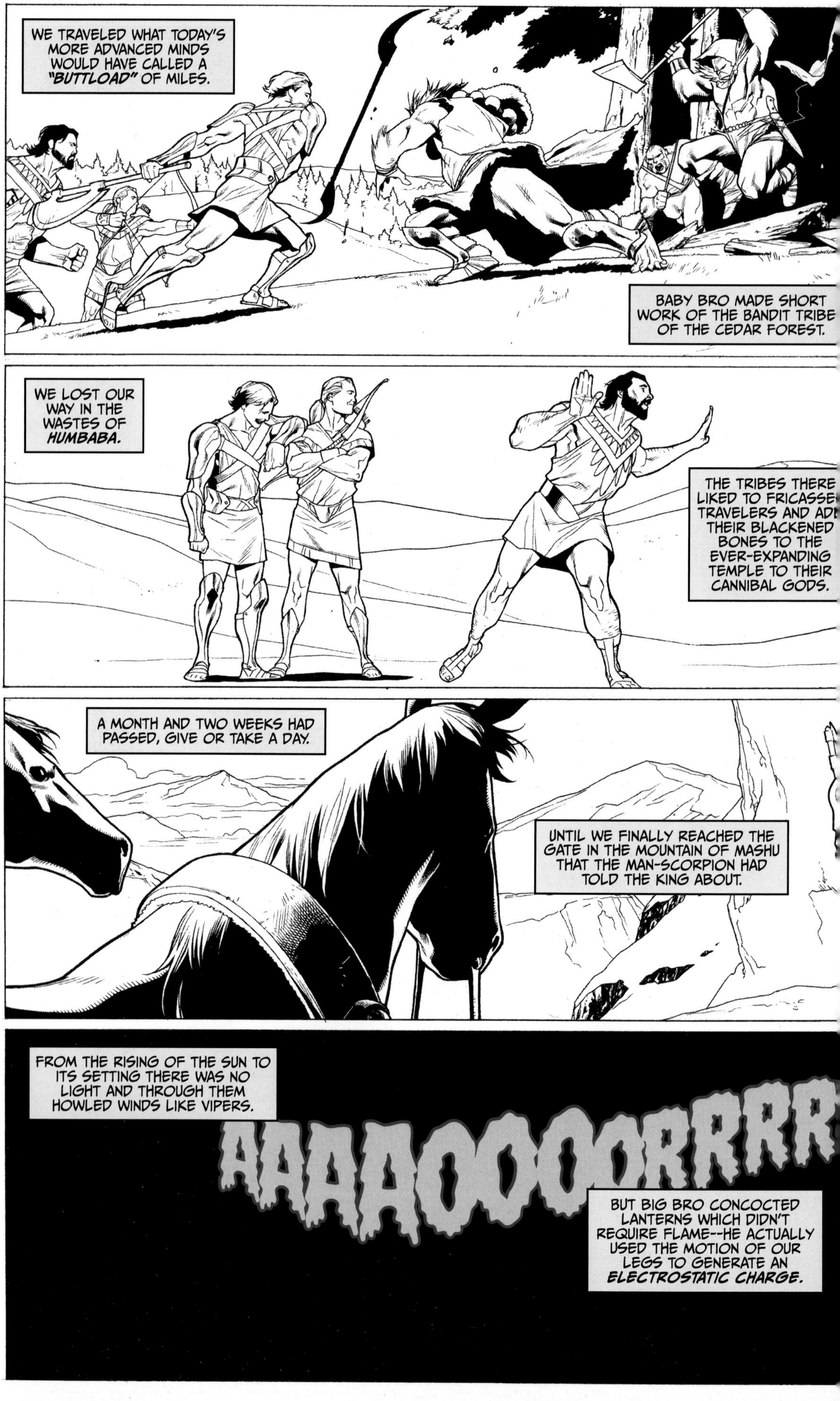

WE TRAVELED WHAT TODAY'S MORE ADVANCED MINDS WOULD HAVE CALLED A "BUTTLOAD" OF MILES.
BABY BRO MADE SHORT WORK OF THE BANDIT TRIBE OF THE CEDAR FOREST.
WE LOST OUR WAY IN THE WASTES OF HUMBABA.
THE TRIBES THERE LIKED TO FRICASSE TRAVELERS AND AD THEIR BLACKENED BONES TO THE EVER-EXPANDING TEMPLE TO THEIR CANNIBAL GODS.
A MONTH AND TWO WEEKS HAD PASSED, GIVE OR TAKE A DAY.
UNTIL WE FINALLY REACHED THE GATE IN THE MOUNTAIN OF MASHU THAT THE MAN-SCORPION HAD TOLD THE KING ABOUT.
FROM THE RISING OF THE SUN TO ITS SETTING THERE WAS NO LIGHT AND THROUGH THEM HOWLED WINDS LIKE VIPERS.
AAAAOOOORRRR
BUT BIG BRO CONCOCTED LANTERNS WHICH DIDN'T REQUIRE FLAME--HE ACTUALLY USED THE MOTION OF OUR LEGS TO GENERATE AN ELECTROSTATIC CHARGE.

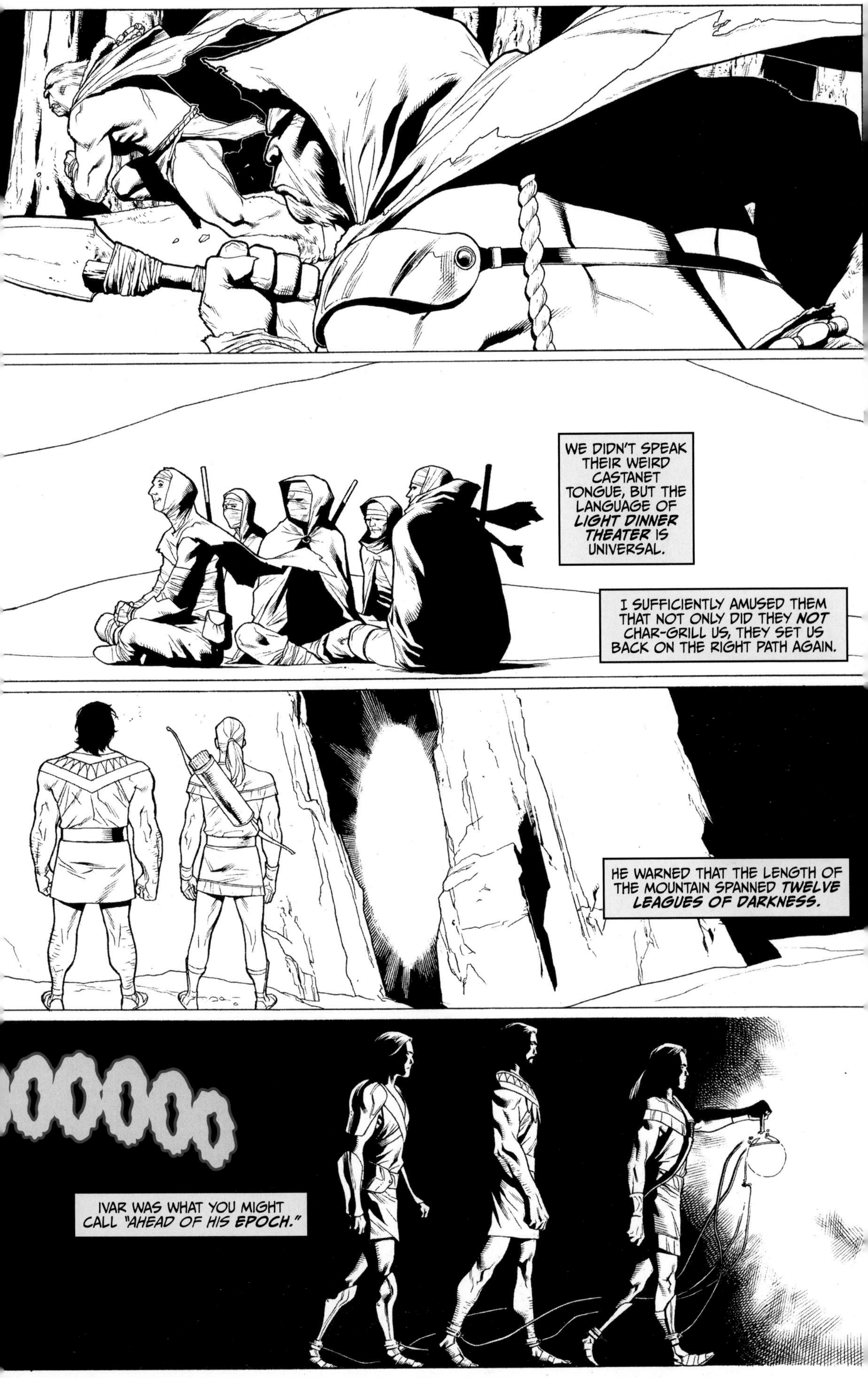
WE DIDN'T SPEAK THEIR WEIRD CASTANET TONGUE, BUT THE LANGUAGE OF *LIGHT DINNER THEATER* IS UNIVERSAL.
I SUFFICIENTLY AMUSED THEM THAT NOT ONLY DID THEY *NOT* CHAR-GRILL US, THEY SET US BACK ON THE RIGHT PATH AGAIN.
HE WARNED THAT THE LENGTH OF THE MOUNTAIN SPANNED *TWELVE LEAGUES OF DARKNESS.*
OOOOOO
IVAR WAS WHAT YOU MIGHT CALL *"AHEAD OF HIS EPOCH."*

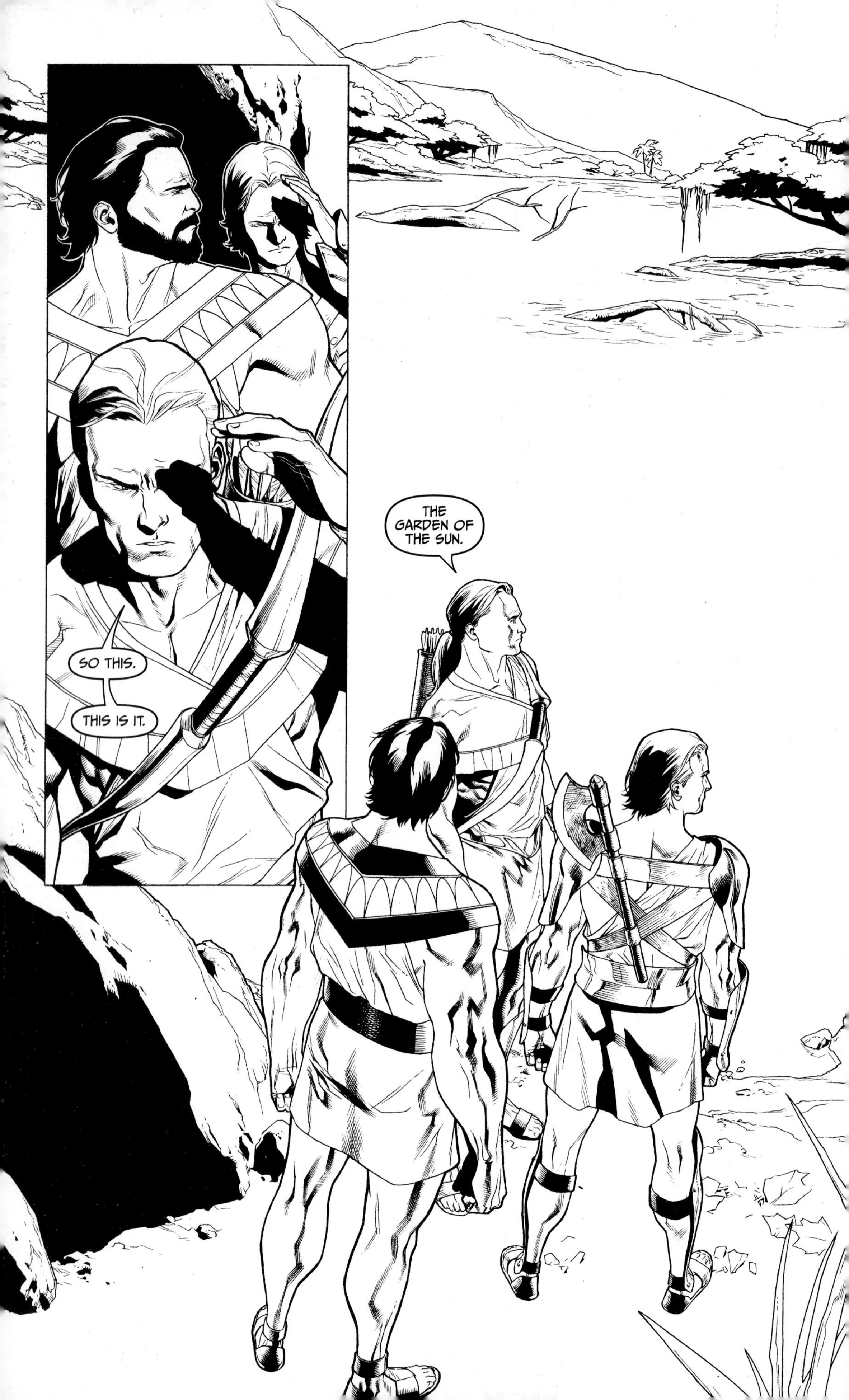
SO THIS.
THIS IS IT.
THE GARDEN OF THE SUN.

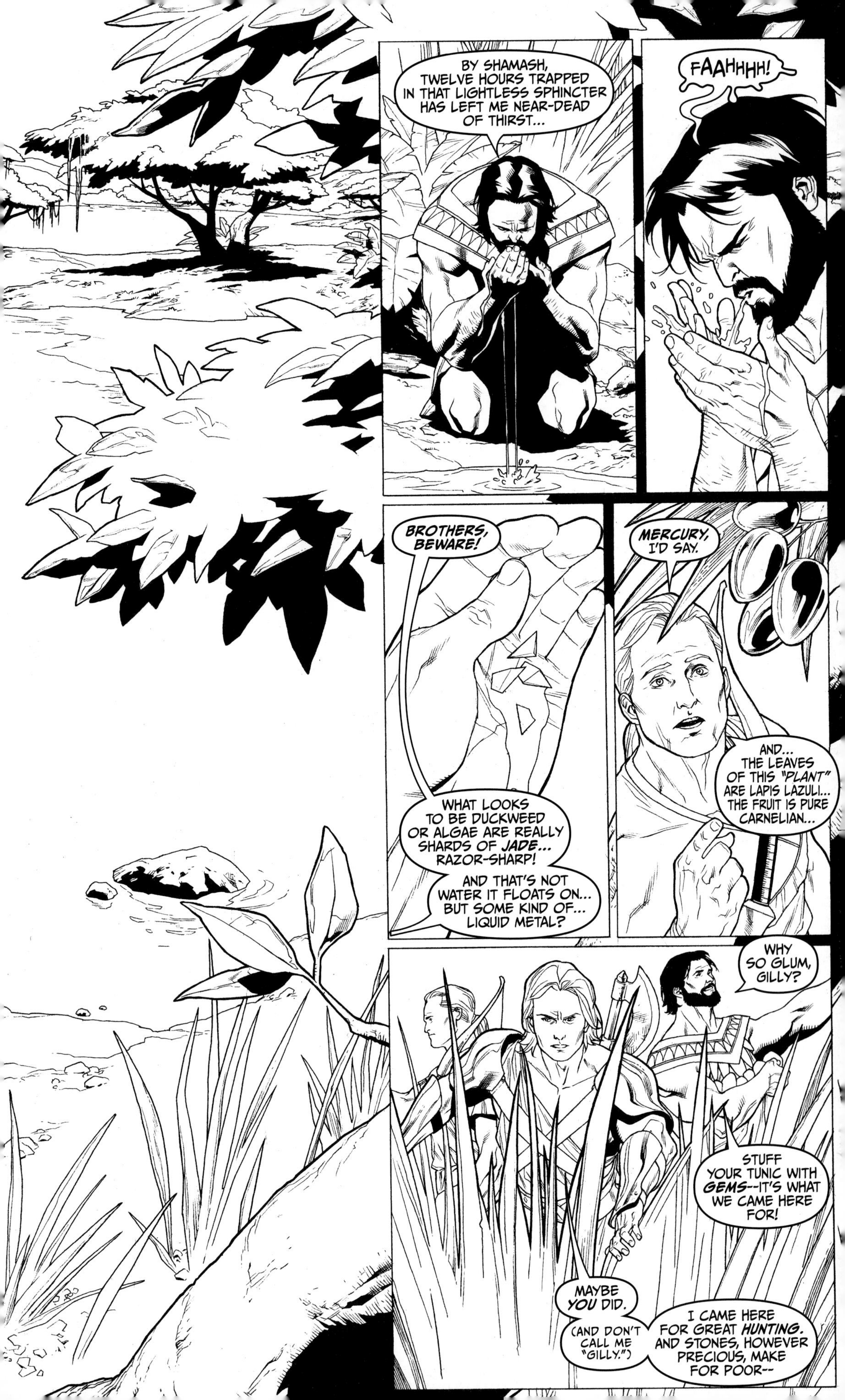
BY SHAMASH, TWELVE HOURS TRAPPED IN THAT LIGHTLESS SPHINCTER HAS LEFT ME NEAR-DEAD OF THIRST...
FAAHHHH!
BROTHERS, BEWARE!
WHAT LOOKS TO BE DUCKWEED OR ALGAE ARE REALLY SHARDS OF JADE... RAZOR-SHARP!
AND THAT'S NOT WATER IT FLOATS ON... BUT SOME KIND OF... LIQUID METAL?
MERCURY, I'D SAY.
AND... THE LEAVES OF THIS "PLANT" ARE LAPIS LAZULI... THE FRUIT IS PURE CARNELIAN...
WHY SO GLUM, GILLY?
STUFF YOUR TUNIC WITH GEMS--IT'S WHAT WE CAME HERE FOR!
MAYBE YOU DID.
(AND DON'T CALL ME "GILLY.")
I CAME HERE FOR GREAT HUNTING. AND STONES, HOWEVER PRECIOUS, MAKE FOR POOR--

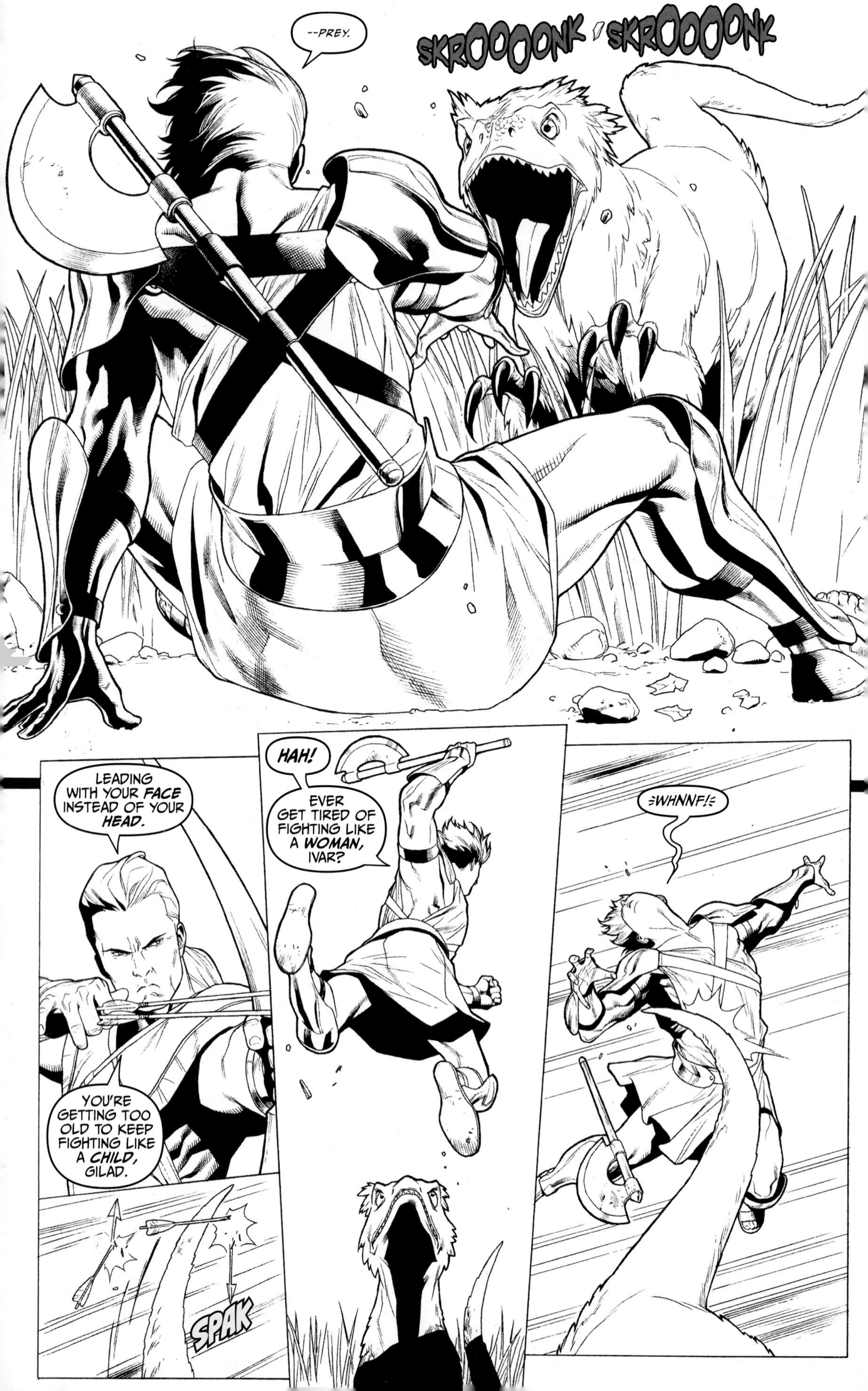
--PREY.
SKROOOOONK! SKROOOOONK
LEADING WITH YOUR FACE INSTEAD OF YOUR HEAD.
YOU'RE GETTING TOO OLD TO KEEP FIGHTING LIKE A CHILD, GILAD.
SPAK
HAH!
EVER GET TIRED OF FIGHTING LIKE A WOMAN, IVAR?
WHNNF!

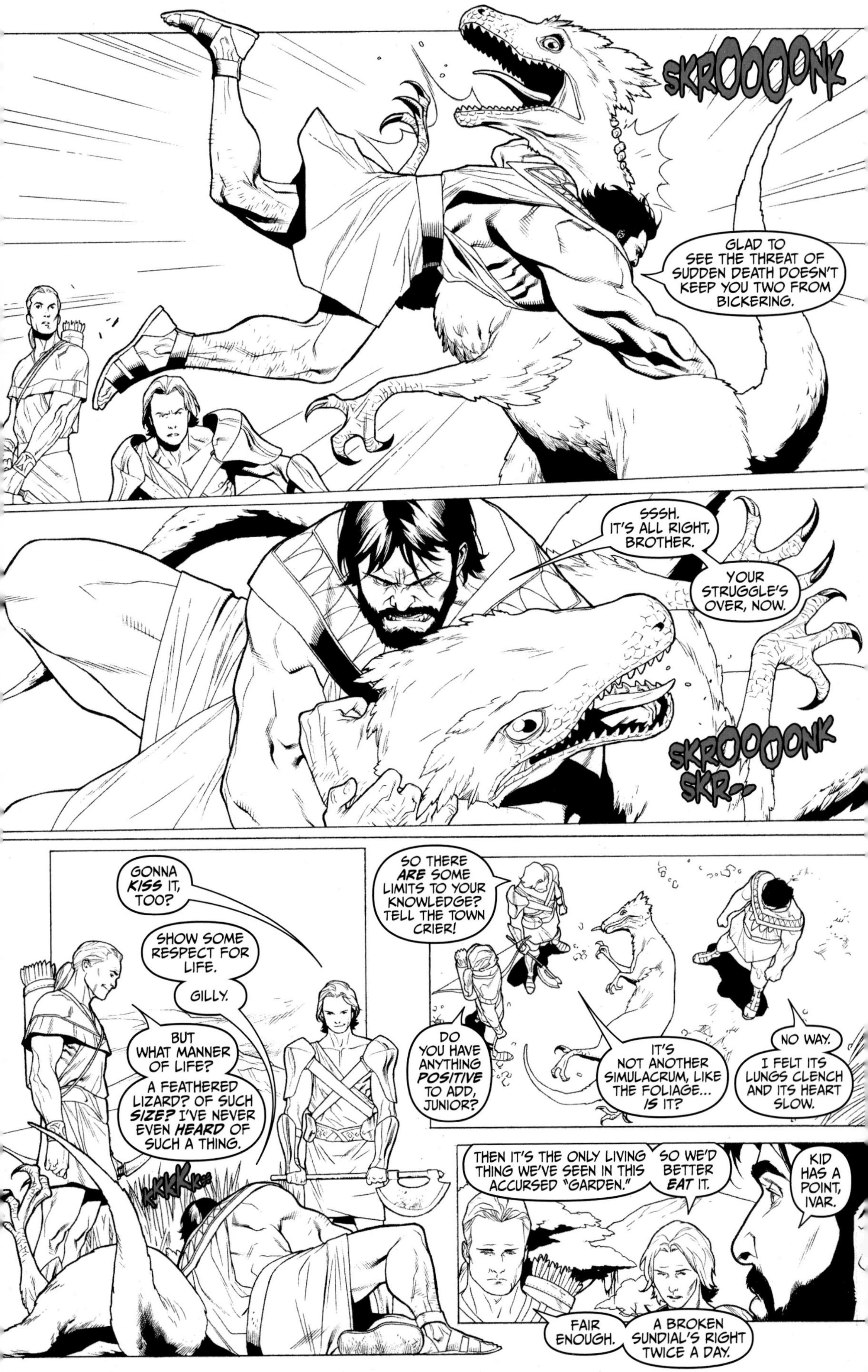
SKROOOONK
GLAD TO SEE THE THREAT OF SUDDEN DEATH DOESN'T KEEP YOU TWO FROM BICKERING.
SSSH. IT'S ALL RIGHT, BROTHER.
YOUR STRUGGLE'S OVER, NOW.
SKROOOONK SKR--
GONNA KISS IT, TOO?
SHOW SOME RESPECT FOR LIFE.
GILLY.
BUT WHAT MANNER OF LIFE?
A FEATHERED LIZARD? OF SUCH SIZE? I'VE NEVER EVEN HEARD OF SUCH A THING.
KKKKK
SO THERE ARE SOME LIMITS TO YOUR KNOWLEDGE? TELL THE TOWN CRIER!
DO YOU HAVE ANYTHING POSITIVE TO ADD, JUNIOR?
IT'S NOT ANOTHER SIMULACRUM, LIKE THE FOLIAGE... IS IT?
NO WAY.
I FELT ITS LUNGS CLENCH AND ITS HEART SLOW.
THEN IT'S THE ONLY LIVING THING WE'VE SEEN IN THIS ACCURSED "GARDEN."
SO WE'D BETTER EAT IT.
KID HAS A POINT, IVAR.
FAIR ENOUGH.
A BROKEN SUNDIAL'S RIGHT TWICE A DAY.

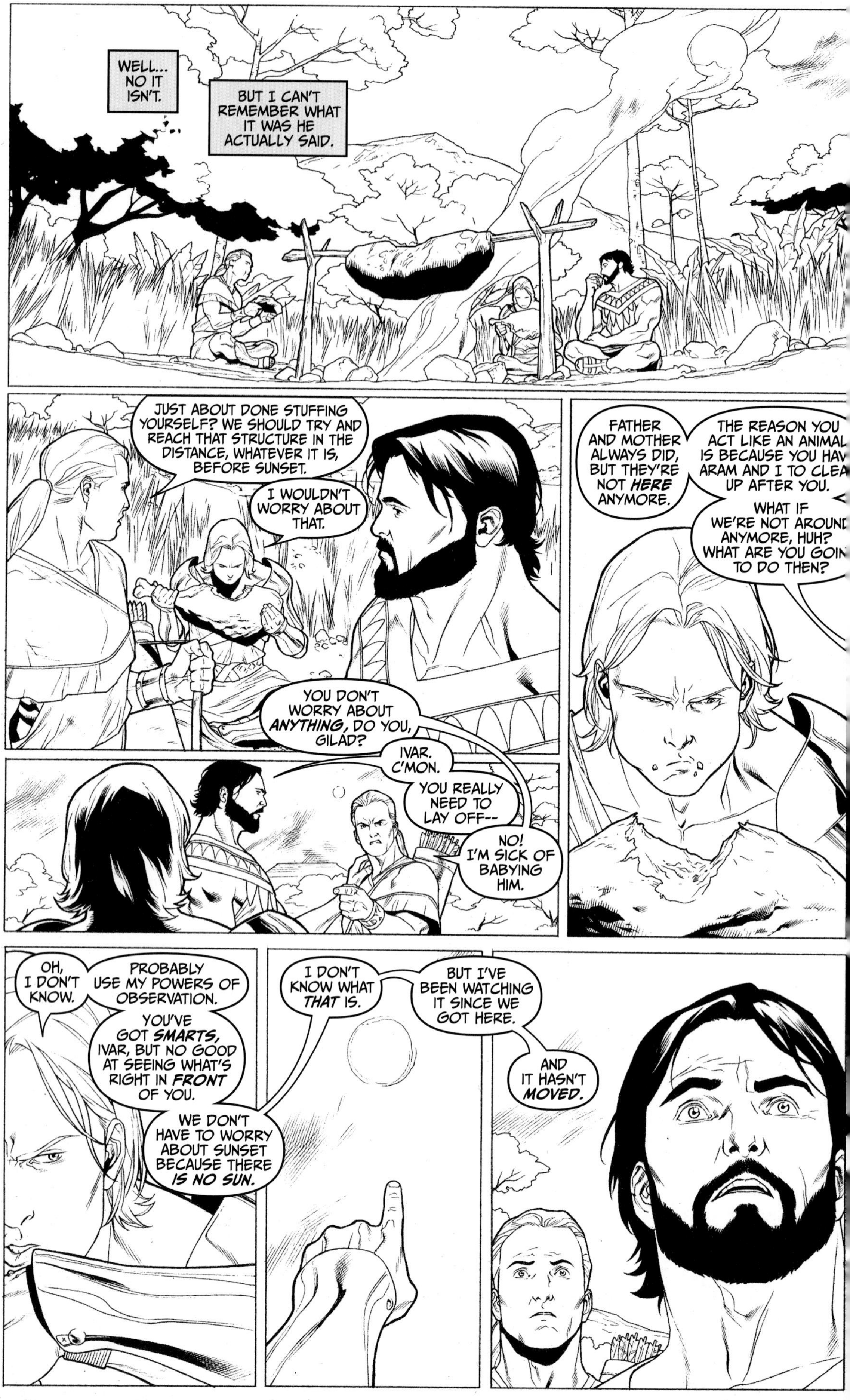

WELL... NO IT ISN'T.
BUT I CAN'T REMEMBER WHAT IT WAS HE ACTUALLY SAID.
JUST ABOUT DONE STUFFING YOURSELF? WE SHOULD TRY AND REACH THAT STRUCTURE IN THE DISTANCE, WHATEVER IT IS, BEFORE SUNSET.
I WOULDN'T WORRY ABOUT THAT.
YOU DON'T WORRY ABOUT *ANYTHING*, DO YOU, GILAD?
IVAR. C'MON.
YOU REALLY NEED TO LAY OFF--
NO! I'M SICK OF BABYING HIM.
FATHER AND MOTHER ALWAYS DID, BUT THEY'RE NOT *HERE* ANYMORE.
THE REASON YOU ACT LIKE AN ANIMAL IS BECAUSE YOU HAV ARAM AND I TO CLEA UP AFTER YOU.
WHAT IF WE'RE NOT AROUND ANYMORE, HUH? WHAT ARE YOU GOIN TO DO THEN?
OH, I DON'T KNOW.
PROBABLY USE MY POWERS OF OBSERVATION.
YOU'VE GOT **SMARTS,** IVAR, BUT NO GOOD AT SEEING WHAT'S RIGHT IN *FRONT* OF YOU.
WE DON'T HAVE TO WORRY ABOUT SUNSET BECAUSE THERE ***IS NO SUN.***
I DON'T KNOW WHAT *THAT* IS.
BUT I'VE BEEN WATCHING IT SINCE WE GOT HERE.
AND IT HASN'T ***MOVED.***

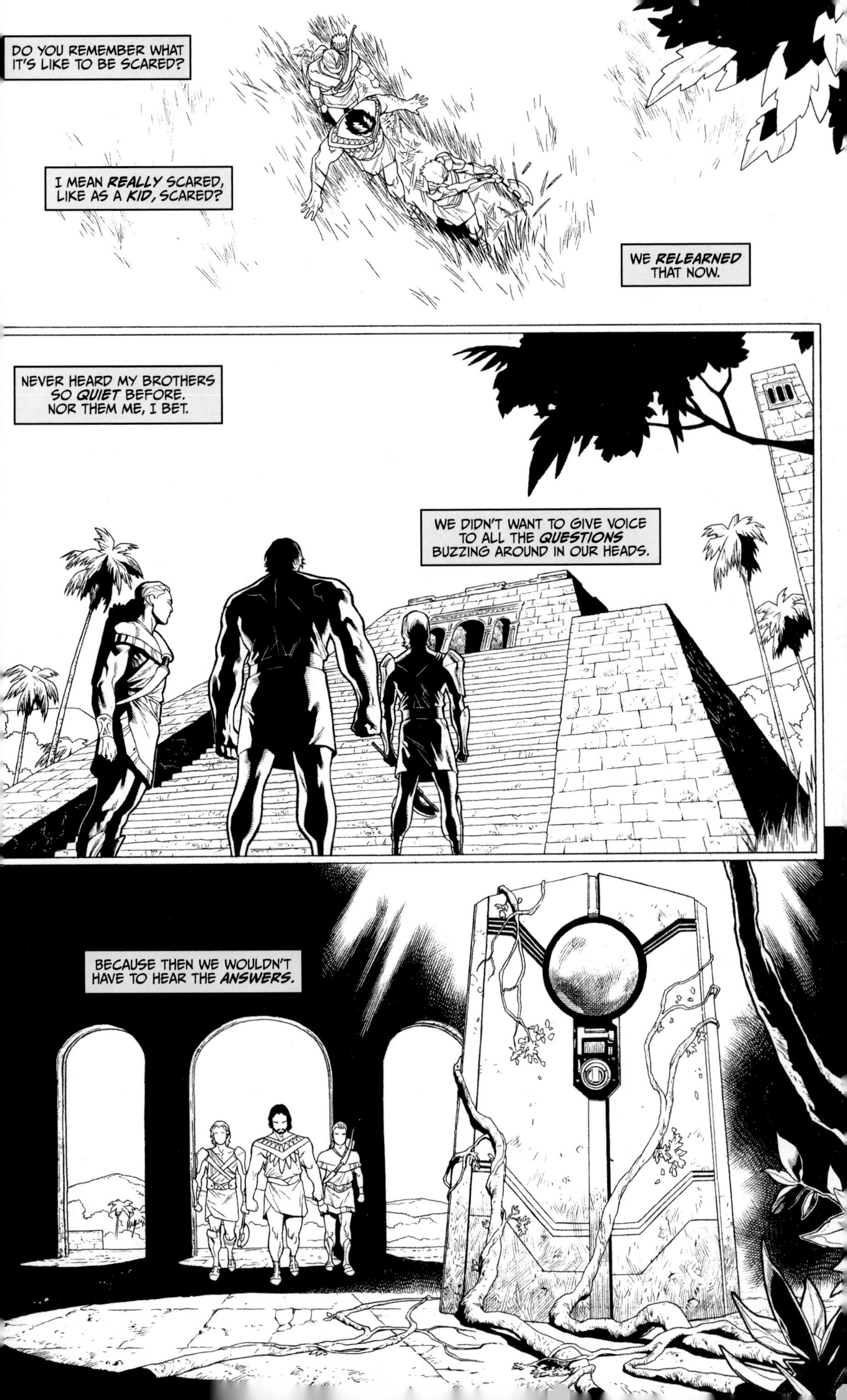
DO YOU REMEMBER WHAT IT'S LIKE TO BE SCARED?
I MEAN *REALLY* SCARED, LIKE AS A *KID*, SCARED?
WE *RELEARNED* THAT NOW.
NEVER HEARD MY BROTHERS SO *QUIET* BEFORE. NOR THEM ME, I BET.
WE DIDN'T WANT TO GIVE VOICE TO ALL THE *QUESTIONS* BUZZING AROUND IN OUR HEADS.
BECAUSE THEN WE WOULDN'T HAVE TO HEAR THE *ANSWERS.*

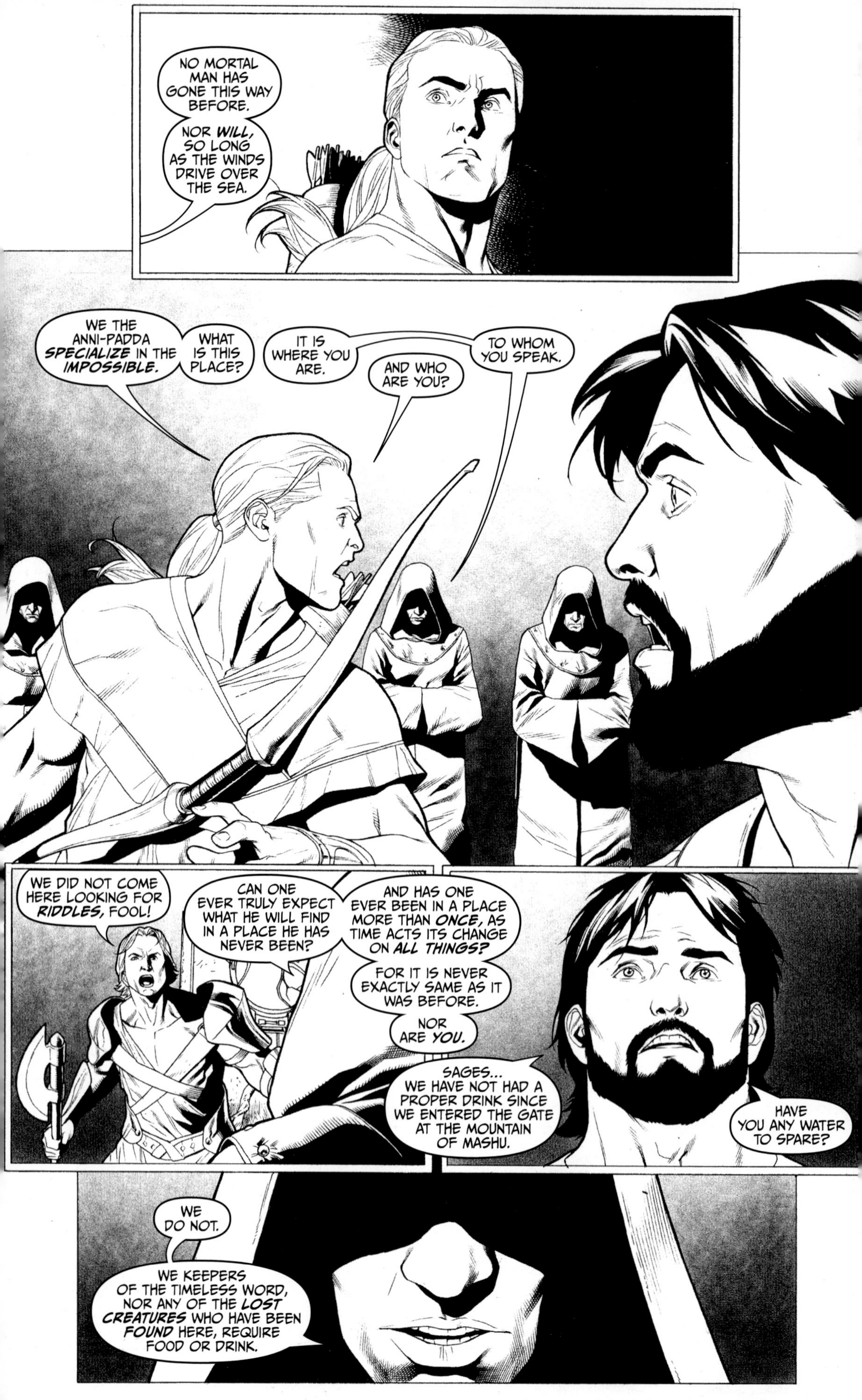
NO MORTAL MAN HAS GONE THIS WAY BEFORE.
NOR *WILL,* SO LONG AS THE WINDS DRIVE OVER THE SEA.
WE THE ANNI-PADDA *SPECIALIZE* IN THE *IMPOSSIBLE.*
WHAT IS THIS PLACE?
IT IS WHERE YOU ARE.
AND WHO ARE YOU?
TO WHOM YOU SPEAK.
WE DID NOT COME HERE LOOKING FOR *RIDDLES,* FOOL!
CAN ONE EVER TRULY EXPECT WHAT HE WILL FIND IN A PLACE HE HAS NEVER BEEN?
AND HAS ONE EVER BEEN IN A PLACE MORE THAN *ONCE,* AS TIME ACTS ITS CHANGE ON *ALL THINGS?*
FOR IT IS NEVER EXACTLY SAME AS IT WAS BEFORE.
NOR ARE *YOU.*
SAGES... WE HAVE NOT HAD A PROPER DRINK SINCE WE ENTERED THE GATE AT THE MOUNTAIN OF MASHU.
HAVE YOU ANY WATER TO SPARE?
WE DO NOT.
WE KEEPERS OF THE TIMELESS WORD, NOR ANY OF THE *LOST CREATURES* WHO HAVE BEEN *FOUND* HERE, REQUIRE FOOD OR DRINK.

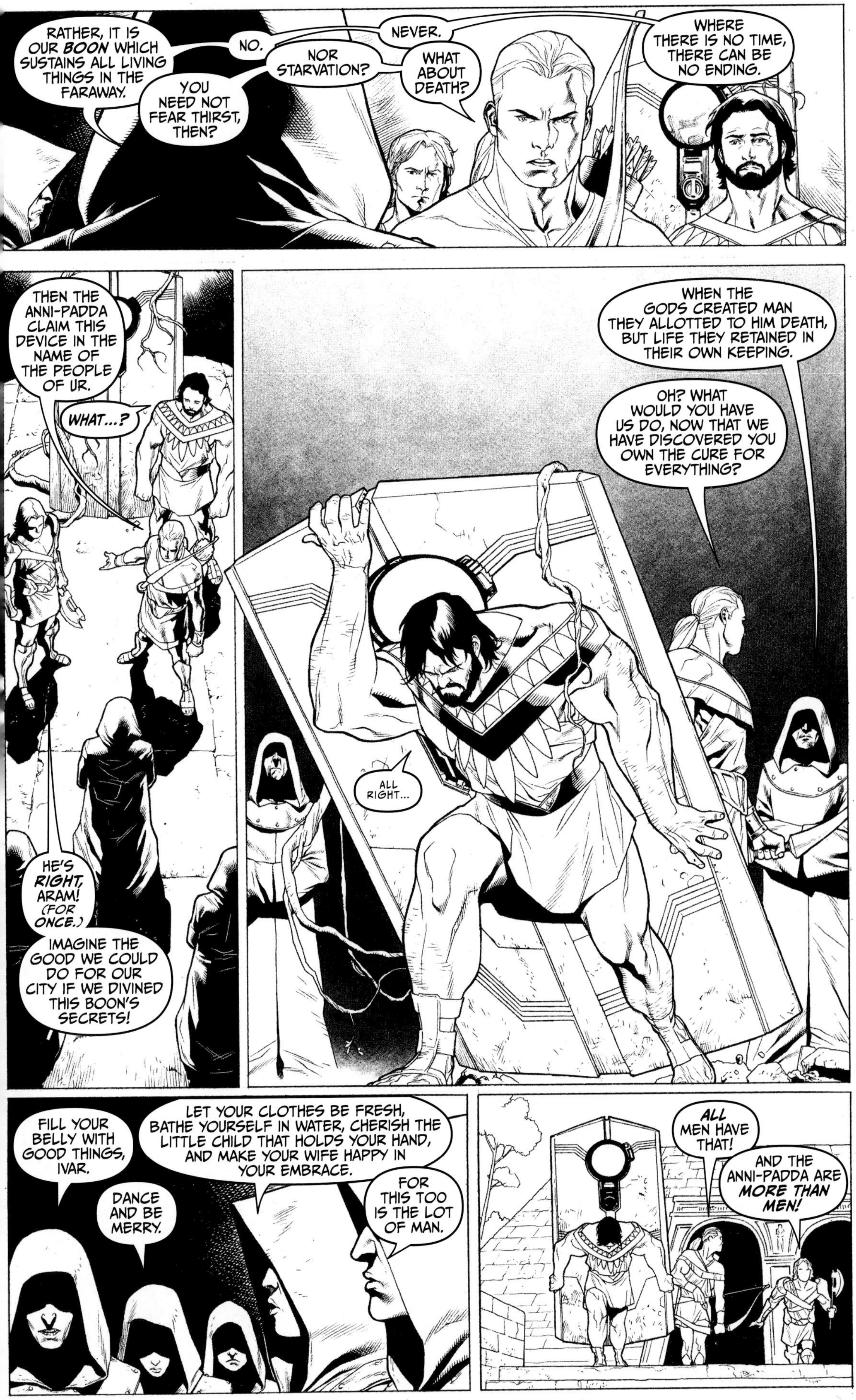
RATHER, IT IS OUR BOON WHICH SUSTAINS ALL LIVING THINGS IN THE FARAWAY.
YOU NEED NOT FEAR THIRST, THEN?
NO.
NOR STARVATION?
NEVER.
WHAT ABOUT DEATH?
WHERE THERE IS NO TIME, THERE CAN BE NO ENDING.
THEN THE ANNI-PADDA CLAIM THIS DEVICE IN THE NAME OF THE PEOPLE OF UR.
WHAT...?
HE'S RIGHT, ARAM! (FOR ONCE.)
IMAGINE THE GOOD WE COULD DO FOR OUR CITY IF WE DIVINED THIS BOON'S SECRETS!
WHEN THE GODS CREATED MAN THEY ALLOTTED TO HIM DEATH, BUT LIFE THEY RETAINED IN THEIR OWN KEEPING.
OH? WHAT WOULD YOU HAVE US DO, NOW THAT WE HAVE DISCOVERED YOU OWN THE CURE FOR EVERYTHING?
ALL RIGHT...
FILL YOUR BELLY WITH GOOD THINGS, IVAR.
DANCE AND BE MERRY.
LET YOUR CLOTHES BE FRESH, BATHE YOURSELF IN WATER, CHERISH THE LITTLE CHILD THAT HOLDS YOUR HAND, AND MAKE YOUR WIFE HAPPY IN YOUR EMBRACE.
FOR THIS TOO IS THE LOT OF MAN.
ALL MEN HAVE THAT!
AND THE ANNI-PADDA ARE MORE THAN MEN!

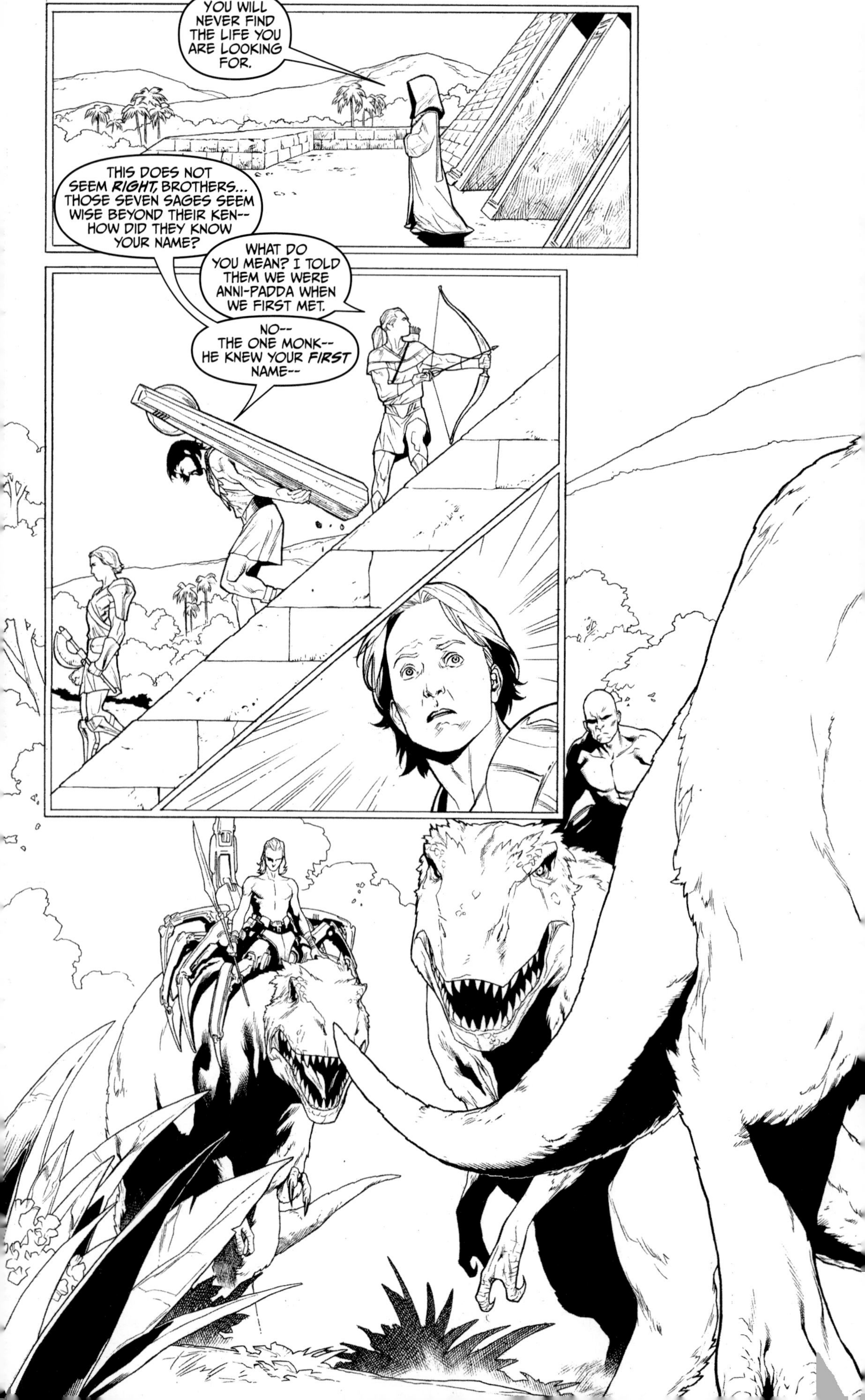
YOU WILL NEVER FIND THE LIFE YOU ARE LOOKING FOR.
THIS DOES NOT SEEM *RIGHT*, BROTHERS... THOSE SEVEN SAGES SEEM WISE BEYOND THEIR KEN-- HOW DID THEY KNOW YOUR NAME?
WHAT DO YOU MEAN? I TOLD THEM WE WERE ANNI-PADDA WHEN WE FIRST MET.
NO-- THE ONE MONK-- HE KNEW YOUR *FIRST* NAME--

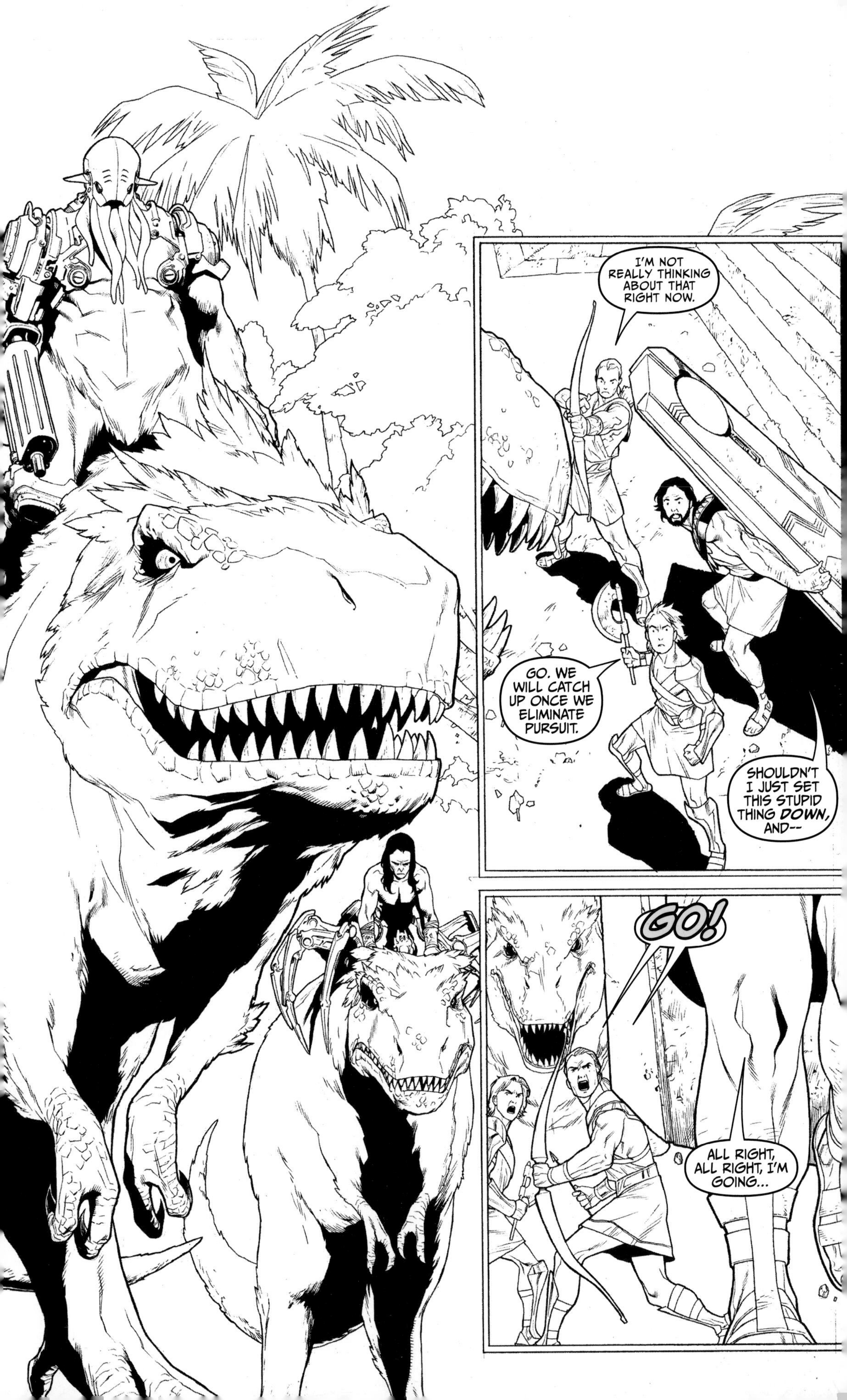
I'M NOT REALLY THINKING ABOUT THAT RIGHT NOW.
GO. WE WILL CATCH UP ONCE WE ELIMINATE PURSUIT.
SHOULDN'T I JUST SET THIS STUPID THING *DOWN*, AND--
GO!
ALL RIGHT, ALL RIGHT, I'M GOING...

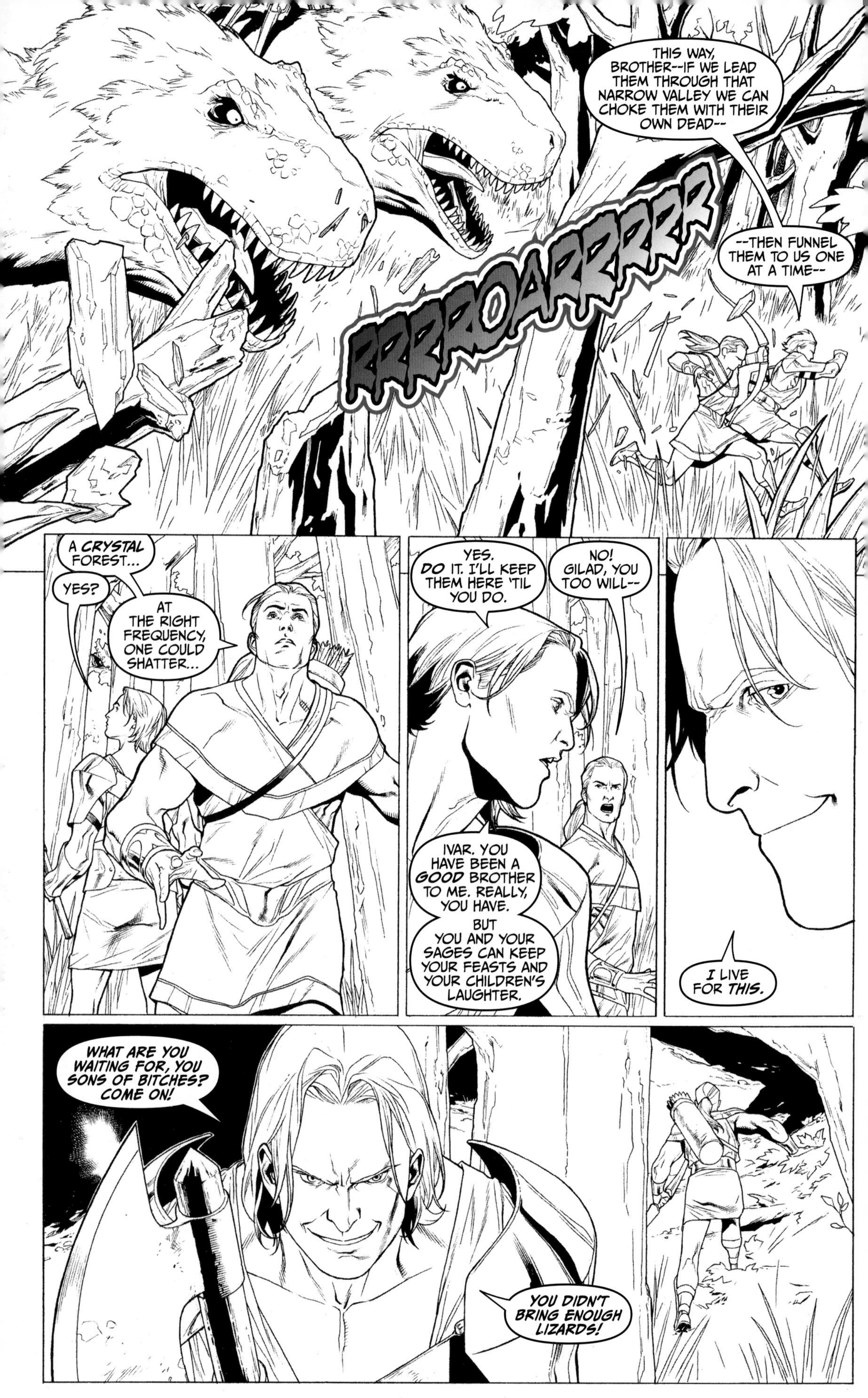
THIS WAY, BROTHER--IF WE LEAD THEM THROUGH THAT NARROW VALLEY WE CAN CHOKE THEM WITH THEIR OWN DEAD--
RRRROARRRRR
--THEN FUNNEL THEM TO US ONE AT A TIME--
A CRYSTAL FOREST...
YES?
AT THE RIGHT FREQUENCY, ONE COULD SHATTER...
YES. DO IT. I'LL KEEP THEM HERE 'TIL YOU DO.
NO! GILAD, YOU TOO WILL--
IVAR. YOU HAVE BEEN A GOOD BROTHER TO ME. REALLY, YOU HAVE.
BUT YOU AND YOUR SAGES CAN KEEP YOUR FEASTS AND YOUR CHILDREN'S LAUGHTER.
I LIVE FOR THIS.
WHAT ARE YOU WAITING FOR, YOU SONS OF BITCHES? COME ON!
YOU DIDN'T BRING ENOUGH LIZARDS!

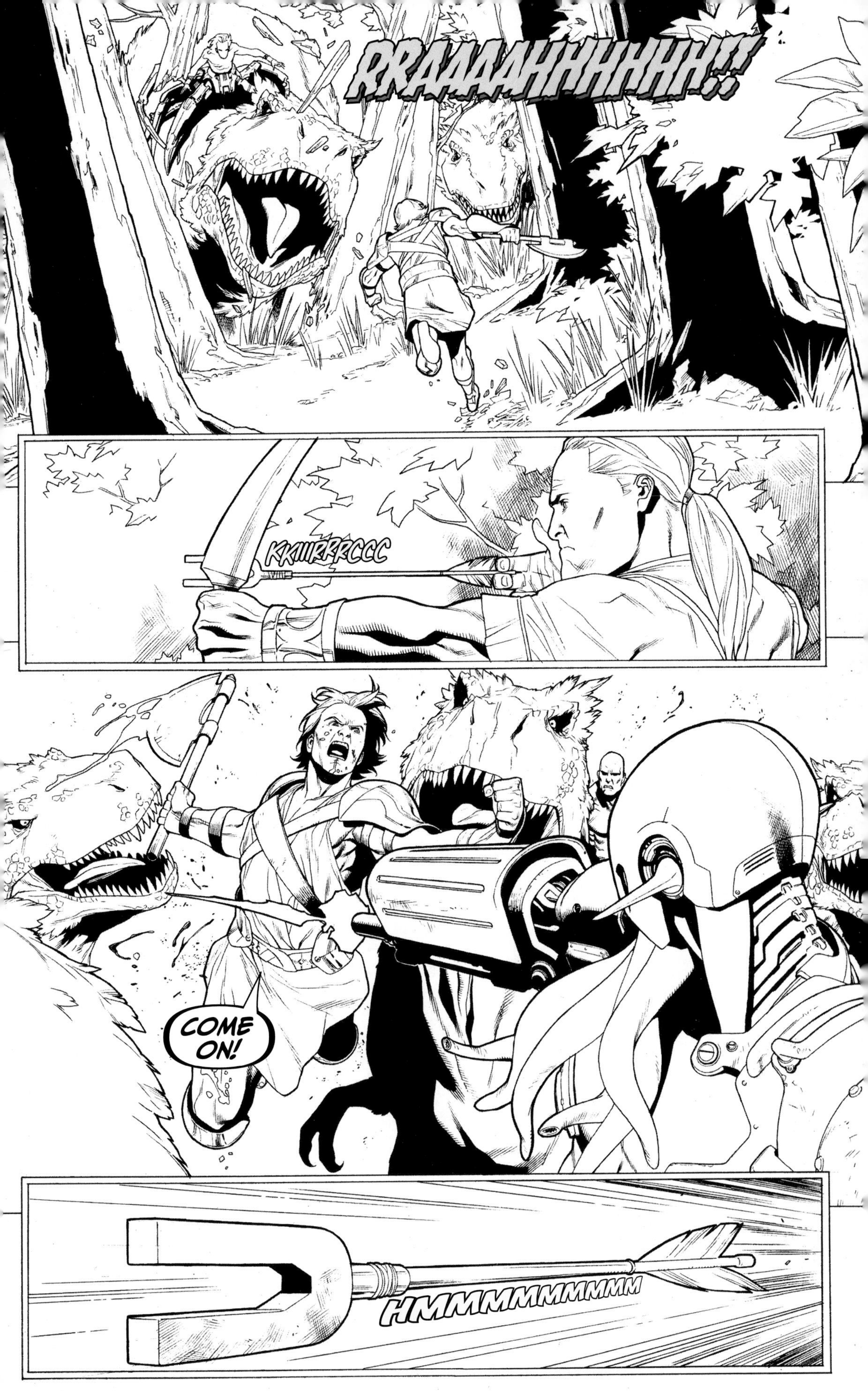
RRAAAAHHHHHH!!
KKIIIRRRCCC
COME ON!
HMMMMMMMMMM

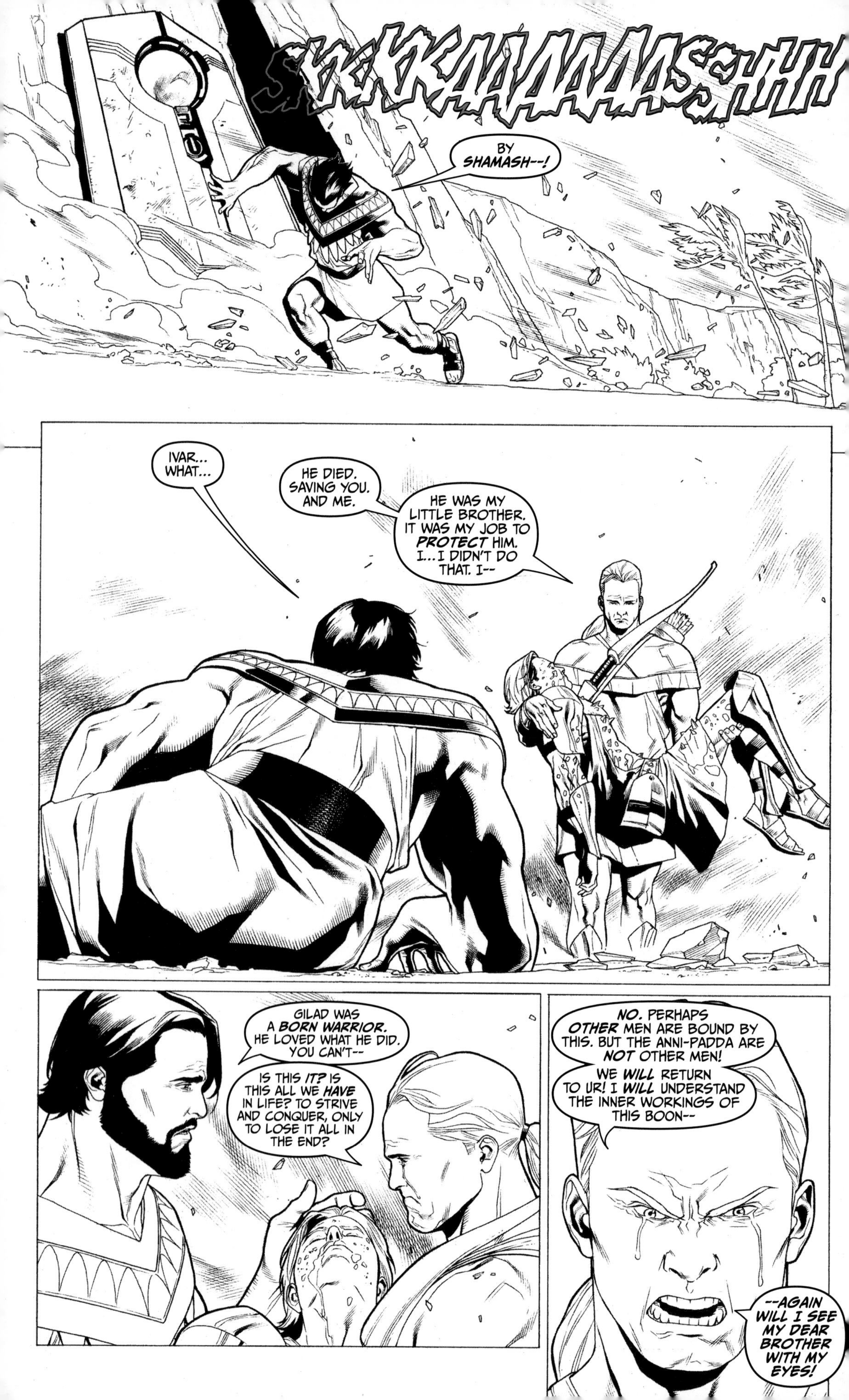
SKKKAAAAAASHHH
BY SHAMASH--!
IVAR... WHAT...
HE DIED. SAVING YOU. AND ME.
HE WAS MY LITTLE BROTHER. IT WAS MY JOB TO PROTECT HIM. I...I DIDN'T DO THAT. I--
GILAD WAS A BORN WARRIOR. HE LOVED WHAT HE DID. YOU CAN'T--
IS THIS IT? IS THIS ALL WE HAVE IN LIFE? TO STRIVE AND CONQUER, ONLY TO LOSE IT ALL IN THE END?
NO. PERHAPS OTHER MEN ARE BOUND BY THIS. BUT THE ANNI-PADDA ARE NOT OTHER MEN!
WE WILL RETURN TO UR! I WILL UNDERSTAND THE INNER WORKINGS OF THIS BOON--
--AGAIN WILL I SEE MY DEAR BROTHER WITH MY EYES!

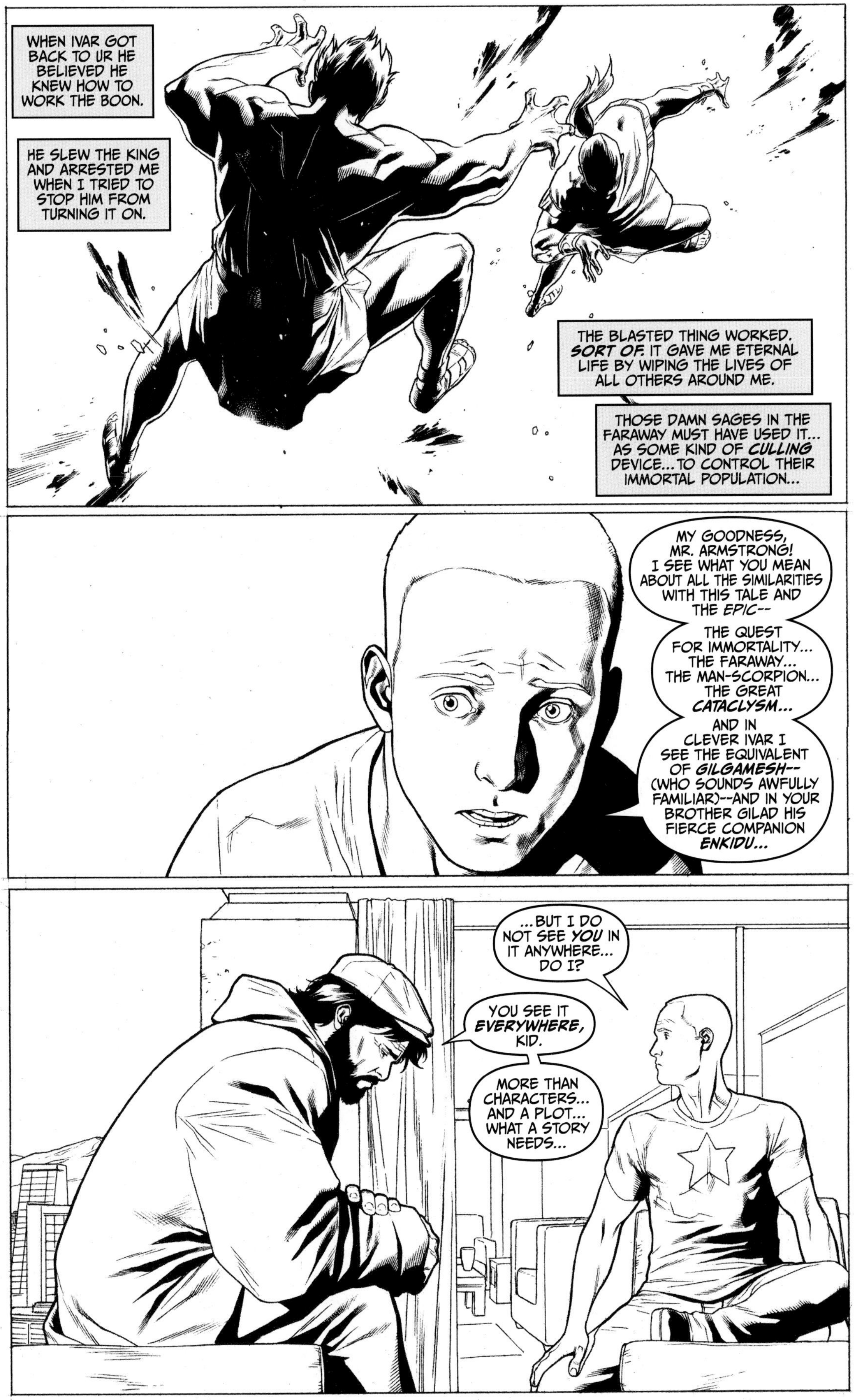
WHEN IVAR GOT BACK TO UR HE BELIEVED HE KNEW HOW TO WORK THE BOON.
HE SLEW THE KING AND ARRESTED ME WHEN I TRIED TO STOP HIM FROM TURNING IT ON.
THE BLASTED THING WORKED. SORT OF. IT GAVE ME ETERNAL LIFE BY WIPING THE LIVES OF ALL OTHERS AROUND ME.
THOSE DAMN SAGES IN THE FARAWAY MUST HAVE USED IT... AS SOME KIND OF CULLING DEVICE...TO CONTROL THEIR IMMORTAL POPULATION...
MY GOODNESS, MR. ARMSTRONG! I SEE WHAT YOU MEAN ABOUT ALL THE SIMILARITIES WITH THIS TALE AND THE EPIC--
THE QUEST FOR IMMORTALITY... THE FARAWAY... THE MAN-SCORPION... THE GREAT CATACLYSM...
AND IN CLEVER IVAR I SEE THE EQUIVALENT OF GILGAMESH-- (WHO SOUNDS AWFULLY FAMILIAR)--AND IN YOUR BROTHER GILAD HIS FIERCE COMPANION ENKIDU...
...BUT I DO NOT SEE YOU IN IT ANYWHERE... DO I?
YOU SEE IT EVERYWHERE, KID.
MORE THAN CHARACTERS... AND A PLOT... WHAT A STORY NEEDS...

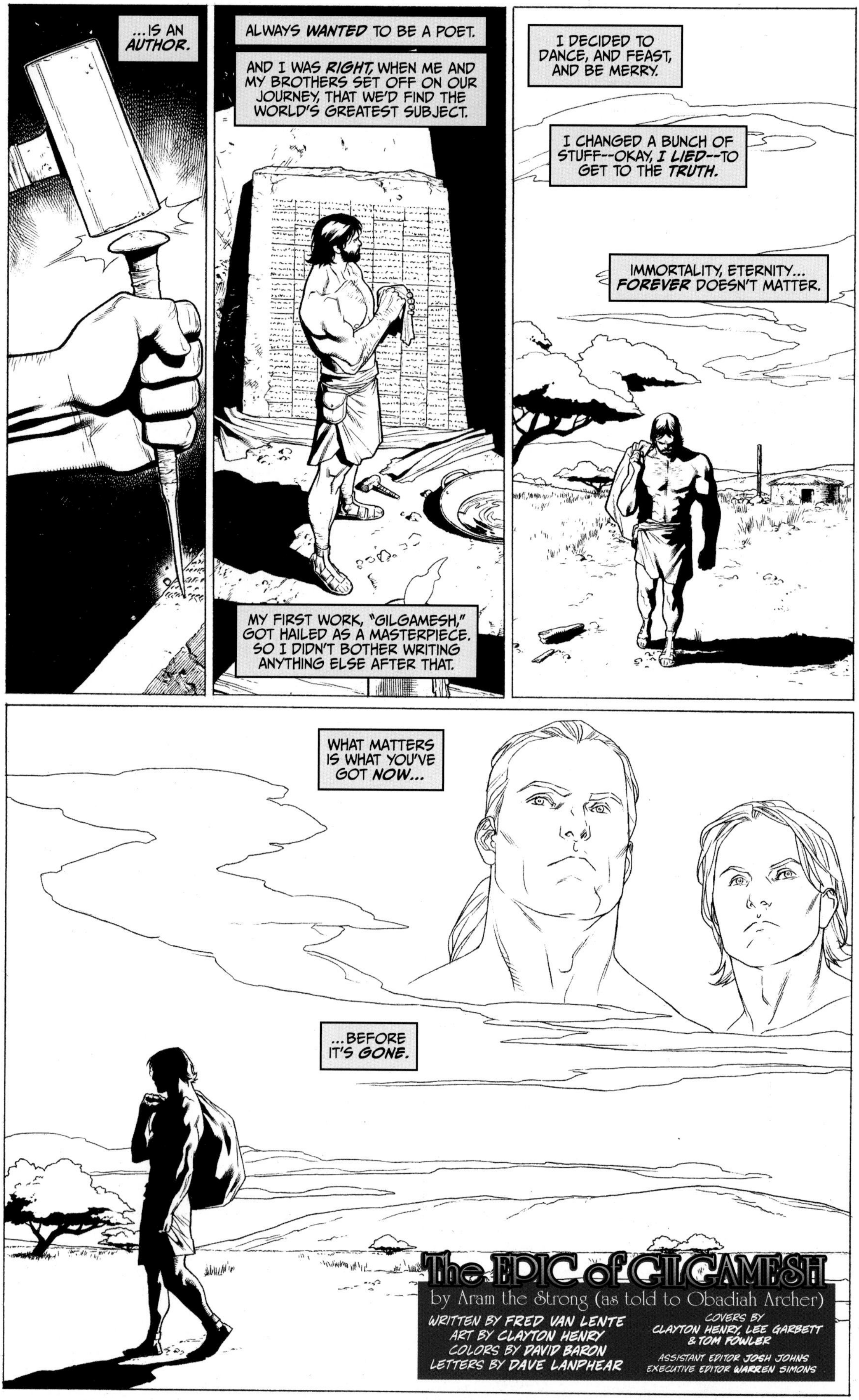
...IS AN AUTHOR.
ALWAYS WANTED TO BE A POET.
AND I WAS RIGHT, WHEN ME AND MY BROTHERS SET OFF ON OUR JOURNEY, THAT WE'D FIND THE WORLD'S GREATEST SUBJECT.
MY FIRST WORK, "GILGAMESH," GOT HAILED AS A MASTERPIECE. SO I DIDN'T BOTHER WRITING ANYTHING ELSE AFTER THAT.
I DECIDED TO DANCE, AND FEAST, AND BE MERRY.
I CHANGED A BUNCH OF STUFF--OKAY, I LIED--TO GET TO THE TRUTH.
IMMORTALITY, ETERNITY... FOREVER DOESN'T MATTER.
WHAT MATTERS IS WHAT YOU'VE GOT NOW...
...BEFORE IT'S GONE.
The EPIC of GILGAMESH
by Aram the Strong (as told to Obadiah Archer)
WRITTEN BY FRED VAN LENTE
ART BY CLAYTON HENRY
COLORS BY DAVID BARON
LETTERS BY DAVE LANPHEAR
COVERS BY CLAYTON HENRY, LEE GARBETT & TOM FOWLER
ASSISTANT EDITOR JOSH JOHNS
EXECUTIVE EDITOR WARREN SIMONS

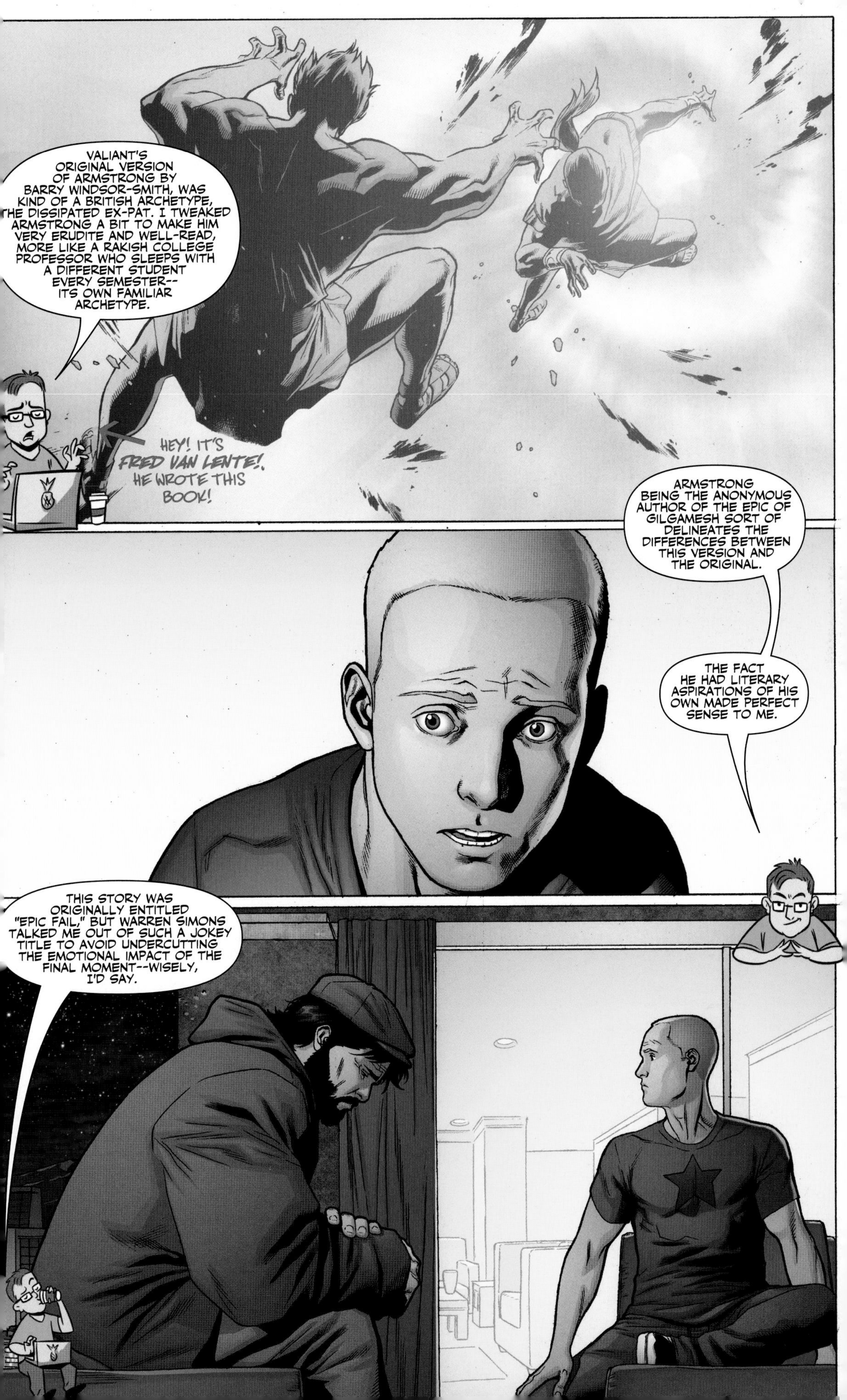
VALIANT'S ORIGINAL VERSION OF ARMSTRONG BY BARRY WINDSOR-SMITH, WAS KIND OF A BRITISH ARCHETYPE, THE DISSIPATED EX-PAT. I TWEAKED ARMSTRONG A BIT TO MAKE HIM VERY ERUDITE AND WELL-READ, MORE LIKE A RAKISH COLLEGE PROFESSOR WHO SLEEPS WITH A DIFFERENT STUDENT EVERY SEMESTER-- ITS OWN FAMILIAR ARCHETYPE.
HEY! IT'S FRED VAN LENTE! HE WROTE THIS BOOK!
ARMSTRONG BEING THE ANONYMOUS AUTHOR OF THE EPIC OF GILGAMESH SORT OF DELINEATES THE DIFFERENCES BETWEEN THIS VERSION AND THE ORIGINAL.
THE FACT HE HAD LITERARY ASPIRATIONS OF HIS OWN MADE PERFECT SENSE TO ME.
THIS STORY WAS ORIGINALLY ENTITLED "EPIC FAIL," BUT WARREN SIMONS TALKED ME OUT OF SUCH A JOKEY TITLE TO AVOID UNDERCUTTING THE EMOTIONAL IMPACT OF THE FINAL MOMENT--WISELY, I'D SAY.

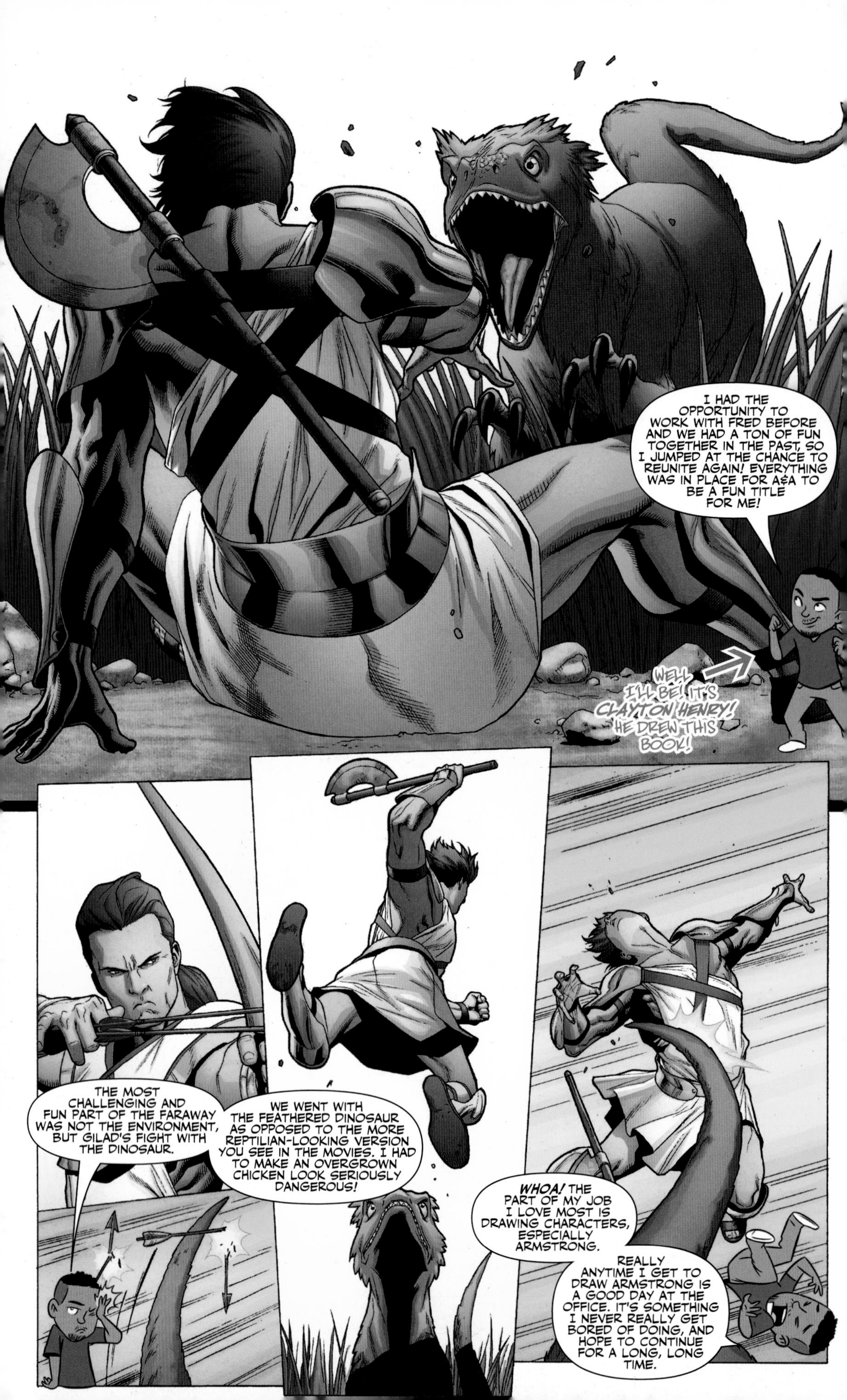
I HAD THE OPPORTUNITY TO WORK WITH FRED BEFORE AND WE HAD A TON OF FUN TOGETHER IN THE PAST, SO I JUMPED AT THE CHANCE TO REUNITE AGAIN! EVERYTHING WAS IN PLACE FOR A&A TO BE A FUN TITLE FOR ME!
WELL I'LL BE! IT'S CLAYTON HENRY! HE DREW THIS BOOK!
THE MOST CHALLENGING AND FUN PART OF THE FARAWAY WAS NOT THE ENVIRONMENT, BUT GILAD'S FIGHT WITH THE DINOSAUR.
WE WENT WITH THE FEATHERED DINOSAUR AS OPPOSED TO THE MORE REPTILIAN-LOOKING VERSION YOU SEE IN THE MOVIES. I HAD TO MAKE AN OVERGROWN CHICKEN LOOK SERIOUSLY DANGEROUS!
WHOA! THE PART OF MY JOB I LOVE MOST IS DRAWING CHARACTERS, ESPECIALLY ARMSTRONG.
REALLY ANYTIME I GET TO DRAW ARMSTRONG IS A GOOD DAY AT THE OFFICE. IT'S SOMETHING I NEVER REALLY GET BORED OF DOING, AND HOPE TO CONTINUE FOR A LONG, LONG TIME.

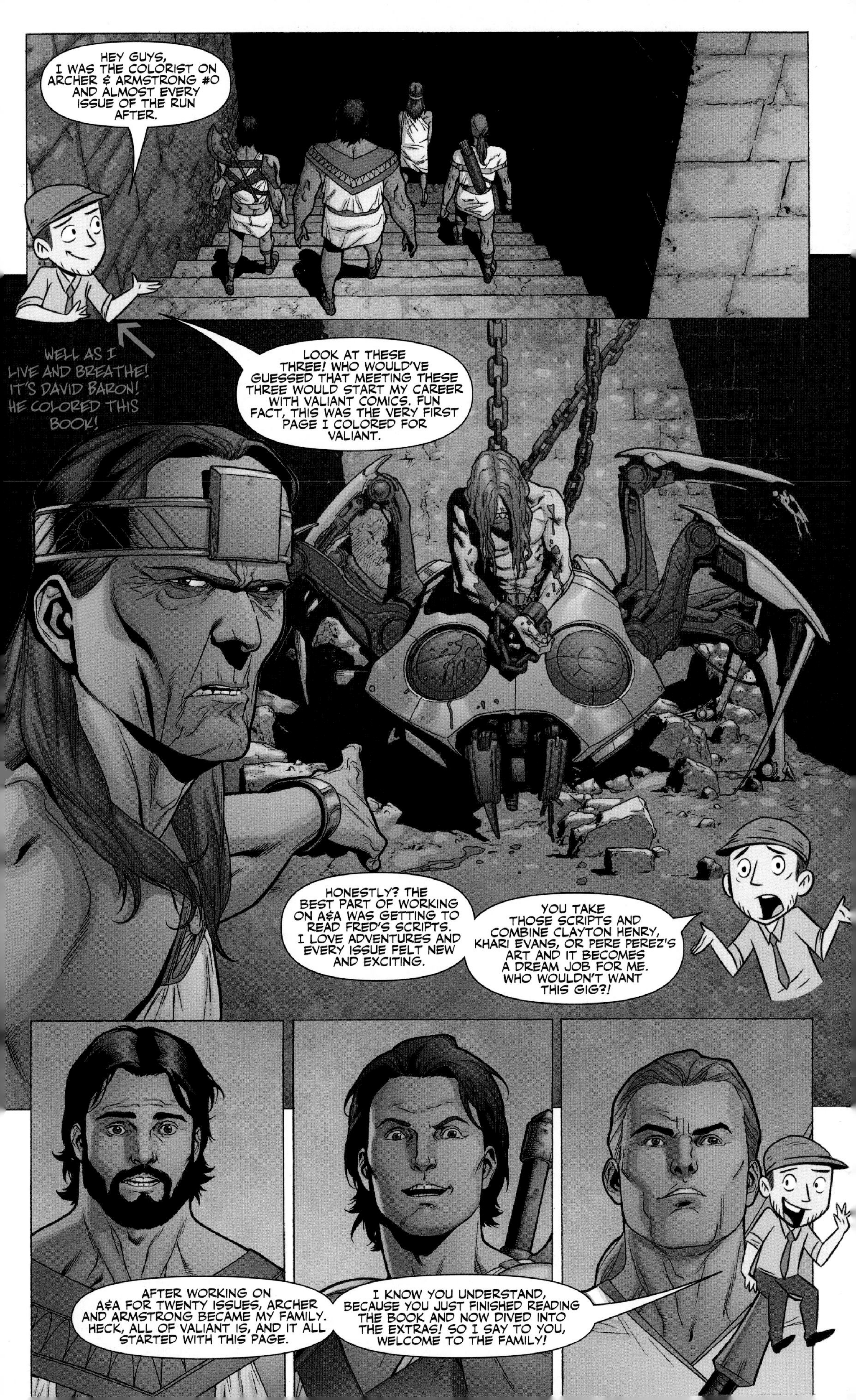
HEY GUYS, I WAS THE COLORIST ON ARCHER & ARMSTRONG #0 AND ALMOST EVERY ISSUE OF THE RUN AFTER.
WELL AS I LIVE AND BREATHE! IT'S DAVID BARON! HE COLORED THIS BOOK!
LOOK AT THESE THREE! WHO WOULD'VE GUESSED THAT MEETING THESE THREE WOULD START MY CAREER WITH VALIANT COMICS. FUN FACT, THIS WAS THE VERY FIRST PAGE I COLORED FOR VALIANT.
HONESTLY? THE BEST PART OF WORKING ON A&A WAS GETTING TO READ FRED'S SCRIPTS. I LOVE ADVENTURES AND EVERY ISSUE FELT NEW AND EXCITING.
YOU TAKE THOSE SCRIPTS AND COMBINE CLAYTON HENRY, KHARI EVANS, OR PERE PEREZ'S ART AND IT BECOMES A DREAM JOB FOR ME. WHO WOULDN'T WANT THIS GIG?!
AFTER WORKING ON A&A FOR TWENTY ISSUES, ARCHER AND ARMSTRONG BECAME MY FAMILY. HECK, ALL OF VALIANT IS, AND IT ALL STARTED WITH THIS PAGE.
I KNOW YOU UNDERSTAND, BECAUSE YOU JUST FINISHED READING THE BOOK AND NOW DIVED INTO THE EXTRAS! SO I SAY TO YOU, WELCOME TO THE FAMILY!

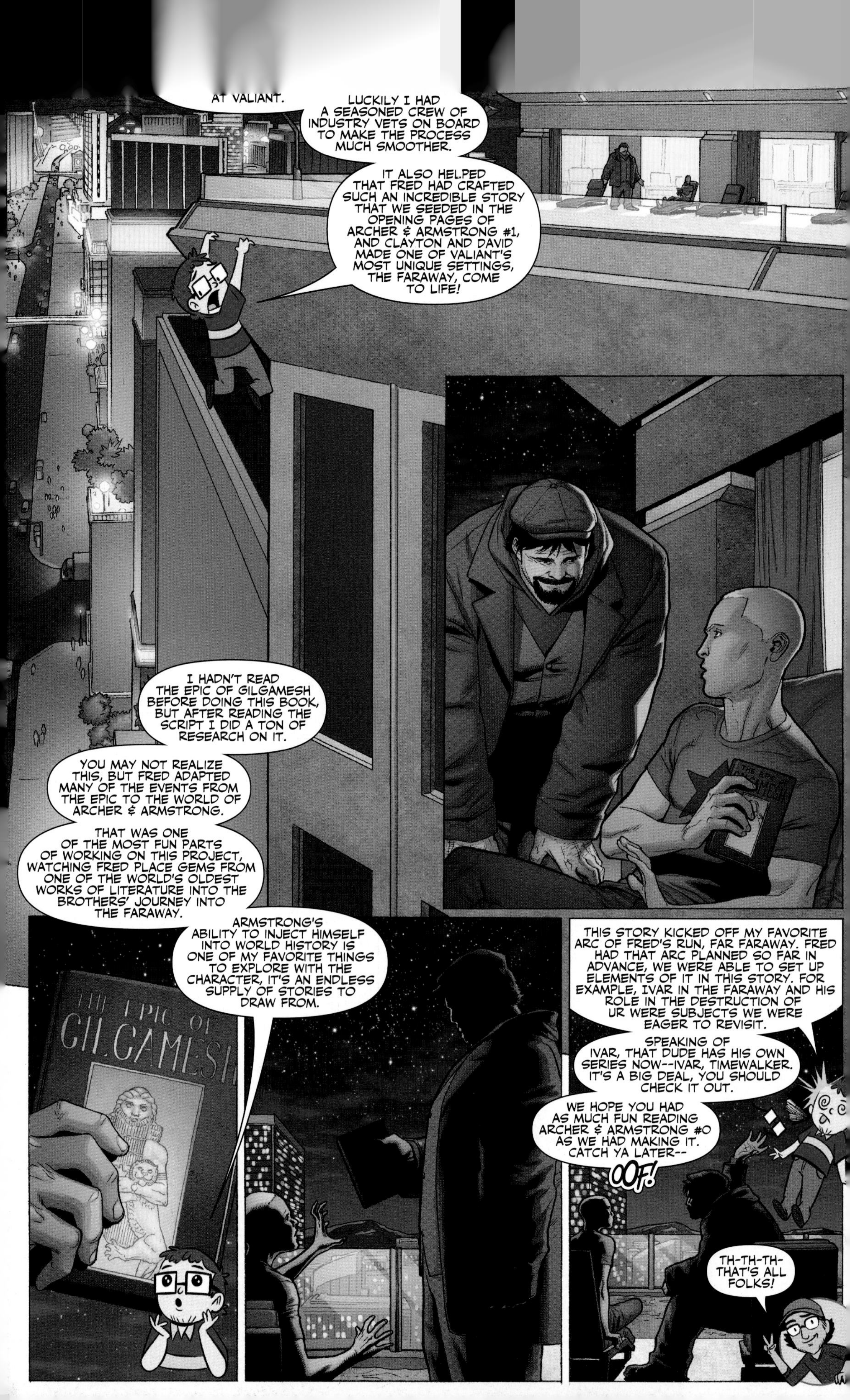

AT VALIANT.
LUCKILY I HAD A SEASONED CREW OF INDUSTRY VETS ON BOARD TO MAKE THE PROCESS MUCH SMOOTHER.
IT ALSO HELPED THAT FRED HAD CRAFTED SUCH AN INCREDIBLE STORY THAT WE SEEDED IN THE OPENING PAGES OF ARCHER & ARMSTRONG #1, AND CLAYTON AND DAVID MADE ONE OF VALIANT'S MOST UNIQUE SETTINGS, THE FARAWAY, COME TO LIFE!
I HADN'T READ THE EPIC OF GILGAMESH BEFORE DOING THIS BOOK, BUT AFTER READING THE SCRIPT I DID A TON OF RESEARCH ON IT.
YOU MAY NOT REALIZE THIS, BUT FRED ADAPTED MANY OF THE EVENTS FROM THE EPIC TO THE WORLD OF ARCHER & ARMSTRONG.
THAT WAS ONE OF THE MOST FUN PARTS OF WORKING ON THIS PROJECT, WATCHING FRED PLACE GEMS FROM ONE OF THE WORLD'S OLDEST WORKS OF LITERATURE INTO THE BROTHERS' JOURNEY INTO THE FARAWAY.
THE EPIC OF GILGAMESH
ARMSTRONG'S ABILITY TO INJECT HIMSELF INTO WORLD HISTORY IS ONE OF MY FAVORITE THINGS TO EXPLORE WITH THE CHARACTER, IT'S AN ENDLESS SUPPLY OF STORIES TO DRAW FROM.
THIS STORY KICKED OFF MY FAVORITE ARC OF FRED'S RUN, FAR FARAWAY. FRED HAD THAT ARC PLANNED SO FAR IN ADVANCE, WE WERE ABLE TO SET UP ELEMENTS OF IT IN THIS STORY. FOR EXAMPLE, IVAR IN THE FARAWAY AND HIS ROLE IN THE DESTRUCTION OF UR WERE SUBJECTS WE WERE EAGER TO REVISIT.
SPEAKING OF IVAR, THAT DUDE HAS HIS OWN SERIES NOW--IVAR, TIMEWALKER. IT'S A BIG DEAL, YOU SHOULD CHECK IT OUT.
WE HOPE YOU HAD AS MUCH FUN READING ARCHER & ARMSTRONG #0 AS WE HAD MAKING IT. CATCH YA LATER--
OOF!
TH-TH-TH-THAT'S ALL FOLKS!

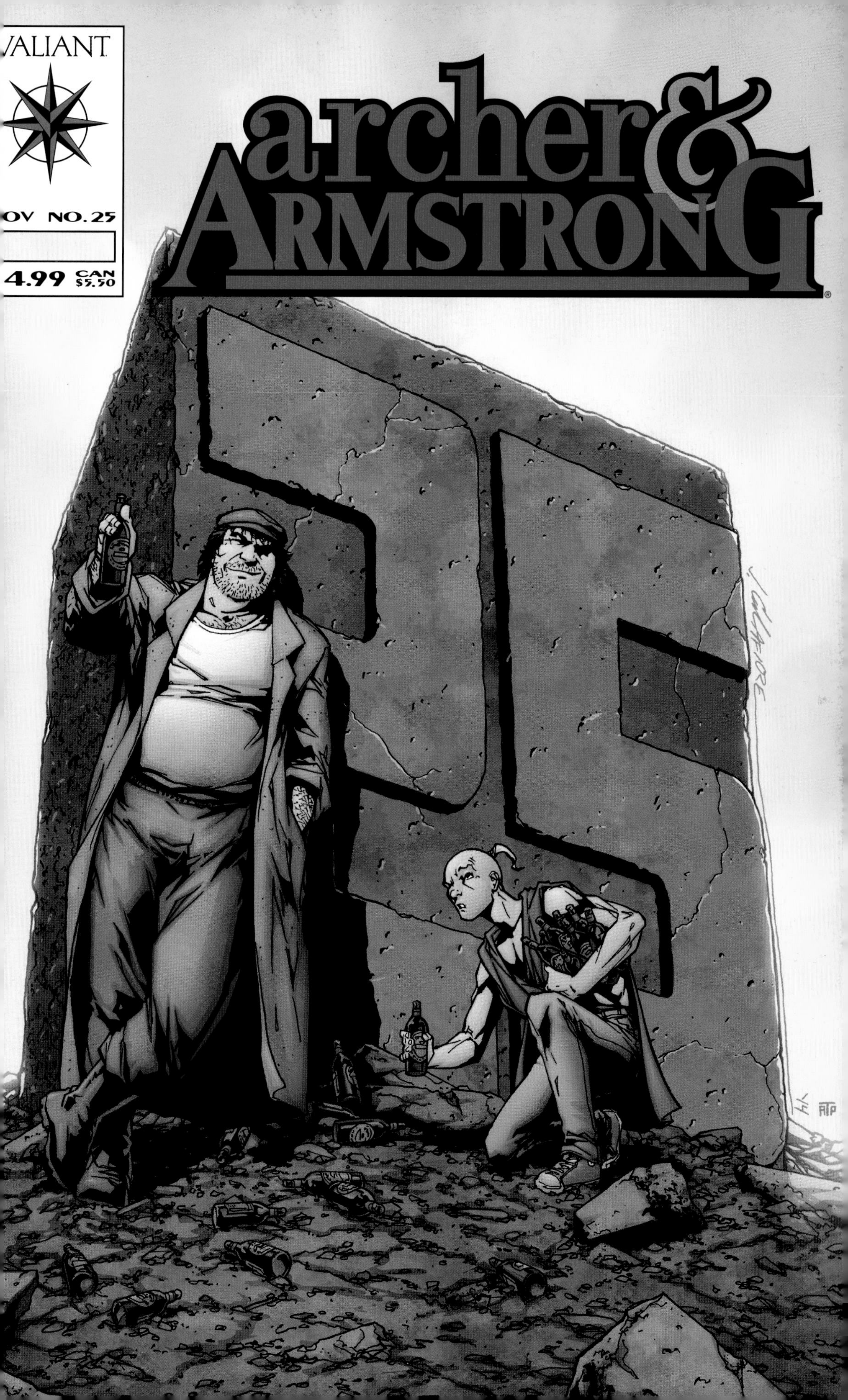
VALIANT
archer & ARMSTRONG
NO. 25
4.99 CAN $5.50

ARCHER & ARMSTRONG COVER GALLERY

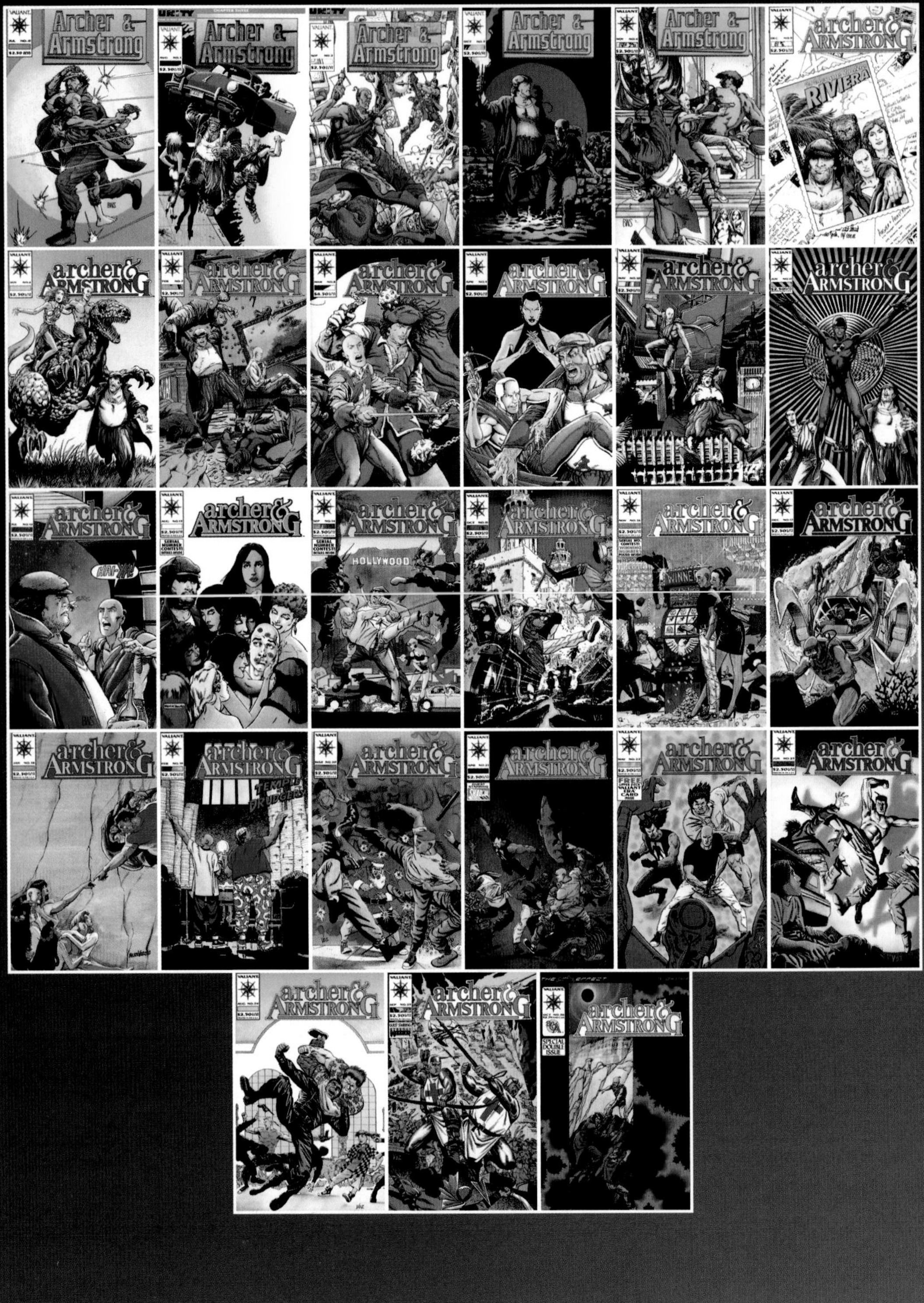

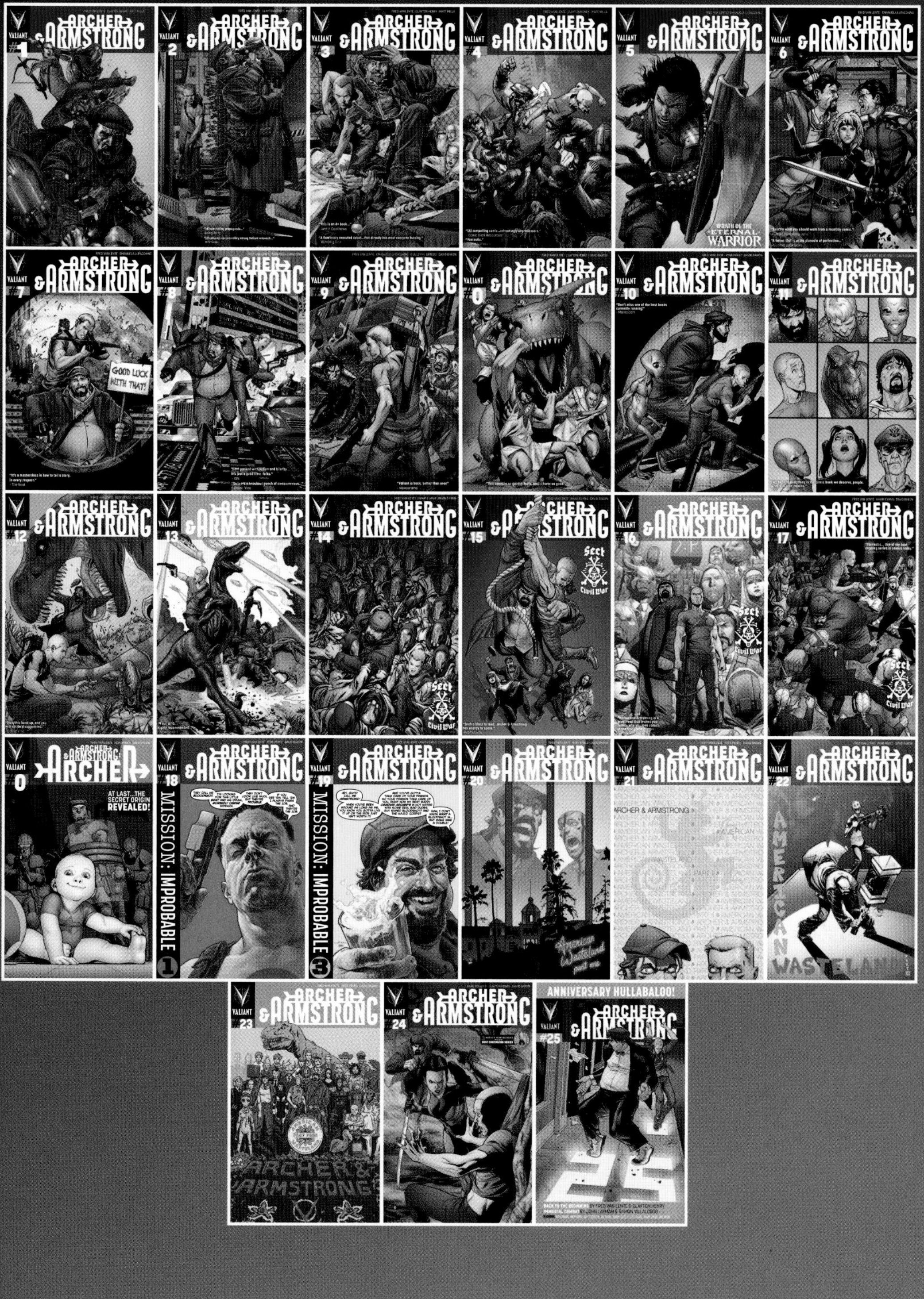

ARCHER & ARMSTRONG
WRATH OF THE ETERNAL WARRIOR
GOOD LUCK WITH THAT!
ARCHER
AT LAST...THE SECRET ORIGIN REVEALED!
MISSION: IMPROBABLE
WASTELAND
ANNIVERSARY HULLABALOO!

ARCHER & ARMSTRONG

Volume 1: The Michelangelo Code
ISBN: 9780979640988

Volume 2: Wrath of the Eternal Warrior
ISBN: 9781939346049

Volume 3: Far Faraway
ISBN: 9781939346148

Volume 4: Sect Civil War
ISBN: 9781939346254

Volume 5: Mission: Improbable
ISBN: 9781939346353

Volume 6: American Wasteland
ISBN: 9781939346421

Volume 7: The One Percent and Other Tales
ISBN: 9781939346537

ARMOR HUNTERS

Armor Hunters
ISBN: 9781939346452

Armor Hunters: Bloodshot
ISBN: 9781939346469

Armor Hunters: Harbinger
ISBN: 9781939346506

Unity Vol. 3: Armor Hunters
ISBN: 9781939346445

X-O Manowar Vol. 7: Armor Hunters
ISBN: 9781939346476

BLOODSHOT

Volume 1: Setting the World on Fire
ISBN: 9780979640964

Volume 2: The Rise and the Fall
ISBN: 9781939346032

Volume 3: Harbinger Wars
ISBN: 9781939346124

Volume 4: H.A.R.D. Corps
ISBN: 9781939346193

Volume 5: Get Some!
ISBN: 9781939346315

Volume 6: The Glitch and Other Tales
ISBN: 9781939346711

BLOODSHOT REBORN

Volume 1: Colorado
ISBN: 9781939346674

DEAD DROP

Dead Drop
ISBN: 9781939346858

THE DEATH-DEFYING DOCTOR MIRAGE

The Death-Defying Dr. Mirage
ISBN: 9781939346490

THE DELINQUENTS

The Delinquents
ISBN: 9781939346513

DIVINITY

DIVINITY
ISBN: 9781939346766

ETERNAL WARRIOR

Volume 1: Sword of the Wild
ISBN: 9781939346209

Volume 2: Eternal Emperor
ISBN: 9781939346292

Volume 3: Days of Steel
ISBN: 9781939346742

HARBINGER

Volume 1: Omega Rising
ISBN: 9780979640957

Volume 2: Renegades
ISBN: 9781939346025

Volume 3: Harbinger Wars
ISBN: 9781939346117

Volume 4: Perfect Day
ISBN: 9781939346155

Volume 5: Death of a Renegade
ISBN: 9781939346339

Volume 6: Omegas
ISBN: 9781939346384

HARBINGER WARS

Harbinger Wars
ISBN: 9781939346094

Bloodshot Vol. 3: Harbinger Wars
ISBN: 9781939346124

Harbinger Vol. 3: Harbinger Wars
ISBN: 9781939346117

EXPLORE THE VALIANT UNIVERSE

KICK ME
QUANTUM AND WOODY
BY PRIEST & BRIGHT
OL 1: KLANG

VALIANT
BATTLE FOR NEW JAPAN
RAI

VALIANT
THE VALIANT

VALIANT
THE DEATH-DEFYING
DOCTOR MIRAGE

VALIANT
DIVINITY

インピリアム
MPERIUM

ume 1: Collecting Monsters
N: 9781939346759

NINJAK

ume 1: Weaponeer
N: 9781939346667

QUANTUM AND WOODY!

ume 1: The World's Worst Superhero Team
N: 9781939346186

ume 2: In Security
N: 9781939346230

ume 3: Crooked Pasts, Present Tense
N: 9781939346391

ume 4: Quantum and Woody Must Die!
N: 9781939346629

QUANTUM AND WOODY BY PRIEST & BRIGHT

me 1: Klang
: 9781939346780

me 2: Switch
N: 9781939346803

me 3: And So...
: 9781939346865

RAI

Volume 1: Welcome to New Japan
ISBN: 9781939346414

Volume 2: Battle for New Japan
ISBN: 9781939346612

Volume 3: The Orphan
ISBN: 9781939346841

SHADOWMAN

Volume 1: Birth Rites
ISBN: 9781939346001

Volume 2: Darque Reckoning
ISBN: 9781939346056

Volume 3: Deadside Blues
ISBN: 9781939346162

Volume 4: Fear, Blood, And Shadows
ISBN: 9781939346278

Volume 5: End Times
ISBN: 9781939346377

Ivar, Timewalker

Volume 1: Making History
ISBN: 9781939346636

UNITY

Volume 1: To Kill a King
ISBN: 9781939346261

Volume 2: Trapped by Webnet
ISBN: 9781939346346

Volume 3: Armor Hunters
ISBN: 9781939346445

UNITY (Continued)

Volume 4: The United
ISBN: 9781939346544

Volume 5: Homefront
ISBN: 9781939346797

THE VALIANT

The Valiant
ISBN: 9781939346605

VALIANT ZEROES AND ORIGINS

Valiant: Zeroes and Origins
ISBN: 9781939346582

X-O MANOWAR

Volume 1: By the Sword
ISBN: 9780979640940

Volume 2: Enter Ninjak
ISBN: 9780979640995

Volume 3: Planet Death
ISBN: 9781939346087

Volume 4: Homecoming
ISBN: 9781939346179

Volume 5: At War With Unity
ISBN: 9781939346247

Volume 6: Prelude to Armor Hunters
ISBN: 9781939346407

Volume 7: Armor Hunters
ISBN: 9781939346476

Volume 8: Enter: Armorines
ISBN: 9781939346551

Volume 9: Dead Hand
ISBN: 9781939346650

EXPLORE THE VALIANT UNIVERSE

VALIANT
HARBINGER
DELUXE EDITION 2

OMNIBUSES

Archer & Armstrong: The Complete Classic Omnibus
ISBN: 9781939346872
Collecting ARCHER & ARMSTRONG (1992) #0-26, ETERNAL WARRIOR (1992) #25 along with ARCHER & ARMSTRONG: THE FORMATION OF THE SECT.

Quantum and Woody: The Complete Classic Omnibus
ISBN: 9781939346360
Collecting QUANTUM AND WOODY (1997) #0, 1-21 and #32, THE GOAT: H.A.E.D.U.S. #1, and X-O MANOWAR (1996) #16

X-O Manowar Classic Omnibus Vol. 1
ISBN: 9781939346308
Collecting X-O MANOWAR (1992) #0-30, ARMORINES #0, X-O DATABASE #1, as well as material from SECRETS OF THE VALIANT UNIVERSE #1

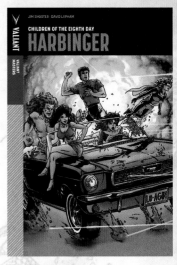

DELUXE EDITIONS

Archer & Armstrong Deluxe Edition Book 1
ISBN: 9781939346223
Collecting ARCHER & ARMSTRONG #0-13

VALIANT
ARMOR HUNTERS
DELUXE EDITION

Armor Hunters Deluxe Edition
ISBN: 9781939346728
Collecting ARMOR HUNTERS #1-4, ARMOR HUNTERS: AFTERMATH #1, ARMOR HUNTERS: BLOODSHOT #1-3, ARMOR HUNTERS: HARBINGER #1-3, UNITY #8-11 and X-O MANOWAR #23-29

Bloodshot Deluxe Edition Book 1
ISBN: 9781939346216
Collecting BLOODSHOT #1-13

Harbinger Deluxe Edition Book 1
ISBN: 9781939346131
Collecting HARBINGER #0-14

Harbinger Deluxe Edition Book 2
ISBN: 9781939346773
Collecting HARBINGER #15-25, HARBINGER: OMEGAS #1-3, and HARBINGER: BLEEDING MONK #0

Harbinger Wars Deluxe Edition
ISBN: 9781939346322
Collecting HARBINGER WARS #1-4, HARBINGER #11-14, and BLOODSHOT #10-13

Quantum and Woody Deluxe Edition Book 1
ISBN: 9781939346681
Collecting QUANTUM AND WOODY #1-12 and QUANTUM AND WOODY: THE GOAT #0

Q2: The Return of Quantum and Woody Deluxe Edition
ISBN: 9781939346568
Collecting Q2: THE RETURN OF QUANTUM AND WOODY #1-5

JAMES ASMUS TOM FOWLER MING DOYLE
KANO JORDIE BELLAIRE DAVE LANPHEAR
VALIANT
QUANTUM AND WOODY!
DELUXE EDITION 1
MEH!

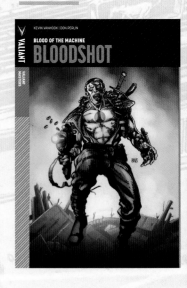

Shadowman Deluxe Edition Book 1
ISBN: 9781939346438
Collecting SHADOWMAN #0-10

Unity Deluxe Edition Book 1
ISBN: 9781939346575
Collecting UNITY #0-14

X-O Manowar Deluxe Edition Book 1
ISBN: 9781939346100
Collecting X-O MANOWAR #1-14

X-O Manowar Deluxe Edition Book 2
ISBN: 9781939346520
Collecting X-O MANOWAR #15-22, and UNITY #1-4

JIM SHOOTER | DAVID LAPHAM
VALIANT
CHILDREN OF THE EIGHTH DAY
HARBINGER
VALIANT MASTERS

VALIANT MASTERS

Bloodshot Vol. 1 - Blood of the Machine
ISBN: 9780979640933

H.A.R.D. Corps Vol. 1 - Search and Destroy
ISBN: 9781939346285

Harbinger Vol. 1 - Children of the Eighth Day
ISBN: 9781939346483

Ninjak Vol. 1 - Black Water
ISBN: 9780979640971

Rai Vol. 1 - From Honor to Strength
ISBN: 9781939346070

Shadowman Vol. 1 - Spirits Within
ISBN: 9781939346018

KEVIN VANHOOK | DON PERLIN
VALIANT
BLOOD OF THE MACHINE
BLOODSHOT
VALIANT MASTERS

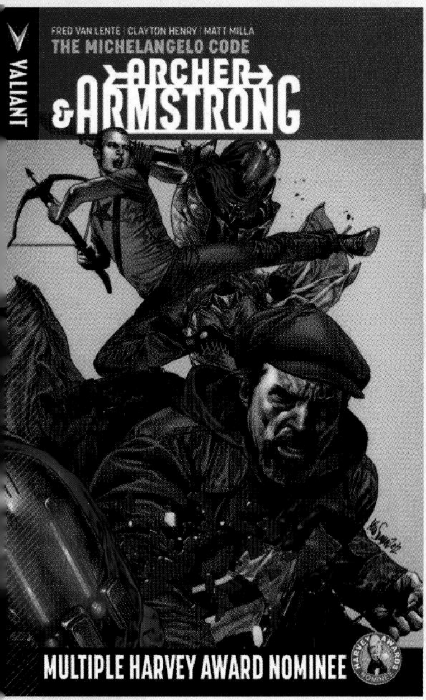
VALIANT
FRED VAN LENTE | CLAYTON HENRY | MATT MILLA
THE MICHELANGELO CODE
ARCHER & ARMSTRONG
MULTIPLE HARVEY AWARD NOMINEE

Archer & Armstrong Vol. 1: The Michelangelo Code

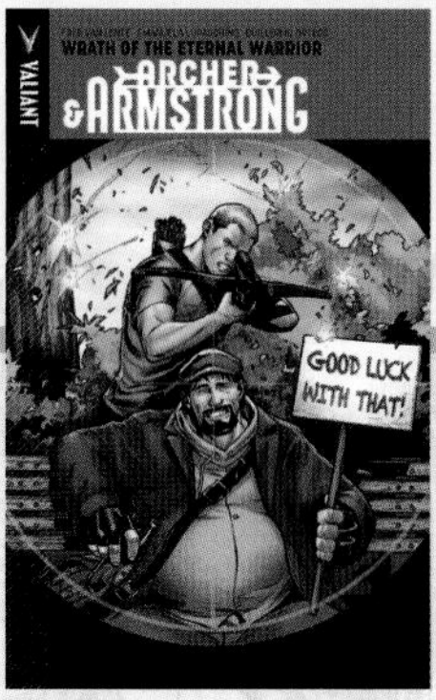
VALIANT
WRATH OF THE ETERNAL WARRIOR
ARCHER & ARMSTRONG
GOOD LUCK WITH THAT!

Archer & Armstrong Vol. 2: Wrath of the Eternal Warrior

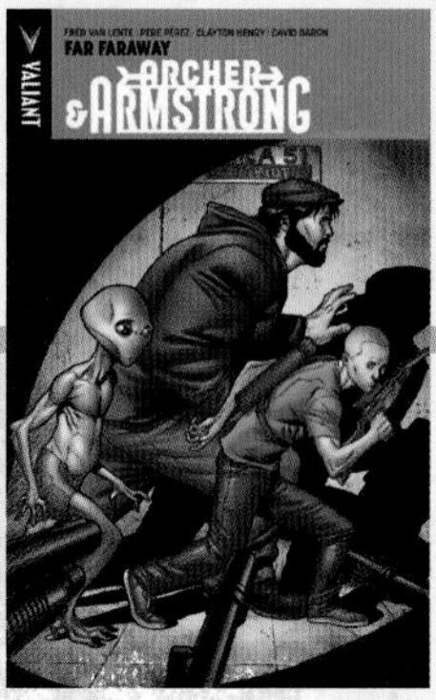
VALIANT
FAR FARAWAY
ARCHER & ARMSTRONG

Archer & Armstrong Vol. 3: Far Faraway

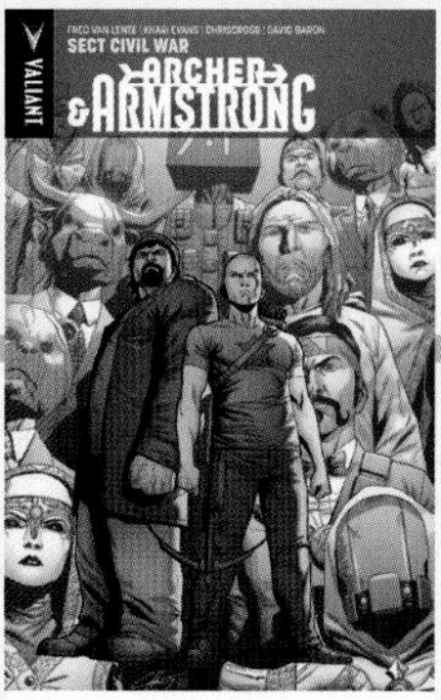
VALIANT
SECT CIVIL WAR
ARCHER & ARMSTRONG

Archer & Armstrong Vol. 4: Sect Civil War

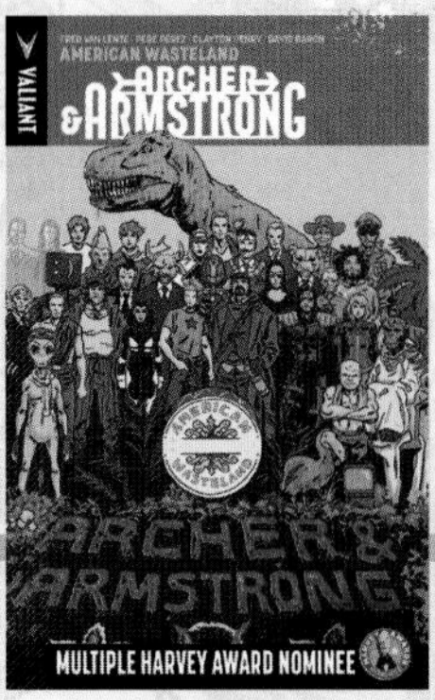
VALIANT
AMERICAN WASTELAND
ARCHER & ARMSTRONG
MULTIPLE HARVEY AWARD NOMINEE

Archer & Armstrong Vol. 6: American Wasteland

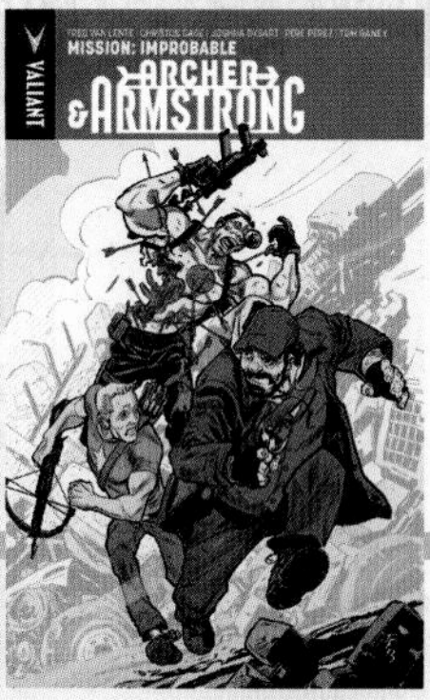
VALIANT
MISSION: IMPROBABLE
ARCHER & ARMSTRONG

Archer & Armstrong Vol. 5: Mission: Improbable

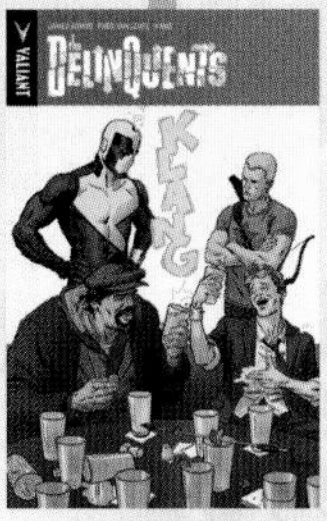
VALIANT
DELINQUENTS

The Delinquents **(OPTIONAL)**

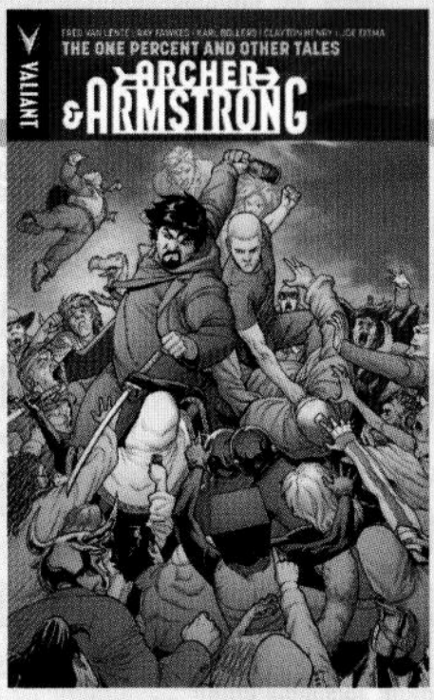
VALIANT
THE ONE PERCENT AND OTHER TALES
ARCHER & ARMSTRONG

Archer & Armstrong Vol. 7: The One Percent and Other Tales

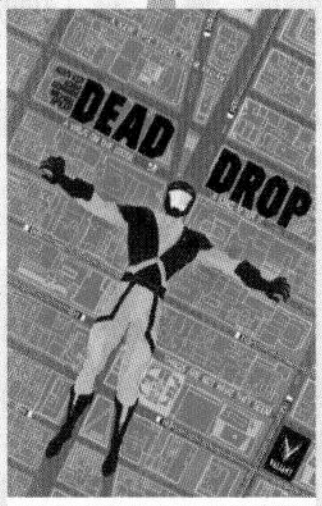
DEAD DROP

Dead Drop **(OPTIONAL)**

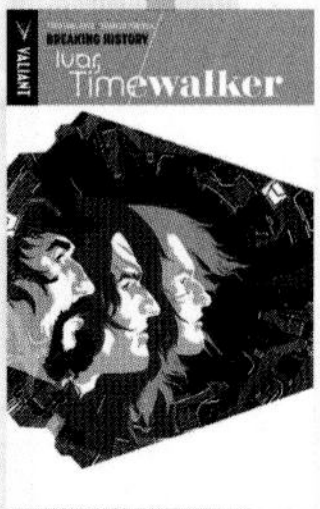
VALIANT
BREAKING HISTORY
Ivar, Timewalker

Ivar, Timewalker Vol. 2: Breaking History **(OPTIONAL)**

'10 out of 10... This is a comic in perfect harmony and is a must-read..." - Newsarama

'Archer & Armstrong is the best damn comic... More of you need o be reading it." -io9

Follow the critically acclaimed adventures of Valiant's conspiracy-busting duo!
From New York Times best-selling writer
FRED VAN LENTE
And all-star artists
CLAYTON HENRY, PERE PÉREZ, and
EMANUELA LUPACCHINO

VALIANT

Ivar, Timewalker

VOLUME ONE: MAKING HISTORY

FROM THE DAWN OF THE DINOSAURS...TO THE BATTLE OF TRAFALGAR... TO THE END OF TIME ITSELF...THE FIRST CENTURY-SPANNING ADVENTURE OF *IVAR, TIMEWALKER* STARTS HERE!

FRED VAN LENTE / CLAYTON HENRY / BRIAN REBER
MAKING HISTORY
VALIANT
Ivar, Timewalker

At this very moment in Geneva, Switzerland, history is being made. A thousand meters underground, inside the Large Hadron Collider, researcher Neela Sethi is about to discover time travel - and jeopardize her life in the process. But she doesn't know that yet. Ten minutes from now, every deadbeat chrononaut, wannabe conqueror, and misguided protector of the timestream will be banging down her door. Good thing that the legendary Ivar, Timewalker, got there first... right? Now it's down to history's most jaded, most tempestuous time traveler to stop the worst of everything that is, was, and will be... before time runs out!

New York Times best-selling creators Fred Van Lente (ARCHER & ARMSTRONG, *The Amazing Spider-Man*) and Clayton Henry (HARBINGER, *The Incredible Hercules*) begin a clock-stopping odyssey into the distant past, far future, and every moment in-between right here with the first volume of Valiant's latest epic! Collecting IVAR, TIMEWALKER #1-4.

TRADE PAPERBACK
ISBN: 978-1-939346-63-6

Ivar, Timewalker

VOLUME TWO: BREAKING HISTORY

A LITTLE CONFUSED BY TIME TRAVEL? DON'T WORRY, THESE GUYS DON'T REALLY UNDERSTAND IT EITHER. SO THEY'RE *BREAKING HISTORY*!

FRED VAN LENTE / FRANCIS PORTELA
BREAKING HISTORY
VALIANT
Ivar, Timewalker

With the universe on the brink of destruction, Ivar must turn to his closest relatives - Armstrong and Gilad Anni-Padda - to save Neela Sethi from the machinations of the Prometheans! The problem? These three guys couldn't be further apart. Time doesn't heal all wounds as the assault on Oblivi-1 begins!

Join New York Times best-selling writer Fred Van Lente (ARCHER & ARMSTRONG) and rising star Francis Portela (*Green Lantern Corps*) as they kick off the next volume of the series that io9 calls "impressively shocking!" Collecting IVAR, TIMEWALKER #5-8.

TRADE PAPERBACK
ISBN: 978-1-939346-83-4

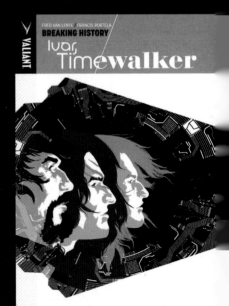